The
Christians

The Christians

Bamber Gascoigne

with photographs by
Christina Gascoigne

Jonathan Cape
Thirty Bedford Square London

First published 1977
Text © 1977 by Bamber Gascoigne
Christina Gascoigne's photographs © 1977
by Christina Gascoigne and Jonathan Cape Ltd

Jonathan Cape Ltd
30 Bedford Square, London WC1

British Library Cataloguing in Publication Data

Gascoigne, Bamber
The Christians.
1. Church History
I. Title II. Gascoigne, Christina
270   BR145.2
ISBN 0-224-01355-6

Printed in England by Jolly & Barber Limited,
Rugby, Warwickshire

Contents

Colour Plates

Preface

The thirteen chapters of this book were written while preparing thirteen pro-grammes on *The Christians* for television. Each chapter therefore covers the same ground as its companion programme, but often it will treat the material in a different way. It is a difficult task to divide Christian history into thirteen brief but equal sections. It poses identical problems in the early stages of preparation for either screen or page. Later, each medium begins to make its own demands. An excellent quotation may have to be dropped on television because there is nothing to illustrate it. An entire sequence may vanish from the book because during it the viewer was invited to sit back and enjoy a succession of absorbing images. But a television series and an illustrated book do share one basic need: to tell the story in concrete terms. To that extent *The Christians* treats the subject differently from a conventional book on Christian history. It is about people, events and places, rather than theory or theology.

The planning of a television series is a group activity, with a great many people pooling their ideas and skills. Those who have contributed to the shaping of *The Christians* are far too numerous to be described or thanked in a brief preface. At the end of the book there is a detailed account of the large team of which, for three exhilarating years, we have formed a part.

B. and C. G.

CHAPTER ONE

A Peculiar People

FOR the first fifty years of what we now call the Christian era, not a word survives in any document about Christ or his followers. During the next fifty years, the Christians themselves wrote down most of the books that now make up the New Testament. But still not a word, with one small exception, from any outside writer. And then, in the second century, Roman authors began to comment:

> There is a group, hated for their abominations, called Christians by the people. Christus, from whom the name comes, suffered the extreme penalty during the reign of Tiberius at the hands of one of our officials, Pontius Pilate.   (*Tacitus*) [1]

> The Christians are a class of men given to a new and wicked superstition.   (*Suetonius*) [2]

> They worship to an extravagant degree this man who appeared recently. They are like frogs holding a symposium round a swamp, debating which of them is the most sinful.   (*Celsus*) [3]

> The poor wretches have convinced themselves that they are going to be immortal and live for all time, by worshipping that crucified sophist and living under his laws. Therefore, they despise the things of this world, and consider them common property. They receive these doctrines by tradition, without any definite evidence. So if any charlatan or trickster comes among them, he quickly acquires wealth by imposing upon these simple folk.   (*Lucian*) [4]

> It is their habit, on a fixed day, to assemble before daylight and to recite by turns a form of words to Christ as a God. The contagion of this perverse and extravagant superstition has penetrated not the cities only, but the villages and the country. Yet it seems possible to stop it and set it right.   (*Pliny the Younger*) [5]

How wrong they were, those Romans. Well it's easy to say so eighteen hundred years later, when Christianity has spread throughout the world. But St Clement, the fourth pope, was confident even then:

> God chose our Lord Jesus Christ, and us through him to be a peculiar people. [6]

* * *

The earliest of the gospels to be written down, that of St Mark, begins in the Palestinian desert — with the baptism of Jesus. Immediately after it, he gathers up his first disciples, and begins his brief three years of preaching and healing. It was the serious beginning of the Christian story and the desert, west of the Dead Sea, seems the right setting for a message of repentance. It's an uncompromising place, with its own harsh method of cleansing. And the river Jordan is near by for a more ritual purification, the washing away of sins

John the Baptist seems more than a little eccentric as he appears in the gospels — wandering around the desert, dressed in camel's hair, eating locusts. But in his own day there were plenty of others like him, living in this landscape which denies so dramatically the comforts of everyday life: and sets the mind dreaming, perhaps, of higher things. We happen to know a great deal about one such group of holy men because of a lucky accident in 1947. Some Bedouin Arabs were smuggling goats into what was then Palestine (it sounds improbable, but seems to have been the case) and they were passing through the Qumran area on their way towards Bethlehem when one of the goats strayed. Already it has a biblical

12

Opposite: *The cliffs at Qumran in which the Dead Sea Scrolls were found.*

Previous pages: *'The Light of the World': reading the Bible in the Church of the Holy Sepulchre, Jerusalem.*

ring to it. A boy clambered along the cliffs to retrieve the animal. Idly he threw a stone into one of the caves. There was a sound of something breaking. Inside the cave he found tall clay jars containing bundles of manuscripts, sewn together in long scrolls and wrapped in linen. They had belonged to a group of Jewish monks, known as Essenes, who lived in a near-by monastery at the time of Christ. It was probably in about A.D. 70, when the Roman army was systematically destroying Jewish culture in Palestine, that the monks hid their sacred books in the caves. They are what we now know as the Dead Sea Scrolls.

When the precious scrolls had been gently unrolled, they revealed that the Essenes were in the desert for the same reason as John the Baptist. They too were awaiting a Messiah — and Christ is only the Greek for Messiah. Both words mean 'the anointed one'. (Jesus, his personal name, means 'God saves'.) The Essenes even relied on precisely the same verse from the Old Testament as John the Baptist. In the Book of Isaiah:

> The voice of him that crieth in the wilderness, Prepare ye the way of the Lord, make straight in the desert a highway for our God. [7]

Four dots in the Essene manuscript replace the name of God, which for the Jews was too holy even to be written. Those four dots say a great deal about the difference between the Jewish and Christian religions — at any rate in their beginnings. The original god of the Old Testament was a distant, an awe-inspiring figure. If he appeared on earth, it was only to speak to prophets — and then, as likely as not, from inside a burning bush. The god of the Muslims, Allah, would be equally remote.

But the Christians went to another extreme. It was a most startling change. A human being, they said, had given birth to God: not a princess, not long ago, not

The star in the Church of the Nativity at Bethlehem, to show the pilgrims where Jesus was born.

Virgin and Child, *by Bernardino Fungai,* c. *1500 (National Gallery, London).*

far away in some distant land: but a simple girl, quite recently, near by. It was, they insisted, an historical event — the sort of thing that in other times you would read about in your local paper. And it was certainly, as they described it, an event that was highly sympathetic.

In all the best newspaper stories X marks the spot. We all want to know exactly where and how it happened. Through the centuries, at Bethlehem, a great church has grown up, constantly patched and added to, around what was believed to be the original manger. The doorway has been altered by Byzantine emperors, by crusader knights, and again more recently; and you can still follow centuries of pilgrims, down through each layer of the past, to rediscover the actual place from that actual time. The first day, in the Christian calendar, of the first year. The year dot.

It doesn't much matter that modern scholarship, in its spoilsport way, has decided that Jesus must have been born in about 4 B.C. – or even that many scholars now believe that the choice of Bethlehem itself is a later invention, to fulfil the Old Testament prophecy which said the Messiah would come from here. Not many Christians today would insist on every part of the nativity scene being precisely true. Of the four gospels, only Luke includes the shepherds; only Matthew has the wise men; and Mark and John don't even mention the Virgin Birth or the infant Jesus. Yet the elements of this story are, and always have been, irresistibly attractive.

Each age has been able to find in the Nativity the elements which most appeal to it: from the magic of the moving star to the warm everyday reality of the mother and new-born child; from the exotic silks and turbans of the wise men to the humdrum clothes of the shepherds; from the angel, who alone in the cast understands everything, to the patient cattle, robbed of their manger, who understand nothing. Even the unusual farmyard setting has its compelling touch of social drama — no room at the inn, so this spectacular event is relegated to the stables.

The human elements in Christianity may have made it, at times, the most sentimental of religions. Yet they have also given it its greatest strength — the close link between God and man which is implicit in a religion where God becomes man. If Jesus was a man and yet was the Son of God, then God can by extension be seen as father to every man. 'Our Father, which art in heaven' is a more intimate way of addressing the deity than is common in other religions.

It was only after his baptism in the Jordan, when he was about thirty, that Jesus began his brief ministry; two or three years spent finding disciples, preaching, healing. His background was that of hard-working country people. Members of his own family are mentioned in Christian documents up to the third century. They seem to have remained fairly humble peasant farmers. And it was among such people that he found his disciples. What made ordinary people follow him? Christians can answer simply that they followed him because he was God, or through some sense of his divine power. But history must look for a more ordinary answer. And the gospels give a clear impression, above all, that it was because people believed he could work miracles. Luke says that even St Peter followed Jesus for this reason. Peter had caught nothing in his net when Jesus told him to put it out once more. This time he brought up so many fish that the boat almost sank.

> When Peter saw it, he fell down at Jesus' knees, saying: Depart from me, for I am a sinful man, O Lord. And Jesus said, Fear not; from henceforth thou shalt catch men.[8]

No type of miracle is more persuasive than a healing miracle. Perhaps it requires faith to be healed: certainly it creates faith to see someone healed. And the gospels are full of the sick, the lame, the blind and even the dead being returned to health by Jesus. If word gets round that a miracle-worker can cure illness, he will find followers.

This basic appeal is confirmed in a delightful legend which grew up around the first king to be converted to Christianity. He was King Abgar, who in about 200 ruled the small kingdom of Edessa in what is now south-eastern Turkey. In the process of story-telling, the event was pushed back to the reign of an earlier Abgar, roughly contemporary with Christ, and soon letters were circulating which had supposedly passed between the two:

> Abgar to Jesus, greeting. As the report goes, thou makest blind men to see again, lame to walk, and cleansest lepers. Either thou art a God come down from heaven, or a Son of God that doest these things. Come to me and heal the affliction which I have. I have heard that the Jews wish to do thee hurt. I have a very little city, but comely, which is sufficient for us both.

The reply was more business-like, but it powerfully conjures up the period when disciples were travelling far and wide making converts. Their precise and difficult task was to persuade people of the reality of a departed man-god, no longer visible, for whose recent existence there was only their own solemn word to go by.

> Jesus to Abgar. Blessed art thou that hast believed in me, not having seen me. I will send thee one of my disciples, to heal thine affliction and give life to thee and them that are with thee.[9]

What Jesus did was attractive; what he said was equally so, especially to the poor. Nothing in the Sermon on the Mount is exclusively original to Christ, for this was a time when religious sects were proliferating under the distress of the Roman occupation of Palestine, and other teachers or rabbis were offering similar consolation. But that didn't make the message any less attractive.

Blessed are the meek, for they shall inherit the earth — a statement almost dotty in its unworldliness, but music in the ears of those who have no choice but to be meek. Blessed are the poor in spirit, for theirs is the kingdom of heaven. This is given more briefly by Luke as 'blessed be ye poor', and to many people it has seemed the most reactionary side of Christianity; don't worry about the poor, their reward will come later. But it wasn't so at the beginning. Jesus preached the same message as John the Baptist. So did St Paul. Repent, and trust to God's mercy, for the kingdom of heaven is at hand. Literally at hand. According to the gospels, Jesus had told his followers that the end of the world would come during their lifetime. And when they marched with him towards Jerusalem, Luke says they believed the kingdom of God was about to begin. No wonder they were in high spirits. Their turn had come.

In political terms Galilee was well known as the centre of resistance to Roman rule and to the Jewish authorities who collaborated with Rome. Whatever Jesus's intention, his march on Jerusalem inevitably had political overtones. And the gospels suggest that when his followers reached the capital city, they were already in a high state of excitement. Jesus himself went straight to the Temple, and began breaking up the stalls of the traders who worked in the courtyard. The priests asked him, 'By what authority are you acting like this?' He replied in mysterious parables, informed the priests that tax-gatherers and prostitutes would enter the kingdom of God before them, and prophesied for good measure that their Temple would be destroyed.

It is hardly surprising that the Jewish authorities made plans to arrest and silence this troublesome Jesus. In his own terms, they had no choice because the scriptures had to be fulfilled. But a sentence in one of the four gospels led to Christianity's least attractive feature — its long tradition of anti-Semitism. The Jewish crowd, wrote St Matthew, clamoured for the death of Jesus with the words: 'His blood be on us, and on our children'. Only in 1974 did the Vatican finally announce that the Jewish people were no longer to be held collectively responsible for the crucifixion.

Christianity is the only major religion to have as its central event the suffering and degradation of its god. Crucifixion was a barbarous death, chiefly used for agitators, for pirates and for slaves. Part of the victim's punishment was to be whipped, and then to carry the heavy cross-beam to the place of his own death. When the cross was raised, a notice was pinned to it giving the culprit's name and crime. INRI in this case. *Iesus Nazarenus Rex Iudaeorum*. Jesus of Nazareth, King of the Jews.

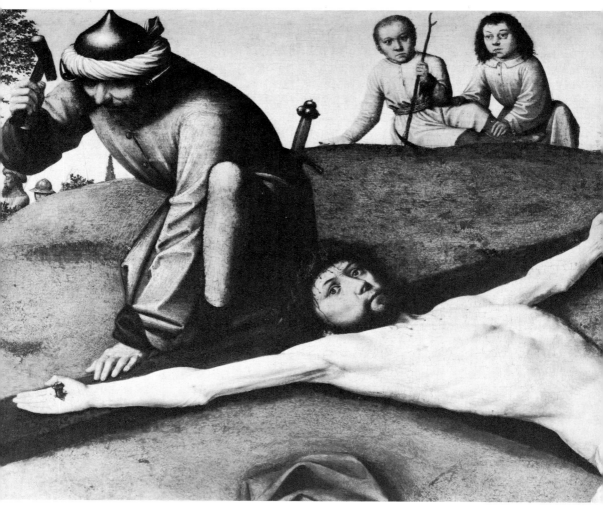

Christ nailed to the Cross: detail of a painting by Gerard David (National Gallery, London).

Opposite: *Good Friday in Jerusalem.*

However familiar the Crucifixion may be, it remains a profoundly moving subject — an inspiration over the centuries to many of Europe's greatest artists. But its familiarity does prevent our noticing quite how remarkable this scene is as an image of God. When a Jesuit missionary told the story of the Crucifixion to an Indian emperor, the emperor was shocked that the god of the Christians should have allowed this to happen to him. By the standards of most religions his surprise is understandable. But the power of this scene is part of that same humanity of the gospel story — that sense of sympathy, even intimacy, which is made possible by a god who is also a man. Devout Christians of all periods have wept tears of pity for their god, and that in itself is unusual.

In the Church of the Holy Sepulchre: priests at the stone slab on which Jesus's body is said to have been anointed before burial.

Jesus's body was put in a rock tomb on the Friday; and by Sunday, all sides agreed, it had vanished. The Jewish authorities were sure the disciples had stolen it. The disciples were sure that Jesus had risen from the dead. And so, with the Resurrection, the suffering of Good Friday gives way to the joyful renewal of Easter Sunday.

An early Christian tradition fixed on a spot just outside the old city wall of Jerusalem as the location for both the Crucifixion and the tomb. There has been a church on the site since the fourth century (the Church of the Holy Sepulchre, altered over the centuries out of all recognition), and here, every Easter, they celebrate the Resurrection with the symbolism of light and darkness. All the candles in this and other churches are put out while the Greek patriarch is enclosed, alone, in the Holy Sepulchre. Inside, so the faithful believe, his torch ignites by a miracle. He emerges with it ablaze, and people struggle to be the first to light their candles from it. The sacred flame is passed from worshipper to worshipper until the body of the church is alive with light, and torches are carried in a hectic and highly competitive race to altars in other churches. It is the perfect image of the spread of the gospel or 'good news'. 'I am the light of the world,' said Jesus. The story of Christ gives way to the story of Christianity.

In the ancient Christian village of Malula, in Syria, the old men still speak the language that Jesus spoke — Aramaic. In his time this was the common language of the Middle East. It remained so for centuries, until it was replaced by Arabic, and it stretched eastwards from Palestine over a vast area, right into the Persian empire. But that was not, as it turned out, the direction that Christianity was to take. Nor was Aramaic the language in which it would spread.

After the Resurrection, and because of it, the disciples came to believe that

The patriarch emerges from the Sepulchre with the Holy Fire.

Jesus was the Son of God. Whether they were right or wrong is a matter of opinion; something that you can no more prove than disprove. All that matters, in terms of history, is that those first Christians believed Jesus was God; and that this faith gave them the strength to spread a new religion, eventually throughout the world. But apart from their faith, the disciples were not particularly well equipped for the task. St Peter would have had a lot in common with the people of Malula. Like them he was a countryman; like them he spoke Aramaic, an eastern language. But Christianity was to have its most lasting success moving westwards; converting people in the cities; and using European languages, first Greek and then Latin. For that a different type of apostle was needed, and Christianity found precisely the man in St Paul.

Paul — or Saul in the Hebrew version of his name — was born both a Jew and a Roman citizen. Somehow, and we don't know how, his family had acquired that privileged status of citizenship. He had grown up in Tarsus, a city in Turkey which had long been part of the Greek world. So legally he was a Roman, intellectually he was a Greek, spiritually he was a Jew. Three trump cards for someone hoping to spread any faith through the empire.

The immediate irony was that Paul came from one of the more legalistic Jewish sects that Jesus had often criticized, and one that had done much to bring about his death. He was a Pharisee. He had come from Tarsus to study in Jerusalem under a distinguished rabbi, and he was well on the way to becoming a rabbi himself. So he was as eager as anyone to root out this new heresy of Christianity. Christians, throughout history, have always persecuted each new Christian sect. The Jews were only doing the same to a new Jewish sect. It is easy to see their point of view. When the Messiah came, they believed it would be to restore their promised land. But the Christians said the Messiah had come; and had been crucified, among common criminals, at the request of the rabbis. A scandalous suggestion. Paul was on his way to suppress those at Damascus who were spreading this sort of subversive rumour, when he experienced his sudden conversion.

Instead of using Jewish law to convict the local Christians, Paul preached in the synagogues of Damascus that the Messiah had arrived. Eventually the Jewish authorities laid plans to rid themselves of this heretic, much as they had with Jesus. Paul got away when his friends lowered him in a basket from the walls. It was the first of his many clashes with synagogues on his travels through the Roman empire.

The empire was already vast. You could march all round the Mediterranean without ever leaving Roman soil. In this huge area little Palestine was an un-important outpost, yet a minor heresy from that one small area was to become the religion of the empire. Much of how Christianity spread is only tradition and guesswork. Damascus and Antioch had small Christian communities within a few years of the Crucifixion. Alexandria, an important early centre, was said — without any historical justification — to have been converted by St Mark in about the year 60. But the missionary travels of St Paul are authentic history, and are amazing.

His three great journeys would be hard work even today. His letters are the

An Aramaic-speaker at Malula in Syria.

Jews of the most extreme Orthodox sect, as legalistic as Saul the Pharisee, praying at the Western Wall in Jerusalem.

earliest writings in the New Testament and they give a vivid picture of his life as a missionary; founding little communities, writing letters to keep them up to the mark, trudging onwards, whipped from time to time by synagogues as a dangerous heretic. At Athens, Paul the Greek intellectual was able to debate in classic style, among equals, but his principle was to go to the synagogues first. After all, he was a Jew preaching about a Jew. But when they ejected him, he would reply: 'My conscience is clear; now I shall go to the Gentiles.'[10] Gentiles included everyone outside the Jewish faith and community — the rest of the world. It was a significant new direction for Christianity, which thus became free to take its place as one of the many religions filtering through the empire, spreading along those convenient Roman roads and competing for converts. A group of people whom Paul met in Ephesus give an intriguing glimpse of one such potential religion developing — and one that Paul nipped quickly in the bud. They turned out to be followers of John the Baptist. Paul said to them:

> 'Did you receive the Holy Spirit when you became believers?' 'No,' they replied, 'we have not even heard that there is a Holy Spirit.' He said, 'Then what baptism were you given?' 'John's baptism,' they answered. Paul then said, 'John told the people to put their trust in one who was to come after him, that is, in Jesus.' On hearing this they were baptised into the name of the Lord Jesus.[11]

Opposite: *The hillside below Bethlehem.*

Overleaf: *The Sea of Galilee.*

Opposite: *Jerusalem: a Jew of the most strictly Orthodox sect.*

Paul's travels brought him to Jerusalem to justify himself at headquarters. He had been bringing Gentiles into the Church — on what basis? The argument centred on circumcision. Circumcision was, and still is, the ritual entry of a male child into the Jewish community, God's chosen people. But it raised the question: what is a Christian? If he was a more enlightened type of Jew, then clearly every Christian must either be a Jew or become a Jew. And that meant being circumcised — an experience which Paul's average serious-minded middle-aged Gentile convert didn't relish. Or was being a Christian something new, quite separate from being Jewish, in which case circumcision was unimportant? This was what Paul passionately believed.

Peter agreed, though a little reluctantly, and their view prevailed in Jerusalem.

St Paul, lowered in a basket from the walls of Damascus: twelfth-century mosaic in the Capella Palatina, Palermo.

25

A letter was sent to the Greek Christians, announcing that they need not undergo circumcision. 'When it was read,' says the New Testament account, 'they all rejoiced at the encouragement it brought.'[12] It was a symbol of the way Paul was taking the church. In his own words: 'There is no such thing as Jew and Greek, slave and freeman, male and female; for you are all one in Christ Jesus.'[13]

Paul's last great journey was to Rome; but he came as a prisoner. The Jewish authorities in Jerusalem had complained of him, just as they had of Jesus — and the words of the New Testament make it plain that they still regarded Christianity as a dangerously radical movement.

> We have found this man a pestilent fellow, an agitator among all the Jews throughout the world, and a ringleader of the sect of the Nazarenes.[14]

It was a tribute, at least, to Paul's effectiveness. At his own request, as a Roman citizen, he was sent to Rome for his trial. He found a small community of Christians already there. We don't know how they had got there. Some perhaps had been brought from the east as slaves. Others may have heard the news from traders, who have always carried ideas from place to place along with the silks and spices. Nor do we know what judgment was passed on Paul himself, because the Acts of the Apostles comes to a sudden end without telling us. But it is generally assumed that Paul died in Rome, somewhere around the year 63.

Tradition adds that Peter came here too and was martyred here — crucified upside down. So the capital of the empire was able to claim the two greatest saints of the early church; they appear together on the first Christian portraits, made in the third and fourth centuries for pilgrims. They were to give Rome its special position once the original church in Jerusalem had collapsed. In the year 70, Palestine rose against Roman rule and Roman soldiers destroyed the Jewish city. With Jerusalem gone, Christians would increasingly look to Rome and would come to think of Peter as the first pope.

The Christians in Rome were not persecuted quite so frequently as the story books used to suggest, but the first great persecution did take place very early — at around the time of Paul's death. It was under the emperor Nero, whose way of life hardly fitted with the Christian ethic. Nero was said to have fiddled during the great fire which blazed through Rome in the year 64, and soon the rumour spread that he had started the fire himself. The historian Tacitus described what followed:

> To be rid of this rumour, Nero fastened the guilt on a class hated for their abominations, called Christians by the populace. Mockery of every sort was added to their deaths. Covered with the skins of beasts, they were torn by dogs and perished; or were nailed to crosses; or were doomed to the flames. Nero threw open his garden for the spectacle and exhibited a show in the circus.[15]

The early Christians met in secret for their communal meal, and soon it gave rise to all sorts of rumours. They called it an *agape*, or Love Feast, from a Greek word meaning 'brotherly love'. Love Feast! There was talk in no time of sexual orgies in dark and secret places. And word also got around of the Christians eating the flesh and blood of some leader of theirs. Cannibalism now! These, no doubt, were the abominations that Tacitus mentioned. Once again, it is because we are familiar with the sacrament in Christian countries that we don't notice

In the catacomb of St Priscilla, Rome.

how strange it is, in a highly developed religion, that the central ritual should be eating the god. It was something that missionaries in nineteenth-century Africa or Asia found hard to explain to cannibals they were converting from their barbarous ways.

It was the common people of Rome, eagerly repeating scandalous rumours, who were usually more hostile than the imperial authorities: the age-old hostility to any group that is both poor and foreign. The early Christians in Rome spoke Greek — it remained the language of the Roman church until the third century — and they were almost all from the poorest classes, many of them slaves. They ran a tiny welfare state among themselves, looking after widows and orphans. They may even have shared their goods. All most suspicious. In fact, for a few years Christianity remained true to its revolutionary beginnings.

When the famous catacombs were rediscovered in the sixteenth century, it was assumed that the persecuted people must have hidden and even lived down in these dark passages. But they were only burial chambers, with ledges for the 27 coffins and sometimes a little chapel scooped out of the rock where a service could be held. Romans and Jews buried their dead in the same way. Only the subjects of the frescoes reveal that these particular catacombs were used by Christians. The paintings show the communion meal. They show that favourite theme of the gospels; miracles of healing. And they show Jesus as the gentle shepherd of his flock. At this stage Christians never showed him on the cross, for that was still the shameful death, reserved for criminals.

The text of an early Christian tomb-stone suggests very well the feeling of the small community which met down here for funerals.

> My name is Avircius, a disciple of the pure Shepherd who feeds the flocks of sheep on mountains and plains, who has great all-seeing eyes. He taught me faithful scriptures. To Rome he sent me. Everywhere I met with brethren. With Paul before me I followed, and Faith everywhere led the way and served food everywhere, the Fish from the spring — immense, pure, which the pure Virgin caught and gave to her friends to eat for ever, with good wine, giving the cup with the loaf. These things I, Avircius, ordered to be written. I am truly seventy two years old. Let him who understands these things, and everyone who is in agreement, pray for Avircius.[16]

'Him who understands these things'; the world of the early Christian was full of secret symbols. The fish was a specially good secret. Not only do fishes make many appearances in the gospels, and it seems that the earliest communion meals offered fish as well as bread and wine: but the very word had its magic. In Greek

Mosaic of fishes, in the house at Pompeii where the ROTAS *square was found.*

it is ICHTHYS: and the letters were taken to stand for *Iesos Christos Theou Yios Soter*, 'Jesus Christ, Son of God, Saviour'. While playing with letters, the early Christians had an even more elaborate game:

```
R O T A S
O P E R A
T E N E T
A R E P O
S A T O R
```

This square of letters has been found in several places, including Pompeii in Italy and even far-away Cirencester in England. It appears to be meaningless, but a little rearrangement will work wonders. 'I am Alpha and Omega, the beginning and the ending, saith the Lord.' If we remove A and O, twice over, we are left with a group of letters which can be reorganized to spell *Pater Noster*, Our Father, also twice over and in the shape of a cross. So the answer, for those in the know, is:

```
                    A

                    P
                    A
                    T
                    E
                    R
A   P A T E R N O S T E R   O
                    O
                    S
                    T
                    E
                    R

                    O
```

   Christianity was far from being the only religion with special secrets. Mystery cults of various sorts were popular in the Roman empire, partly because the official religion was so very unmysterious. It involved a public ritual of sacrificing large animals for the sake of good luck — impressive but not very imaginative — and it meant acknowledging the emperor as a god, even if only one among many. Naturally the Christians refused to do so, and this was the only official reason why they were persecuted. Other people were more pliable. They shared in the sacrifice, made the necessary nod to the emperor's statue, and then retired to a private place for their own more stimulating ritual.

   Gradually three religions pulled ahead of the field, all of them from the east. From Persia, the god Mithras who killed and ate a sacred bull; from Syria, the worship of Sol, the sun; and from a little farther west, Jesus Christ. By the third century it seemed certain that if Rome adopted a new state religion it would be one of these — or a combination of elements from all three.

Roman sacrificial rites: a detail from Trajan's column.

It was a time of chaos in the empire. Emperors followed each other in a bewildering and rapid progression. Twelve successive emperors reigned an average of three years each, and not one of them died in his bed. The Romans had a collector's attitude to religion and every aspiring ruler was on the look-out for any new god powerful enough to help him grab and then hold on to the throne. In 274 Aurelian believed that the sun-god had brought him victory in Syria. He set up a state cult to Sol Invictus, the unconquered sun: and announced that the birthday of the sun, a day of special festivity, was December 25th. The sun's halo, as well as the date of his birthday, would later be borrowed by Christianity. A little later Diocletian declared Mithras, who was very popular with the army, to be the god who was 'protector of the empire'. After slaying the bull, Mithras made a sacrificial meal of it; and his followers re-enacted this with a ritual of bread and wine. The Christians, understandably, were outraged at this infringement of their rites.

The instability of third-century Rome had been gradually reduced by emperors as strong as Aurelian and Diocletian. It was finally brought to an end by Constantine — seen, in his most authentic portrait, in a massive form which deliberately expresses his power but hardly exaggerates it. The god that Constantine chose to help him in battle was the Christian god. With his conversion Christianity turned the crucial corner from heresy to orthodoxy. The peculiar people were about to become normal, and some regret it to this day (in that it involved the religion becoming 'official'). There had been no such event in Christian history since the conversion of St Paul. Even the occasion had the same dramatic quality as that blinding flash on the road to Damascus.

An altar to the Syrian sun god, first century A.D. *(Capitoline Museum, Rome).*

32 *Gigantic head, six-foot high, of the emperor Constantine (Palazzo dei Conservatori, Rome).*

Opposite: *The Christ of the Byzantine emperors: twelfth–century mosaic in the Capella Palatina, Palermo.*

At the end of his life Constantine was to be more securely in control of the empire than anyone had been for a couple of centuries, but he had been born the son of a common soldier and, it was said, a barmaid — though we now know the barmaid as St Helena. His father rose through the ranks to become one of four emperors, ruling jointly. When his father died, in 306, Constantine was in the extreme north-west of the empire, at York, in England. The Roman soldiers acclaimed the young man emperor in his father's place; and six years later he was in a position to march on Rome, to capture it from one of his rivals. Like many other aspiring emperors, he worshipped the sun — and hoped to borrow some of its strength. But one day, as he was in the Italian countryside marching south, he saw a sign imposed on the sun — a monogram of the letters CH and R (the Chi-Rho), and the words *In hoc signo vinces*, 'In this sign shalt thou conquer'. It was a message, he believed, from the god of the Christians.

When he captured the city of Rome, Constantine decided that he had found his patron. And so had the Christians. From now on the empire, and Rome, was to be theirs. Little Palestine was in the limelight, and was destined to remain so.

The last word on Constantine's victory and conversion can go to Eusebius, a bishop who was a friend of his and who wrote his life:

> Throughout the world a bright and glorious day, an unclouded brilliance,
> illuminated all the churches of Christ with a heavenly light.[17]

Opposite: *The trappings of imperial Christianity: Russian Orthodox bishops in a church service at Zagorsk, near Moscow.*

CHAPTER TWO

The Christian Empire

ARCHBISHOP or President Makarios is an oddity in the twentieth century: church and state in one person. It is strange to us to see a cleric stand at the rostrum of the United Nations and argue his country's case. It is strange to see a head of state swinging a censer in his own cathedral on a Sunday morning. The Turks of Cyprus often refer to Makarios as 'His Byzantine Beatitude'. It is meant as a hostile joke, but historically it has a kernel of truth. Makarios is the heir of a Christian tradition which stretches back across sixteen centuries to the beginnings of the Byzantine empire.

The link between Christianity and the state, between God and Caesar, began with Constantine. He had seen his vision in the sky of Christ's monogram in the year 312. Soon afterwards he captured Rome and made himself emperor. Christ and the empire in quick succession: the result was predictable, a Christian empire.

Along with its new religion, Constantine provided the Roman world with a new capital city. The empire's enemies tended to gather in the east (the Goths pressing down on the Balkans, and farther away mighty Persia): an increasing amount of trade was with the east; and now the official religion was eastern. A move to the east was natural. The site chosen by Constantine could hardly have been more perfect for a city which would grow rich through trade. The narrow neck of the Bosporus is a natural cross-roads between Asia and Europe, either by land or by water. A new suspension bridge now spans the gap where caravans, bringing the riches of the east, have for centuries been ferried from shore to shore. Beneath that bridge must pass every boat plying between the Black Sea and the Mediterranean. Neatly placed to one side of the straits is an ideal natural

Previous pages: *The domes of Orthodoxy: St Basil's cathedral, Moscow.*

Archbishop Makarios, during the 1950s, when he was leading Cyprus's fight for independence from Britain.

The Golden Horn, with Santa Sophia in the background.

harbour, narrow enough for a chain to be stretched across it in the old days to keep out intruders — the Golden Horn, though the modern pool of oily water and rusting hulks no longer deserves that romantic description. There had already been a town here for some centuries. Byzantium it had been called, until the day in 330 when Constantine was ready to inaugurate his new city. Exactly 1600 years later, in 1930, the Turks changed its name to Istanbul. But for the greater part of its long history the place has been known as Constantine's city, Constantinople.

The founding of the city was celebrated with a day of chariot races. This was still a Roman city, but with a difference. Beside the circus, where there would have been a temple to the gods, there was now a church to the One God, or Three-in-One: Santa Sophia, the great central church of the Christian empire, the cathedral of Byzantium. Constantine founded the first church on the site, but in the sixth century it was burnt in a riot and was replaced by the present   37

building. In its massive domed interior the emperors were baptized, crowned, married — the central figures in the Christian liturgy, which was now the ritual of the empire.

But does one ruler, adopting Christianity, lead to a genuinely Christian community? Well, the answer is yes. History has shown it again and again. But it takes time. The first part of a community to adopt the new ideology is the Civil Service. With Constantine's conversion, Christianity became for the first time a positive advantage in furthering a career, instead of a private and potentially dangerous commitment. Constantine offered special concessions to Christians. Soon the rich were flocking into the church for the sake of tax concessions, or to avoid wearisome service on city councils. At a humbler level, while Christians in the army were in church on a Sunday morning, their pagan colleagues were marched on to a parade ground to offer up generalized prayers for Constantine and his family. No doubt it was more comfortable in church.

Opposite: *The great domed interior of Santa Sophia.*

The emperor Theodosius presiding at a chariot race: base of obelisk in the hippodrome, Istanbul.

By 380 rewards for Christians had given way to penalties for non-Christians. In that year the emperor Theodosius made belief in Christianity a matter of imperial command:

> It is Our Will that all the peoples We rule shall practise that religion which the divine Peter the Apostle transmitted to the Romans. We shall believe in the single Deity of the Father, the Son, and the Holy Spirit, under the concept of equal majesty and of the Holy Trinity.
>
> We command that those persons who follow this rule shall embrace the name of Catholic Christians. The rest, however, whom We adjudge demented and insane, shall sustain the infamy of heretical dogmas, their meeting places shall not receive the name of churches, and they shall be smitten first by divine vengeance and secondly by the retribution of Our own initiative, which We shall assume in accordance with divine judgement. [1]

Theodosius takes for granted the close link between his own will and God's, and in that same year he even allowed himself to be described as 'the visible God'. It was a connection which was implicit from the start of the Christian empire. Constantine, for example, had prepared his own tomb in a church dedicated to the Holy Apostles. Monuments to the twelve apostles were arranged in two rows of six, with his own resting place in the middle. He was to be the thirteenth apostle, though the arrangement did somehow suggest that he was the first and he liked to be referred to as *Proto-Apostolos* (had not the Lord himself promised that the last should be first?).

Churches of the Christian empire were carefully designed to emphasize the new hierarchy of Christ and emperor. The style was borrowed from the east. A Greek traveller visited Persia in the second century and described a palace in which there was 'a hall covered with a dome, the inside of which was adorned with sapphires sparkling with a celestial blue brilliance, and standing out against the blue background of the stones were golden images of the gods, glittering like stars in the firmament'. [2] This was to be the pattern for the mosaic-encrusted interiors of Byzantine churches — displaying, if not 'golden images of the gods', at least God and the demi-god who represented him on earth.

If Santa Sophia still had its original interior, this would be the place to see the spectacular hierarchy of the Christian empire. Justinian, who rebuilt it in the sixth century, was the most powerful emperor since Constantine, and when he entered the completed church he felt able to boast: 'Solomon, I have surpassed thee.' But time has dealt cruelly with Santa Sophia. Christian iconoclasts had hacked nearly all its mosaics from the walls long before Muslims turned it into a mosque. Today one of the few surviving images acknowledges the foundation of the city and the building of the church (in one of the entrance passages the Virgin Mary is offered the city by Constantine and the church by Justinian), but for the real glories of Byzantium one needs to go elsewhere — to Ravenna, on the coast of Italy.

Images of the Orthodox empire. Opposite: *A monk in St Catherine's, Sinai, a monastery founded by Justinian.* Overleaf: *The grand finale: the skyline of cathedrals in the Kremlin, Moscow.* Facing page 41: *One of the monasteries at Meteora in Greece.*

Justinian and Constantine with the Virgin and Child: entrance to Santa Sophia.

With the capital of the empire established in the east, Ravenna became a place of importance as the chief seaport on the journey from Rome to Constantinople. By a series of lucky accidents the city has escaped the ravages both of war and of iconoclasm. Elsewhere there are only a few scattered examples of Christian paintings and mosaics which survive from the early centuries — some in Rome, 41 in Thessalonica, in Sinai. But hidden among the everyday streets of Ravenna there are no less than six churches which were built and lavishly decorated before the year 600.

Christianity has made more use of images than any other religion, and in the early centuries they were specifically used to emphasize the majesty of the emperor and of his powerful colleague above. The relationship can best be seen in the church of San Vitale, which was built in Ravenna while Justinian was emperor. Its mosaics sum up the Christian empire.

Above sits Christ, enthroned on a circle representing the universe. He is accompanied by his archangels and saints. He still has the fresh, clean-shaven face of the Jesus of the early Christians; but he is sitting now in majesty, holding the law. As the centuries pass he will become a sterner figure, more emperor than friend, staring down from the dome of Eastern Orthodox churches. Christ Pantocrator, he was called: Christ the Ruler of Everything.

Below, to one side, is the emperor: Justinian. Like Christ he has a halo. To match Christ's title, he called himself Cosmocrator, Ruler of the Universe. Ruler of everything and ruler of the universe; there was little to choose between them. Roman emperors had called themselves Cosmocrator and had been seen with

The emperor Justinian with his bishop, Maximian, and retinue: sixth-century mosaic in San Vitale, Ravenna.

42

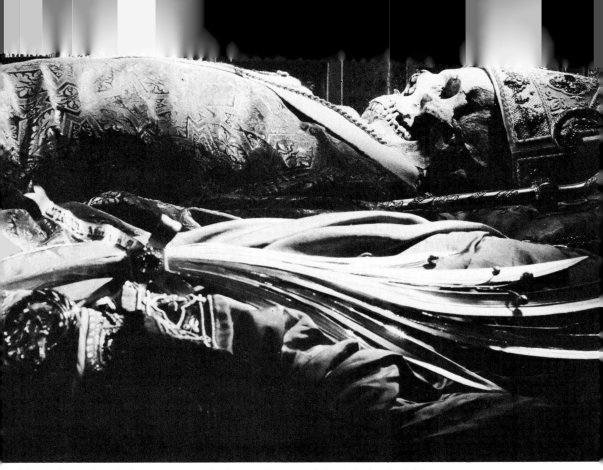

The skeleton of St Ambrose in episcopal robes, in the crypt of Sant' Ambrogio, Milan.

haloes long before they were Christian. From their point of view it was Christ, not them, who was the new member of this club. And as Jesus has his archangels and saints, so the emperor has his bishop, Maximian, and his priests and his soldiers. His court is the earthly reflection of Christ's. From time to time Justinian even entertained his bishops and other dignitaries to a version of the Last Supper. And it was he, rather than the bishop, who played the central role.

Maximian, standing obediently beside his emperor, was to be typical of bishops in the Christian empire of Constantinople — the bishop as imperial servant. But not all prelates, particularly in the west, could be relied on to accept this role. And the most distinguished of those who rejected it was St Ambrose, the bishop of Milan.

One event in the life of Ambrose became famous as an example of how a bishop could tame a prince. In the year 390 there was a riot in a city in Greece — all because a popular charioteer had been put in prison — but during the riot the governor of the city was killed. The emperor Theodosius was in Milan at the time, and he sent orders for a brutal punishment. Several thousand fans of the charioteer were invited into their local circus to see a special performance. Once they were in, the gates were closed and the emperor's soldiers set about killing

43

Medieval image of St Ambrose enthroned as bishop, engraved inside a silver bowl (Treasury, Sant' Ambrogio, Milan).

them. The massacre lasted three hours, more than 5,000 died. When Ambrose heard the news, he told the emperor that he could not give him Communion until he had done public penance for the crime. For a while Theodosius stayed away from church, but in the end he accepted Ambrose's terms. In front of a crowded congregation he took off his splendid imperial robes and asked pardon for his sins. He had to do so on several occasions until at last, on Christmas Day, Ambrose gave him the sacrament.

It seems natural enough to us that a priest should object if one of his parishioners kills 5,000 people, but it required remarkable courage to humiliate in this way a Byzantine emperor. Ambrose had hit upon the weapon — the threat of excommunication — which the western church would later use again and again to bring rulers to heel. But at the centre of the Christian empire, in Constantinople, no bishop ever stepped so far out of line. The simple pottery bowl from which Ambrose used to eat was later enclosed in a silver one, on which there was carved a picture of him sitting on his throne — an image of absolute spiritual authority. It was an idea of the bishop which rulers in the west grudgingly came to accept.

Today, in the Milan church named after St Ambrose, the services are Roman Catholic — recognizably different from the form of worship associated with the Byzantine emperors, which we now know as Greek Orthodox. But orthodox merely means correct; catholic is a word for universal. We might equally well refer to them as Greek Catholic and Roman Orthodox. It was just a case of each side, east and west, claiming to have the right form of Christianity. But in the Christian empire, where politics and religion were almost the same thing, heresy became a form of treason. If the empire was to hold together, the emperor had to make sure that everyone accepted his interpretation of Christian doctrine. In small modern countries, with easy communications, we find it impossible to agree among ourselves on matters of politics. So what chance was there, in the vast Christian empire, of everybody agreeing on that incomparable mystery at the heart of Christianity, the nature of the Trinity?

The amazing variety of ways in which painters have tried to depict the Trinity suggests how hard the concept is to grasp. Three gods in a religion which insists that it has only one, Three in One and One in Three, each identical and yet different? Even one of the greatest of medieval saints, St Bernard, described it as incomprehensible. And the best known of the three, a Being begotten not made,

Different interpretations of the Trinity: fifth-century mosaic in the baptistry at Albenga, and painting by El Greco (Prado, Madrid).

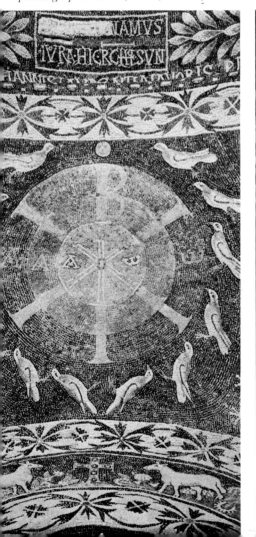

wholly human and yet wholly divine? With such mysteries to disagree upon, it was not long before everyone was calling somebody else a heretic.

As early as the fourth century, a bishop described Constantinople itself as seething with precisely these topics of discussion:

> If in this city you ask anyone for change, he will discuss with you whether God the Son is begotten or unbegotten. If you ask about the quality of bread, you will receive the answer that 'God the Father is greater, God the Son is less.' If you suggest that a bath is desirable, you will be told that 'there was nothing before God the Son was created'.[3]

The debate can be heard continuing in the theological treatises of these early centuries:

> If the Father begat the Son, he that was begotten had a beginning of existence; hence it is clear that there was a time when the Son was not.[4]

> No. The Son has been always with the Father, not only since time began, but before all time. For the Father could not have been so named unless he had a Son; and there could be no Son without a Father.[5]

> If you say that the Holy Spirit proceeds from the Father as the Son does, why do you not say that he is the brother of the Son? If he proceeds from the Son, why do you not say he is the grandson of the Father?[6]

> The Son is not the Father, but is what the Father is; nor is the Spirit the Son, but is what the Son is. These Three are One if you look at the divinity, and the One is Three if you take account of their distinguishing characteristics. Nor are the Three split up by these modern pestiferous dividings.[7]

The difficulty was that the gospels mention the Father, the Son and the Holy Spirit, but not the concept of the Trinity. That was developed later to answer criticisms that Christianity seemed to have more than one god. I suspect that most Christians today accept the Trinity without troubling themselves too much over the details: something so long established can be treated as a piece of sublime mysticism. But in the early years it had the more nagging quality of a piece of unfinished research, something about which the facts were still to be fully discovered. In the third century Origen described the matter as work in progress:

> With regard to the Holy Spirit it is not yet clearly known whether he is to be thought of as begotten or unbegotten, or as being himself a Son of God or not, but these are matters which we must investigate to the best of our power from holy scripture.[8]

The fourth century produced the basic formula that there were three divine persons in one divine essence, but that left a great deal still to be argued about. (Even today typography reveals continuing inequalities: some books refer to both Son and Holy Spirit as 'He', others reserve 'He' for Jesus and let the Holy Spirit make do with 'he'.) And within the Trinity there were further problems. Jesus is both God and man. Had he existed as long as God his father? Did he cease to be God during the brief period of the incarnation? Could he perhaps be better described as God taking on the appearance of man? Or as a man so perfect that he resembles God? Vast sections of the empire would differ from Constantinople, and from each other, on these matters. Nestorians in Syria believed that Jesus had two quite separate natures; Monophysites in Egypt insisted that he only had one; and Rome was increasingly going her own way on the matter of his relationship with the Holy Spirit. Heresy was the regionalism of a theological age. Today the Church of the Holy Sepulchre in Jerusalem is a tiny microcosm of these tensions within the Christian empire, a miniature battlefield on which the struggle still continues between those sects which deviated from the orthodoxy of Constantinople. The building is shared by the six regional churches which in the fifth century were already establishing themselves as separate branches of Christianity: Greek, Roman, Armenian, Syrian, Egyptian, Ethiopian. The priests of these six churches find it almost impossible to agree among themselves even on repairs to their building, the holiest in Christendom. Every corner where an image might stand or an icon hang has been fought over with a tenacity usually reserved for principalities and kingdoms. The name of the present arrangement between the groups, the *Status Quo*, suggests that it is no more than a cease-fire. If the claims of territory and theology can be so divisive within one Christian shrine, there was small likelihood of agreement within the Christian empire.

Each sect naturally regarded itself as orthodox, and the central orthodoxy was that of the centre of empire — Greek Orthodoxy. But during the eighth century one of the most characteristic features of Greek Orthodoxy, its veneration of icons, was itself branded a heresy in Constantinople. Even the emperors, who had made such an effective display of the Christian hierarchy, now began to take seriously the Bible's second commandment: 'Thou shalt not make unto thee any graven image, or any likeness of any thing that is in heaven above, or that is in the earth beneath, or that is in the water under the earth.'[9] Image-breaking, or iconoclasm, became official policy. Mosaics were gouged from the walls, icons were daubed with whitewash. More than a hundred years of destruction explains the complete absence of early Christian art today in Constantinople. Ravenna escaped only by a lucky chance. At one point an iconoclast fleet was lying off shore, waiting to capture the city and destroy its mosaics. The ships were prevented from landing. But for that stroke of good fortune, we should know little of the splendour of early imperial Christian art: and, but for the ultimate victory of the image, Christianity itself would have followed a far less colourful course. But in 843 the empress Theodora restored the official veneration of icons. Her most powerful opponent, the patriarch of Constantinople, greeted the news with a final gesture of defiance. He took an icon and cut out its eyes. Oriental potentates have usually much enjoyed making the punishment fit the crime, and it is surprising the patriarch was not blinded himself. He was merely flogged. But the day on which the icons triumphed is still celebrated each year in the Greek church as the Feast of Orthodoxy.

Military losses, as well as heresies, whittled away the great empire of Constantine and Justinian. Hordes of barbarians in the west were followed by the rise of Islam in the east. In the late Middle Ages the original territories of Greek Orthodoxy were reduced to western Turkey, the Balkans and Cyprus. In 1453 even Constantine's city itself fell to the Turks. After eleven centuries, the original Christian empire was at an end and the Christians became a minority in a community run by Muslims. Without an emperor at their head, they looked to the patriarch for political guidance. For centuries he had stood obediently beside 47

One of the few surviving mosaics inside Santa Sophia, with shafts of sunlight like the whitewash of the iconoclasts.

the emperor in the Christian hierarchy, like Maximian beside Justinian on the wall of San Vitale at Ravenna. After 1453 the patriarchs were acknowledged by both Muslims and Christians as the leaders of the Christian community. It was a natural development of the old Christian empire, and one that leads equally naturally to the present role of Makarios in Cyprus.

Today only Greece and half Cyprus are still Greek Orthodox, out of the vast empire which was diverted into Christian paths by Constantine. But Orthodox Christianity had found one new area to expand into. In spite of pressures from Roman Catholic Europe in the west and from Islam in the east, a narrow funnel remained open to the north. Boris, king of the Bulgarians, was converted in the ninth century; Vladimir, grand prince of Kiev and of all Russia, in the tenth. The domes and delicacies of Byzantine architecture marched north, becoming ever more fanciful as they went and reaching an improbable peak in distant Moscow.

Opposite: *The sixteenth-century domes of St Basil's, in Moscow.*

Opposite: *A new Christian empire in the west; reliquary head of Charlemagne (Cathedral Treasury, Aachen).*

The earliest Russian chronicle tells a story of how Vladimir sent out envoys to report on the different religions of the world. They saw western Christianity in Germany, and found it unimpressive. They decided that Judaism would not suit the Russian people. On Islam, the prince cut them short when they came to the Prophet's views on alcohol. 'It is the Russians' joy to drink,' he said, 'this we cannot forgo.' But the envoys who had been to a service in Santa Sophia left him in no doubt:

> The Greeks led us to the edifices where they worship their God and we knew not whether we were in heaven or on earth. For on earth there is no such splendour or such beauty, and we are at a loss how to describe it.[10]

Russia was to make the aesthetic glories of Orthodox Christianity very much her own — so much so that the Greek word 'icon' is often thought of today as meaning a Russian painting. And gradually Moscow began to see herself as the leader of the Orthodox world. A theory grew up that there had been one Rome, in Italy, which had fallen to the barbarians and to the Roman Catholic heresy. There had been a second Rome: Constantinople. And when that fell to the Turks, there was a third Rome: Moscow. The emperor took his title from the first Rome — czar is the same word as Caesar — just as he had taken his religion from the second. In the year 1512 a monk wrote to the czar:

> Two Romes have fallen, but the third stands, and a fourth there will not be. Thou art the only Christian sovereign in the world, the lord of all *faithful* Christians.[11]

Cathedrals towering above the Kremlin walls, Moscow.

It is not only the onion domes of the east which make the Kremlin look so unusual as a European seat of government. What other country has a castle which contains within its walls no less than three cathedrals? Here, visibly, the emperor and his patriarch ruled side by side from a shared fortress; here the old themes of Constantinople and of Orthodoxy lived on. In the twentieth century, up to 1917, it was still possible to observe in Moscow the peculiarly Byzantine characteristics of an all-powerful Christian tyrant — and to savour the rich and evocative ritual which had so long expressed, and bolstered up, that almost divine authority.

From the start of the Christian empire there had been another great tradition, deliberately unlike the opulence of the imperial cult. A crumbling cliff in the Egyptian desert contains a group of caves in which there lived, in the fourth century, the man who is now regarded as the first Christian monk: St Anthony. The emperors were offering the most spectacular form of Christianity. The desert fathers who followed the example of St Anthony went to the opposite extreme. They did so partly out of protest against a society in which Christianity was becoming rather too fashionable, but they also had a deeper motive — to grapple with the devil. Jesus had been tempted by Satan in the wilderness and had overcome him. Every monk hoped to do the same. It was this side of St Anthony's life, his lurid temptations, which became a favourite theme for painters. The details they illustrated were given by Athanasius, a contemporary of Anthony's, who wrote his life:

> The enemy would suggest filthy thoughts, but Anthony would dissipate them by his prayers. The wretched devil even dared to masquerade as a woman by night. It was as though demons were breaking through the four walls of the little chamber and bursting through them in the forms of beasts and reptiles. All at once the place was filled with the phantoms of lions, bears, leopards, bulls, of serpents and asps, of scorpions and wolves. Anthony said: 'It is a sign of your helplessness that you ape the forms of brutes.'[12]

One might think Anthony and his followers were uncomfortable enough in their caves, but others soon outdid them. Hermits in Syria chose to live on the top of pillars — the famous stylites. The first, St Simeon, spent the last twenty years of his life on a column fifty feet high with nothing but a railing round the top to prevent him falling off. His fame was such that people came to visit him from as far away as the Atlantic coast, from Spain, even from Britain. Every afternoon a crowd would gather at the base of his pillar. People would shout up to him their problems, their fears, their worries, and the saint would yell back his advice. It was the original agony column. And soon there were people standing on pillars all over the Syrian desert. Even asceticism goes in fashions.

But the real contribution of monks in Christian history was to come not from individual hermits, however dramatic their particular form of isolation, but from monks gathered together in monasteries. It was in Egypt, during the life of St Anthony, that the first Christian monasteries were founded. Below the rocky hillside where he had his cave there has been for fifteen centuries a monastery

A street of monks' houses in St Anthony's monastery.

named after him: St Anthony's, standing in the desert like a walled fortress against Satan. Until recently the only way to get inside the great walls was to be hauled over the top on a winch.

The earliest monasteries were formed by hermits who chose to live near each other and to emerge from their caves on Sundays for communal worship and for a meal. Life in St Anthony's still shows traces of this pattern. The high walls enclose a pleasant oasis of palm trees and gardens. The buildings look much like any small Christian village, with several little streets grouped round the church, and in these streets each monk has his own house in which he prays, eats, sleeps —a distant descendant of the hermit's cave. The only formal gathering takes place each morning and evening, when the monks drone and mumble their way through the divine office in their tiny smoke-begrimed church.

By twentieth-century standards life in St Anthony's is very simple, but St Anthony himself would have considered it the height of luxury. There is only one country in the world today, which has been Christian almost from the start, and in which one can still find monks living with something of the early simplicity: Ethiopia.

Until 1974 Ethiopia was still essentially its own small Christian empire, with a tradition longer than any. Christianity had penetrated its mountain fastnesses as early as about 340. The imperial title 'Lion of Judah' is one of the phrases used for Christ himself in Revelation, and Haile Selassie — the name which Ras Tafari chose for himself in 1930 — means 'Might of the Trinity'. As with the empire of Constantinople, the Christian faith remained to the end an almost automatic requirement for high office even though only half the population were Christian (the others now being Muslim), and thriving communities of primitive monks still dot the rugged Ethiopian landscape as profusely as they once did the Egyptian desert. The monks live in the two most natural forms of isolation: on top of great rocks, and on islands. The earliest monastery, Debra Damo, consists of a village on a table-top of rock which rises sheer on all sides from the surrounding countryside. It is the same concept as St Anthony's, except that here the walls have been provided by nature and there has never been any winch to help the visitor: even today he must climb a fifty-foot rope to reach the door of the monastery. In keeping with the original monastic tradition, the monks have their own cells or houses (depending on their status) and only gather together in the church for worship. There are even more primitive monasteries on the many separate islands of Lake Tana. It may be inescapable poverty rather than principle which keeps the monks on the smaller islands at such a level of physical deprivation, but the result is certainly as close as it is possible to come to the daily lives of St Anthony and his followers.

Within the territories of the original empire, among the splendours of Byzantium, monasticism increasingly lost its early simplicity. The icons, which the monks themselves had painted over the centuries, turned each monastery into a treasure-house far removed from the lodging of the desert fathers or the stylites. What the Greek Orthodox monks did preserve from the original tradition was a

St Anthony and St Paul of Thebes, patron saints of desert monasticism, on a doorway in St Anthony's monastery.

A monk from one of the monasteries of Lake Tana.

Opposite: *The rope which leads up into the rock monastery of Debra Damo (the nuns in the foreground would be forbidden access, as women, even if they could climb the rope).*

greater separation from the everyday world than became common among monks in western Europe. Mount Athos, on which not even a female animal may set hoof or paw, is the best-known example of this isolation. But at Meteora, in central Greece, there are still monasteries which look like latter-day descendants of the stylites, each house perched on top of a massive pinnacle of rock. In this landscape entire communities have been able to follow, in rather greater comfort, the ancient calling of a hermit among the clouds. Only a few of them survive today (pestered by, and yet supported by, the intruding chara-bancs), but their intoning of the liturgy among a profusion of icons is a distant echo of the Christian empire, like a stone dropped into a well that is centuries deep.

55

CHAPTER THREE

The Birth of Europe

A Latin poet travelled through the south of France in about the year 415 and reported that the rocky islands off the coast were inhabited by a strange new breed: scruffy fellows, clad in squalid garments, who had turned their backs on worldly pleasures. Fifteen and a half centuries later there are still monks (rather less scruffy) on the island of Lérins. It is Europe's oldest surviving monastery.

The man who founded it was St Honoratus. Like most early monks in the west, he had probably been inspired by reading the life of St Anthony, the original Christian hermit in his cave in the Egyptian desert. Honoratus himself seems to have spent several years in Egypt, and when he came back to Europe he moved into a cave high up in the hills overlooking Lérins. But soon he changed it for a more extreme and literal form of isolation — life on an island.

The year when he probably crossed the water to Lérins was 410, which happened also to be a turning point in western history. In that year an army of barbarians captured Rome. For centuries wild men from the north had been making trouble on the borders of the empire, but the Romans had either tamed them or kept them out. It was nearly 800 years since any foreign enemy had entered Rome. So the fall of the capital city came as a profound shock. An author writing a few years before the disaster was able to take an optimistic view of world history, seeing the Roman empire as the divinely ordained foundation for the empire of Christ:

> What is the secret of Rome's historical destiny? It is that God wills the unity of mankind, since the religion of Christ demands a social foundation of peace and international friendship. Hitherto the whole earth from east to west had been rent asunder by continual strife. To curb this madness God has taught the nations to be obedient to the same laws and all to become Romans. This is the meaning of all the victories and triumphs of the Roman empire: the Roman peace has prepared the road for the coming of Christ. [1]

St Jerome, reacting to the barbarian invasions, wrote with a new pessimism:

> A remnant of us survives not by our merit, but by the mercy of God. Innumerable savage peoples have occupied the whole of Gaul. Who could believe that Rome, on her own soil, fights no longer for glory, but for her own existence; and no longer even fights, but purchases her life with gold and precious things. [2]

The barbarians had much to learn from Rome, but they also had a lively culture of their own. Swirling lines and vigorous animals and warriors provided the ingredients of this nomadic art. Generations of critics have dismissed this as primitive, but our own century has changed that from a word of abuse to one of praise. Today we appreciate the energy, the freshness of those swirling lines — which seem to reflect so accurately the restless movement of the barbarian tribes themselves over the map of Europe.

The climate of the snowbound north bred the toughest people in Europe and gave them the strongest possible reason for moving elsewhere. Goths, Vandals,

Opposite: *Monks on the island of Lérins.*

Previous pages: *A detail from the sarcophagus (Roman, second century) in which Charlemagne chose to be buried (Cathedral, Aachen).*

The animals and swirling patterns of barbarian art: details from the Gundestrup Cauldron, c. 100 B.C. (National Museum, Copenhagen), and from the Jelling Stone, tenth century (Jelling, Denmark).

Angles, Saxons, Danes, Vikings or Normans — all of Europe's most ferocious migrants came from in or near Scandinavia. The Goths began to shift south and east in the second century. The Vandals followed soon after. It was the Goths who reached Rome and sacked it in 410. The Vandals, after moving south through Spain, east along the north coast of Africa, and then briefly up into Italy, reached the same position and sacked the imperial city once again in 455.

No doubt many of the monks coming to join Honoratus on the island of Lérins did so to get away from a Europe that was falling into chaos. What they can't have imagined is that they themselves were building up a monastic tradition which in the long term would restore order to Europe. But over the water, on the north coast of Africa, there was a Christian writer who at this very time was almost predicting that future development.

St Augustine of Hippo was to become the most influential Christian theologian after St Paul. Each successive age would find new inspiration in his book *The City of God*, even though it had been written in response to one very specific event — the sack of Rome in 410. How was it, people were asking, that Rome's walls had been pierced after so many centuries? What had changed, since the great days of the empire? The gods had changed, came the hostile answer. The old gods of the empire had been abandoned. It was Christianity, the empire's new religion, which was to blame. This was a disturbing criticism, and Augustine took up his pen to argue the Christian case. His first line of defence was

60

frankly unconvincing, but one which has always been popular. Everything is God's will, therefore everything must be all for the best.

> The extremity of famine destroyed many Christians in these invasions. Now such as the famine made an end of, it delivered from the evils of this life. Such as it ended not, it taught them a sparing diet and ableness to fast.[3]

You can still find that sort of argument in religious pamphlets today, and it hasn't improved with age. But St Augustine's other defence was far more interesting. The fall of Rome was unimportant, he said, because it was an earthly city. All that mattered was the city of God, and this could never fall because it and all its citizens were immortal. Some were already in heaven. Others, the faithful Christians, were still on earth. While on earth they must play their part in life, but their real home was with God. They were in this world and yet out of it, which would later seem to have been a perfect description of a medieval monk. But that was a long way ahead. When St Augustine died, in 430, the Vandals were besieging his town of Hippo. Five years later they had made it their North African capital. It needed remarkable faith to see anything but darkness in the future.

The two places in Europe where Christianity did manage to hang on are still the fervent Catholic extremities of the Common Market: Italy and Ireland. Italy was understandable. Ireland was odder, and in that strange development Lérins also played its part. St Patrick may have been here while Honoratus was still alive: and when for some reason he decided to take the faith to Ireland (tell it not in Galway, but it seems he was born an Englishman), it was the eastern type of monasticism that he established there. The rocky-island variety, severe and ascetic, in the tradition of St Anthony.

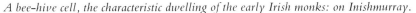

A bee-hive cell, the characteristic dwelling of the early Irish monks: on Inishmurray.

The Irish monks were gluttons for punishment. A monk who misbehaved could be beaten, and the normal position for prayer was with the arms held out in the position of a cross. Try that for more than a few Hail Marys and you will know the meaning of penance. The Irish penitentials (elaborate lists of crimes and punishments) imagined a lurid range of transgressions. The first sentence of the earliest list, from the sixth century, plunges straight in at the deep end:

> A boy who communicates in the sacrament although he has sinned with a beast shall do penance for a hundred days on bread and water.[4]

Among other deadly sins, gluttony before Communion was imagined in even more startling detail:

Holy Island, or Lindisfarne, seen from the coast.

He who vomits the host because of greediness, forty days of penance . . .

If he ejects it into the fire, he shall sing one hundred psalms . . .

If a dog laps up his vomit, he who has vomited shall do penance for one hundred days.[5]

Overheated thoughts, perhaps, from a cold cell on an empty stomach, but one of the more trivial offences does suggest rather well the twin temptations threatening an ascetic monk, lust and drowsiness:

He whose sperm flows whilst he is sleeping in church shall do penance for three days.[6]

Meanwhile these monks were busy with the task which has made them famous — copying and illustrating the sacred texts. The basic craft of the medieval monastery was becoming established, and some of the most beautiful of early Christian manuscripts were produced by Irish monks in their draughty cells. The relentlessly interlacing lines of their favourite type of pattern pick up the swirling energy of barbarian art and carry it one crucial step forward towards sophistication — without losing any of the energy. The scribes may well have grumbled at the conditions in which they worked (indeed from occasional complaints written in the margins we can hear them doing so), but the results were magnificent.

> Twenty days to Easter Monday and I am cold and tired.

> I am Cormach, son of Cosnamach, and there is some devil in this ink.

> Thin ink, bad vellum, difficult text.

> Do not reproach me concerning the letters; the ink is bad, the parchment scanty, the day dark.

Or, on occasion, more cheerfully:

> I have written this book for love of the Irish, because I am myself an Irishman.[7]

The Irish have a habit of leaving Ireland, and the early monks were no exception: in the sixth century the country's chief export seems to have been saints. Their itching feet took them trudging farther and farther from home, until soon they were founding Celtic monasteries as far away as Switzerland and Italy. The first step had been across the Irish sea to Iona, an island off the west coast of Scotland, where St Columba settled in about 563 with twelve monks, echoing the twelve disciples. An island near to the land was still their ideal choice for a monastery, and when Celtic monks later came down from Scotland into Northumbria they found somewhere which seemed perfect — Lindisfarne, also known because of the monks as Holy Island. At high tide it is an island. At low tide you can walk ashore. What could be better for a monk who is both in and out of the world?

Even before Lindisfarne was founded, Irish monks had spread deep into Europe, far from the sea and the safety of islands. In about 590 another party of twelve set sail from Ireland to France. They landed not knowing what was ahead of them, and offering a brand of Christianity that was singularly strict. Yet their success was astonishing. One of the party, Gall or Gallus, reached what is now Switzerland before he found a cave that suited him. A flourishing Swiss town now stands at the place and bears his name: St Gall. The leader of the group, St Columban, went even farther and crossed the Alps. An Italian place-name, Mezzano Scotti, still commemorates the distant time when the Irish were there — and when, to the eternal confusion of schoolboys, the people who lived in Ireland were called Scots. It is near Bobbio, where St Columban established his final monastery. Nothing remains of the monastery today, and even in its own time it was something of an impertinence. Bobbio was only a few hundred miles north of Rome. And the pope in Rome had already launched a counter-offensive, sending monks of his own north and west as the Irishmen moved south and east.

The tradition carried north by the Roman monks was a more gentle one than the rigid discipline of the Irish. It derived from St Benedict, a rich young Italian who retired soon after the year 500 to the valley of Subiaco, forty miles east of Rome. There were already hermits here, and their caves looked down on the ruins of the palace of Nero. It was an apt contrast. Roman imperial authority was no more. In the coming centuries it would be St Benedict's monks who would unify the new Europe; in 1964 Pope Paul declared him the patron saint of Europe. The young Benedict, tradition says, began his monastic life with a self-denial more than sufficient for any Egyptian or Irishman. His cave was so isolated that food had to be lowered to him on a rope. His only companion was a raven, and when teased by a lustful thought he would fling off his rags and leap into a bush of thorns. But his fame as a holy man spread and people came to seek him out — particularly other monks, begging him to organize them in communities. It was this, his ability to create an organization, which was to be his great contribution. In the valley of Subiaco he founded no less than twelve monasteries. The rule which St Benedict devised for them emphasized the change from the harsh ways of Egypt:

A monastery should, if possible, be so arranged that everything necessary — that is, water, a mill, a garden, a bakery — may be available.

For bedding, a mattress, a woollen blanket, a woollen under-blanket, and a pillow shall suffice.

We read that wine is not suitable for monks. But because, in our day, it is not possible to persuade the monks of this, let us agree at least that we should not drink to excess. We believe that one pint of wine a day is enough.

For the daily meal let there be two cooked dishes, so that he who happens not to be able to eat of one may make his meal of the other. Avoid excess — above all things, that no monk be overtaken by indigestion.

When the brothers rise for the service of God, let them gently encourage one another, because the sleepy ones are apt to make excuses.[8]

Europe was ready for this more gentle monasticism. It was Pope Gregory the Great (incidentally the biographer of St Benedict), who first sent monks out as missionaries from Rome. He sent a party of them to distant and barbaric England under Augustine — another St Augustine, who would become known as St Augustine of Canterbury.

Just two details of English history stick in the minds of most of us from those distant centuries, when monks first came from Rome to England. One is a flattering story, Pope Gregory's famous comment on the English:

Gregory saw some boys in Rome for sale, with fair complexions, fine-cut features, and beautiful hair. He enquired from what country they came. 'They come from the island of Britain, where all the people have this complexion.' He then asked whether the islanders were Christians, or whether they were still ignorant heathens. 'They are pagans.' 'Alas', said Gregory with a heartfelt sigh: 'how sad that such bright-faced folk are still in the grasp of the author of darkness, and that such graceful features conceal minds void of God's grace! What is the name of this race?' 'They are called Angles.' 'That is appropriate,' said Gregory, 'for they have angelic faces.'[9]

The other detail at the back of the mind is the name of the English monk who recorded that story – the Venerable Bede. It is typical of Bede that he carefully labelled the unlikely tale of the angelic English boys a 'story, handed down by tradition'. He was a serious historian, and he had a fascinating subject. He was able to look back over more than a century during which the Christianity of Rome had struggled against the Celtic Christianity which had been here before it.

Pope Gregory had sent Augustine and his party of monks to convert the English in 596. Augustine seems to have been a rather timid character. Bede describes how at the last minute he turned back from his journey, complaining that the English were far too 'barbarous, fierce and pagan' to be visited. But Gregory insisted, and when Augustine finally crossed the Channel it all turned out to be surprisingly easy. The king of Kent had a wife, Bertha, who was already Christian. She even had a church in Canterbury. Through her, Augustine was able to settle and to become the first archbishop of Canterbury: and Canterbury acquired, what it has had ever since, the Primacy of All England. But not without a struggle. Gregory appointed Augustine head of the Christians in England, but nobody had consulted the Christians in England. They didn't take kindly to a stranger who arrived and announced that he was their leader: and the Romans were equally horrified to find themselves disobeyed. They complained forcefully about the natives:

> Until we realized the true situation we had a high regard for the devotion both of the Britons and of the Scots. On further acquaintance with the Britons, we imagined that the Scots must be better. We have now, however, learned that the Scots are no different from the Britons in their practices.[10]

The chief disagreement was over the date of Easter, a subject on which Bede himself wrote two learned volumes. It sounds trivial, but the great churches of Rome and Constantinople were to split over equally small matters. In both cases the true quarrel was over who should dominate whom, not over the details — though Easter could cause practical difficulties as well. Bede says that the local royal household in Northumbria was split down the middle. The queen had gone over to Roman customs, the king was still using Celtic ways. As a result, he explains, 'when the King had ended Lent and was keeping Easter, the Queen and her household were still fasting.' Enough to ruin any family Easter. The matter was resolved when the king called a meeting at Whitby, in 664, between the two sides. Oddly they both agreed to accept his decision, and he decided for Rome — or for his wife. Again and again, in the early history of Christianity, it was women who showed the way. The decision was a crucial step towards the centralized Europe of the later Middle Ages. From then on the inspiration of the Celtic church was merged with the organizational advantages of the Roman. When the monks of Lindisfarne came to make their famous gospel, the monastery had already gone over from the Celtic to the Roman rites. The abstract pages still have the restless and primitive interlacing lines, but the human figures are in the realistic style which derived from Rome. The two traditions together would inspire a new generation of monks — the Anglo-Saxon missionaries who converted northern Europe.

The first full account of northern Europe had been written by Tacitus in the year 98. He said it was a place of bristling forests, foul swamps, and sinister practices:

> At a set time, deputations from all the tribes gather in a grove hallowed by immemorial awe. The sacrifice of a human victim marks the grisly opening of their savage ritual. Another observance shows their reverence for this grove. No one may enter it unless he is bound with a cord, by which he acknowledges his own inferiority and the power of the deity.[11]

Various bogs in Denmark seem recently to have proved Tacitus right. The tannic acid in the peat has a remarkable quality of preserving bodies. Over the years these bogs have yielded up a macabre collection of leathery corpses, perfectly preserved, and some of them may well have been sacrificial victims. The man found at Grauballe died (with his throat slit) some 200 years after Tacitus, or more than 1600 years ago: Tollund man, with a noose round his neck, had died before the time of Tacitus.

The most successful English missionaries were Willibrord, known as the Apostle of the Frisians, and Boniface — the Apostle of the Germans. By their time, in the late seventh and early eighth centuries, the human sacrifices had come to an end. But the people still sacrificed animals, and worshipped nature

Contrasting pages from the Lindisfarne Gospel (London, British Library): Celtic decoration for the opening page of St Matthew, and a realistic portrait of St Luke.

The head of Tollund man, 2,000 years old, still with the noose round his neck (Silkeborg Museum).

Opposite: *Detail from the Gundestrup Cauldron, a great bronze bowl used for ritual purposes, c. 100 B.C. (National Museum, Copenhagen).*

spirits among trees or beside water. These were abominable superstitions, and the missionaries reacted accordingly. The most famous incident, but it's only one of many, was when Boniface marched into a shrine in Germany which was sacred to Thor, the god of thunder. The cult object was a massive oak. Boniface, so the story goes, took an axe to it; at the very first stroke there was a mighty breath of wind, from God, and down it fell. The pagans marvelled and were converted, and the saint used the wood to build a chapel to St Peter.

The story, in detail, may be preposterous; but certain elements in it ring true. One is the sheer courage needed to walk into somebody else's holy place and start breaking it up — imagine doing so in a church or mosque today, even in our own rather unreligious age. And the other is the fact that Christian missionaries were not eliminating magic. They were offering to replace it with a superior magic. God blew and the tree fell down: unlikely. But it was the chance of a miracle, or of success in battle, which converted people in those days. Both Willibrord and

Boniface went everywhere with chests full of holy relics, bones of saints, which they had collected from Rome. These were the lucky charms which would replace ancient superstition.

With Rome as their official headquarters, the missionaries could claim to represent a superior and altogether more pleasant culture. A certain bishop of Winchester, sitting comfortably at home, sent Boniface some ideas on how to convince the pagans. One of his suggestions went:

> Ask them, Why have their gods allowed the Christians to possess the countries that are rich in oil and wine and other commodities, and have left them only the frozen lands of the north? The heathens are frequently to be reminded of the supremacy of the Christian world and of the fact that those who still cling to outworn beliefs are in a very small minority.[12]

The great tooth-like rocks of the Externsteine.

The deposition from the Cross, carved in the rock face at Externsteine, twelfth century.

They were not; but they were rapidly becoming so.

Sometimes Christianity came to terms with pagan customs by absorbing them. The dancing procession of St Willibrord is an example, held each year at his monastery town of Echternach in Luxembourg. Or the Christians merely appropriated the pagan shrine. Nowhere suggests the process so powerfully as the Externsteine, in north-west Germany. This is a place of mystery and magic, a natural home for the older gods, with pinnacles of rock rising from water and woods like a few surviving teeth in some primeval jaw-bone.

It is thought that the Saxons had a pagan shrine here at the time of Boniface. And just as he had built a church out of Thor's oak at Geismar, so the Christians here made the Externsteine their own. In the rock face there is carved a relief showing Christ being taken down from the cross. Its mood is essentially part of the new Europe; it could never have existed in Jerusalem, or Constantinople, or ancient Rome. The dead body of Christ sagging over the back and shoulders of the man who lifts him down is far from realistic, but it is intensely expressive. 71

A figure from the Utrecht Psalter, c. 830 (University Library, Utrecht).

The realism of classical sculpture has been distorted by the vigour of primitive art to form what we now call Romanesque — the development of Roman culture which Christianity and the barbarians rescued from the rubble of the empire. The vitality of this compromise had been seen as early as the ninth century in the superb illustrations to the Utrecht Psalter. But it was above all in the more public art of stone-carving, as at Externsteine, that Christian Europe was to express its new identity.

The turning point, for Externsteine, may have come in the year 772. Before then the Saxons had been worshipping the pagan gods who seem the most natural inhabitants of these rocks. But in that year they were invaded by a Christian army which smashed their shrines and stole the gold and silver ornaments of their cult. It was the beginning of a long campaign to convert the Saxons by force.

The leader of the army was Charlemagne, and being converted by him was a very different experience from being converted by Boniface. Refusing to be baptized carried the death penalty in Charlemagne's book of laws. The chronicles say that on one day 4,500 reluctant Saxons were executed for not worshipping the right god. State Christianity, long familiar in the eastern empire, was

Opposite: *The bog at Grauballe in Denmark; and the man who was thrown into it 1,600 years ago, possibly as a sacrificial victim.*
Overleaf left: *Irish Christian carving of the seventh century (White Island, Lough Erne).*
Overleaf right: *Antique cameo of the emperor Augustus set in the cross of Lothair II, c. 1000 (Cathedral Treasury, Aachen).*

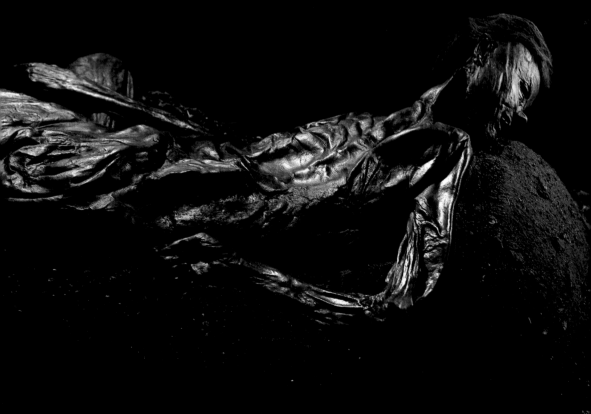

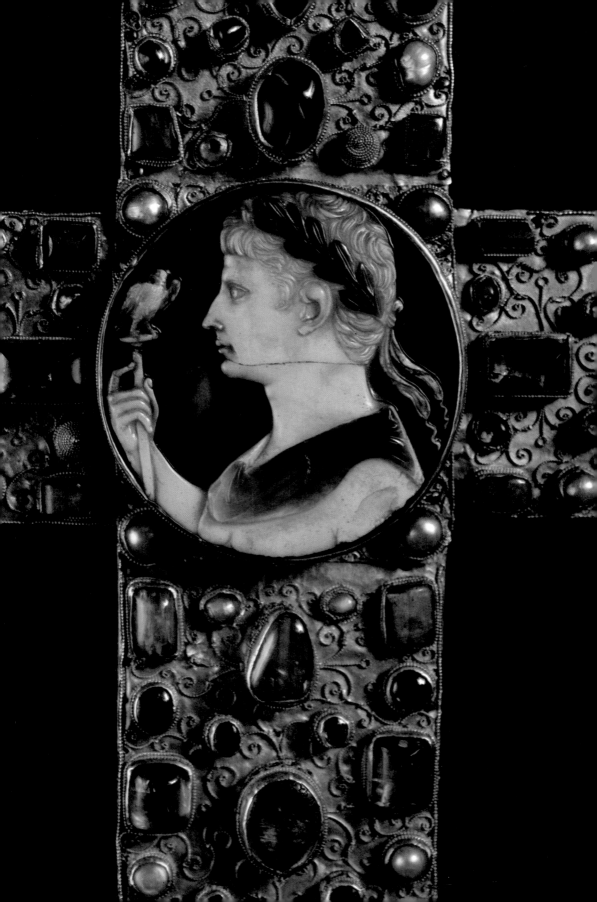

Charlemagne's royal chapel, now part of Aachen cathedral.

Opposite: Thirteenth-century stained glass in the cathedral at Bourges, showing the crafts of various guilds.

returning to Europe. It was the logical step forward. For nearly three centuries there had been hopes of a new Constantine in the west — a ruler who would adopt Christianity and impose the religion on wide territories. Clovis was one of the first rulers to be baptized, in about the year 500. He was a ruthless chieftain, and he was baptized at Rheims with some 3,000 of his warriors, but it was not until Charlemagne that any ruler had the strength or the conviction to spread Christianity through Europe as a matter of policy. Charlemagne was by nature an empire-builder. The bricks of his empire were the usual ones, imperial soldiers: but the mortar was Christianity, a Civil Service of Christian clerics and monks. Church and state were hand in hand again.

A crucial meeting had occurred some twenty miles from Externsteine, in Paderborn, where Charlemagne had built himself a palace. A pathetic figure came here in the year 799 — a pope, Leo III, who had recently been set upon during a religious procession in Rome by a rival bunch of clerics. They had tried to put out his eyes and to cut out his tongue, and had accused him — by way of explanation — of perjury and adultery. He came to Charlemagne for help. Nobody knows what they discussed that summer of 799 in Paderborn, but it is very likely that they made a deal by which Charlemagne would be crowned emperor. Certainly Charlemagne gave Leo his support, and travelled to Rome the following year to show as much. On Christmas Day, 800, he was kneeling at Mass in St Peter's when the pope suddenly popped a crown on his head and the assembled congregation acclaimed him emperor of the Romans. Charlemagne immediately pretended that he knew nothing of this plan, and that he was mildly displeased at what the pope had done. Well, politicians have a way of expressing surprise and shock when some new honour is forced upon them. And though the legal emperor was still the one in Constantinople, Charlemagne's title did reflect the realities of power. The Byzantine emperor, far away, often weak and always suspicious of Rome, was no protector to the pope. Charlemagne was able to protect him, and eager to do so. The phrase Holy Roman Empire was not coined until later. But in Charlemagne and Leo the twin cornerstones of medieval Europe — emperor and pope — were already in place.

Charlemagne's idea of his own dignity involved identifying himself with earlier emperors. In his capital at Aachen (a site chosen largely because he liked to relax in its hot sulphur springs) his palace was based on the Roman imperial palace at Trier and his chapel was a direct imitation of the eastern emperor's church of San Vitale at Ravenna. Even Charlemagne's writers became so classi-cally minded that they were no longer able to describe the reality in front of their eyes. A poem of 799 lists the new buildings going up in Aachen. There is the senate; well, that may be a justifiable bit of translation into Latin. There are marble baths; and these, with Charlemagne's love of the hot springs, there probably were. There is a theatre; odd that we should have heard nothing elsewhere of plays being performed before Charlemagne, but even so, perhaps. And there is a harbour. A harbour? At Aachen? It turns out that the poet was imitating the description of Carthage in Book One of Virgil's *Aeneid*.

It was typical that Charlemagne himself chose to be buried in an antique Roman sarcophagus, which he found in Italy and brought back to Aachen. But it was also typical that no one in later centuries could quite believe that he had been buried in so ordinary a fashion as lying down in a coffin. Charlemagne appears in later medieval art as the ideal ruler, and his legend grew accordingly. You have to go back a thousand years to Alexander, or come forwards a thousand years to Napoleon, to find any European figure of comparable stature. The Czech word for a king, *kral*, is only his name — Karl, Charles. His chariot is up in the heavens as Charles's Wain or Wagon — an old popular name for the Great Bear. And when a later emperor decided to open up his tomb, in the magic year 1,000, even an eye-witness wrote an account which bore no conceivable relationship to reality:

> We entered in unto Charles. He was not lying down, as is the manner with the bodies of other dead men, but was sitting as though he were alive, on a chair. He was crowned with a golden crown and held a sceptre in his hands, the same being covered with gloves, through which the nails had grown. We sank upon our bended knees before him. And straightway Otto the Emperor clad him in white raiment, and cut his nails, and made good all that was lacking about him. But no part of his body had corrupted or fallen away, except a little piece of the end of his nose, which the Emperor caused at once to be restored with gold; and he took from his mouth one tooth, and built up the tabernacle again, and departed.[13]

Charlemagne's favourite book was St Augustine's *City of God*, and he thought of himself as establishing the city of God in this world. His political programme, by which he and the monks would inherit the earth, was in fact like a debased version of St Augustine's dream; and it would be the pattern of the later Middle Ages. But Charlemagne was over-optimistic. Before the Middle Ages settled down, there was to be one further upheaval: a final eruption of yet another wave of barbarians, following the traditional trail down from Scandinavia. When Charlemagne died, the Vikings to the north were already on the move.

Bede's monastery at Jarrow was burnt by the Vikings in 794. Its fate was typical. Monasteries were easy plunder for this new wave of sea-going barbarians. They were full of valuable objects and of fat harmless monks: and their favourite position, on islands or on the coast, now made them more rather than less vulnerable. Lindisfarne had been destroyed a year before Jarrow. Iona would fall just ten years later. And then it was the turn of Ireland. The Christian civilization which had spread east from Ireland through England to northern Europe was now being rolled back along the same route. But Christianity has made a habit of surviving. When the Vikings finally settled among Christian people, they gradually adapted to Christian ways. A proud stone at Jelling in Denmark announces, in 980, that even a Viking homeland has gone Christian:

> King Harald ordered this monument to be made in memory of his father and of his mother: that Harald who won the whole of Denmark for himself and Norway, and made the Danes Christian.[14]

The Vikings had moved as far and as fast as any of the previous hordes of barbarians leaving Scandinavia. They even followed precedent to the extent of sacking Rome, in 1084. But by then they were settling down. And the most powerful of all the Viking groups were no longer known as Vikings, but as Northmen, or Normans.

Durham suggests the strength of the Vikings once they had settled down as Normans and Christians. Castle and cathedral, side by side on top of the powerful riverside cliff: the Christian bishop and the barbarian warrior are finally hand in hand, after a long and often embarrassing courtship. The rounded arches which the English call Norman are part of the wider tradition known in Europe as Romanesque. The last wave of barbarians was safely under the wing of the Christian church and within the traditions of the Roman empire.

When the castle and cathedral were being built at Durham, there was a Benedictine monastery on the hill-top as well. And a citizen of Durham could now travel through Europe finding similar monasteries everywhere. The barbarian love of movement continued in the form of pilgrimage. Along the great pilgrim routes Benedictine monasteries sprang up to cater for both the bodies

Opposite: *Christ on the Cross: one face of the Jelling Stone.*

The nave of Durham cathedral, twelfth century.

and souls of the travellers. The pilgrims and the rich pickings of feudalism brought wealth to the monasteries, and wealth brought the monks an ever more comfortable way of life. Their buildings grew more impressive. The cloisters were invaded by sculptures of those weird and wonderful monsters which had previously so delighted the barbarians. Monkish manuscripts became more fanciful. And the monks spent more and more of each day not in penance, not at work in the fields, but praising God in the glorious language of medieval plainsong — a joy to sing and a joy to listen to. The Benedictine world seemed to have realized the dream of both St Augustine and Charlemagne. Surely this was the city of God on earth: and very pleasant it was. And then, suddenly, a harsh interruption:

> What are these ridiculous monsters doing in the cloisters? What are these filthy apes, ferocious lions, monstrous centaurs doing there? Good God, even if one is not ashamed of these stupidities, one must regret the waste of money.[15]

It was the voice of St Bernard, the most influential monk in the entire Middle Ages. He disliked the Benedictine daily routine of divine worship as much as he disliked their art:

> Arouse yourself, gird your loins, put aside idleness, grasp the nettle, and do some hard work.[16]

St Bernard was a white monk, a Cistercian. It is his order which today occupies the ancient monastery on the island of Lérins. The Cistercians were the last great reforming movement from within the Benedictine order, and with them the final brick fell into place in the building of medieval Europe. They believed that hard work was part of a monk's holy calling. They planted new monasteries in the wild and uncultivated parts of Europe, and largely through them the land was tamed.

Bernard must have been an infinitely persuasive character: his entry into his first monastery proved as much. He was the son of a French nobleman, and his relations did their best to dissuade him from becoming a monk. He argued back. And instead of them keeping him out of the cloister, he took them into it. At the age of twenty-two he knocked on the door of the monastery at Citeaux, accompanied by about thirty of his male relations, including his father, four brothers and an uncle. At that time, in 1112, there was only one Cistercian monastery. Forty years later, at the time of his death, there were 343 dotted all over Europe. And the cause of this amazing expansion was very largely Bernard himself.

His forceful character exactly suited Europe at this high point of the Middle Ages. He stormed around preaching a crusade to the east. He took under his wing the Knights Templar, soldiers for Christ who wore a red cross over their white Cistercian robes. His brand of Christianity also answered the romantic needs of the time. Like any other knight, in this century which invented Courtly Love, he had his lady. And his most famous vision, known as the Lactation of the Virgin Mary, suggests that he won her favour. He was kneeling before a statue of Mary feeding the Holy Child, when the image came to life and squeezed some milk on to Bernard's lips.

St Bernard's fame did much to spread the medieval cult of the Virgin, though

'Filthy ape and ferocious lion': ridiculous monsters carved in the century of St Bernard (Victoria and Albert Museum, London).

he himself notably lacked her qualities of understanding and patience. He was aggressive, he was abusive — when he quarrelled with the bishop of Winchester, he happily referred to him as 'that old whore of Winchester, a thief and a robber' — and he was a devious politician who was quite unscrupulous in the methods he used to bring down his enemies, the most distinguished of whom was Peter Abelard. He had all the vices of a man who is tireless in a cause which he knows to

be right. And that cause was the service of a strong pope in the holy city of Rome, instructing an obedient Europe in the true Christian faith. Bernard may have longed only to meditate in a monastery cell — he frequently said so — but instead he trudged from council to diplomatic parley to private audience, manipulating the ecclesiastical politics of Europe. Three times he crossed the Alps in dead of winter, in his role as the twelfth century's Henry Kissinger.

By now a vast stream of documents was also perpetually on the move through Europe, travelling to and from Rome. Some were on the most trivial topics. How many cows could a particular monastery keep? Could a man be released from his vows because he was drunk when he made them? Others were on matters of high policy: excommunication of kings, or a papal banner sent to encourage one side or another in a battle. William the Conqueror was sent such a banner from Rome before he invaded England, and an arrow fell from the sky into the eye of King Harold. And the documents went on and on. We are not the first to wallow in bureaucracy.

But the remarkable fact was that from the most distant parts of Europe the descendants of Celts and Goths and Franks and Vikings were writing in one language, Latin, to one place, Rome. The language was that of the old Roman empire, the city had been its capital. The barbarians and Rome, through the medium of Christianity, had come to a fruitful compromise. And Rome had a new kind of empire.

The spirit of the age: a few years before the crusades began, this fortified tower was added to the ancient island monastery of Lérins.

CHAPTER FOUR

Faith and Fear

THERE are two conventional images of the Middle Ages. It is a toss-up whether the word 'medieval' first brings to mind a glorious picture, of soaring cathedral and snug walled town, or a darker theme — that same walled town from inside, its narrow crowded streets the home of disease, superstition, a gnawing sense of guilt, fear of death and of damnation.

It is hard to find traces in Europe today of the darker side of the Middle Ages. Our own century can match any in its obsessions and cruelties, but they bear a distinctively modern face. However, in the little village of Verges, in the north of Spain, the people still enact every Good Friday a pageant, which has been performed from beyond memory or written record and which has its roots firmly in the Middle Ages. Men in black tights, painted with white bones, pass convincingly for the skeletons of a Dance of Death as they gyrate with their scythes to the sombre rhythm of a drum. Their movement (turn to one side, pause, hop through 180 degrees to the other side, pause, hop back again to the first position) echoes more than the simple motion of death harvesting mortals with his scythe. It follows the pattern of a new medieval device for measuring time itself — the escapement of a clock. Time is death's relentless ally, reflected in the dance of skeletons at Verges. Repent now, before it is too late and the devil gets his hands on you.

Chartres has long established itself as the symbol of the more glorious side of the Middle Ages — with justification. Its cathedral is almost the earliest and one of the finest of nearly 200 built in the Gothic style in the thirteenth and fourteenth centuries. But each European country can provide its own examples of superb Gothic cathedrals perched above ancient cities. My own favourites outside France are Lincoln and Siena. The architecture of the three cathedrals is very different — Chartres with its spires and a profusion of elegantly elongated stone saints, Lincoln more four-square and chunky, presenting a proud slab of a façade, Siena striped like a zebra — but all three have one thing in common which says a great deal about the Middle Ages. Each of them, built on the highest part of the city, broods protectively over the narrow streets below. You can see the great cathedral as a work of faith, rising serene and confident above a world of superstition and cruelty: or as an astonishingly rich institution diverting the pennies of the people to the greater glory of God. In a sense it was both. And such ambiguities were characteristically medieval.

For the people who lived in these cities the building of a cathedral was more than a matter of pride, or even faith. It was an attempt to appease God. Enthusiasm and a sense of guilt were almost inseparable. People's sense of guilt gave them the energy to build their cathedral. And the cathedral gave them hope. Sometimes the whole community was moved to lend a hand in the great task, but increasingly it was the age of the professionals. Architects travelled Europe, rivalling each other's work and often pushing the technology of arch and buttress beyond its known limits. Independent craftsmen did the same, walking to any new city where there was work. They were a privileged class (the serfs working on the land were not free to move), and so the masons became

Opposite: *Thirteenth-century figures on the north doorway of Chartres cathedral.*

Previous pages: *The dead rise to face their maker on Judgment Day: thirteenth-century relief above the central doorway of Bourges cathedral.*

The cathedrals of Siena (above) and of Lincoln, towering over the surrounding houses.

Sculpture in the fourteenth century: relief by Andrea Pisano for the Campanile in Florence (now in the Museo dell' Opera del Duomo).

known as freemasons, and were able to form themselves into powerful masonic lodges. Craftsmen were aware of their growing wealth and importance. The guilds would happily pay for a window in the new cathedral, depicting some biblical event connected with their trade — and underneath it a little vignette showing themselves at work. The medieval cathedral was in every sense the centre of the community. As well as being a place for worship, it was somewhere to meet, to hold a discussion, or to transact business. It could even be a labour exchange. After Chartres cathedral was finished, its nave remained the place where craftsmen came in the hope of finding their next employer.

The cathedral at Bourges was begun in the same year as Chartres, 1195, and it offers the same dominant image. But here the fields come up almost below the cathedral wall. The medieval peasants who worked in those fields may have been poor and ignorant, but the church offered them one great consolation. Theirs would be the kingdom of heaven — a guarantee denied to the rich, who could enjoy themselves so well on earth. The rich man at Bourges was one of the richest in the whole of France, and one of history's most inspired patrons of art. He was the duke of Berry. He kneels still at prayer, beside an altar at the east end of 87

Bourges cathedral. In real life his prayer book, the *Très Riches Heures du Duc de Berry*, was decorated with a series of superb paintings. Some of them were clearly an aid to devotion. On other pages he could remind himself of his favourite castles, or enjoy portraits of his friends and courtiers. When it came to pictures of the peasants, the duke's artist had the tact to show them remarkably well dressed, but when they were working in the December snow even he could appreciate that their life was not quite like his own. It was not only the weather that was harsh. On the death of a peasant the landlord took his best beast, and the local priest his second best — even if he had only two. The abbot of Burton, in England, after confiscating his villeins' cattle during a dispute, took the opportunity of reminding them that they possessed 'nothing apart from their bellies'. A peasant's cottage in thirteenth-century Yorkshire had the same value as fourteen apple trees. Tenants in some places had to pay their lord a fine if an unmarried daughter became pregnant outside wedlock, quite apart from the girl's making

Opposite: The duke of Berry, kneeling at prayer in Bourges cathedral.

The old traditions continuing: the senior mason at Lincoln cathedral.

88

her own reckoning with God. The legal reason? Compensation for damage to the lord's property. The peasants protested in vain:

We are made men, in the likeness of Christ, but you treat us like savage beasts.[1]

A priest disagreed:

Peasants are coarse, blubbery, gluttonous, rough-skinned, dirty, and their crooked manners are a consequence of their crooked bodies.[2]

It was an attitude reflected in the English language. A churl was a poor freeman and a villein was just a serf. But 'churlish' and 'villainous' — the words still speak for themselves. Not everyone accepted this state of affairs:

Innocent people die of hunger, while the great wolves fill their bellies and pile up wealth. The grain, the corn — these are the blood and bones of the poor which have gone into the land, for which their souls cry to God 'Vengeance'.[3]

For most people it would have to be God's vengeance — not in this world, but in the next.

The most detailed architectural drawing in the duke of Berry's prayer book is the façade of his local cathedral at Bourges, which still stands unchanged. Every time that he, or anyone else, came to worship here they were reminded of a vengeance that threatened them when they were dead. Above the main entrance is a sculpture which make God's judgment all too plain. When the trumpet sounds on that Last Judgment Day, the graves open and naked men and women climb out to hear their fate. They are weighed in the balance and those found wanting are led off by devils to the burning cauldrons. The spikes and prods and bites of devils, the searing marks of pain on naked flesh — this was the scene, more than any other, that gripped the medieval mind.

Most of the people coming to church in the Middle Ages couldn't read: sculpture and paintings were described as 'books for the illiterate'. François Villon, France's great vagabond poet, wrote some lines for his mother:

I am a poor old woman who knows nothing; I never could read. In my parish church I see Paradise painted, with harps and lutes, and Hell, where the damned are boiled. The one frightens me, the other brings joy.[4]

Medieval writers and artists were fascinated by the possibilities of hell. An encyclopaedia of the thirteenth century explained where it was and what it was like:

There is in the middle of the earth a place which is called Hell. Thus much say I to you of this place, that it is full of fire and of burning sulphur. And it is over-hideous, stinking, full of ordure and of all evil adventure. And there is the fire so overmuch ardent, hot and anguishous that our fire and the heat thereof is no more unto the regard of that fire of Hell than a fire painted on a wall is in comparison to our fire.[5]

A soul in torment described herself in a vision to St Bridget:

My feet are as toads, for I stood in sin: a serpent creepeth forth by the lower parts of my stomach unto the higher parts, for my lust was inordinate; therefore now the serpent searcheth about mine entrails without comfort, gnawing and biting without mercy. My breast is open and gnawed with worms, for I loved foul and rotten things more than God. My lips are cut off. My nose is cut off. Mine eyes hang down upon my cheeks.[6]

It was believed that one of the pleasures of the blessed in heaven would be to behold the torment of the damned. A writer in about 1200 enumerated the joys of life hereafter, and listed this as the sixth:

The sixth and last cause of joy will be to behold the damned on the left hand, to whom the Judge will say 'Depart, ye accursed, into everlasting fire!'[7]

And it really was to be everlasting. There was no question of life meaning fifteen years.

One day a French nobleman wondered if the damned in Hell would be freed after 1,000 years, and his reason told him no; he wondered again if after 100,000 years, if after 1,000,000 years, if after as many thousand years as there are drops of water in the sea, and once again his reason told him no.[8]

This remains the official Roman Catholic belief. The *New Catholic Encyclopaedia* (1967) prints an article on hell which states that a dogmatic pronouncement in the year 543 defined the punishment of demons and the damned as unending: it then goes on to dismiss some later speculation (of a more merciful character) with the observation that these views are made untenable by the dogma of 543.

Demons and devils were everywhere in the Middle Ages, though they did have favourite haunts. They liked lettuce, for example, so there was a special

The devils and their cauldron: thirteenth-century relief above the central doorway of Bourges cathedral.

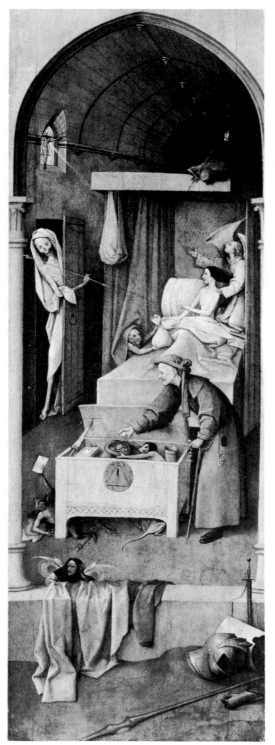

Opposite:
Skeletons dancing in the early hours of Good Friday, in the annual ceremony at Verges.

Death and the Miser, *by Hieronymus Bosch (National Gallery of Art, Washington).*

danger of swallowing one in a salad. But most of all they clustered round a death scene, particularly when it was a rich man clutching still at his money bags. Hieronymus Bosch's *Death of a Miser* is later than the Middle Ages, but it matches perfectly a medieval text:

> The devils haunt us most of all on our death bed. They ride like motes in the sunbeam; they are scattered everywhere like dust; they come down upon us like rain; their multitude fills the whole world; the whole air, the whole air I say, is but a thick mass of devils. Yet they can do nothing against the sign of the Cross. [9]

As the medieval centuries passed, so the obsession with death increased. The Dance of Death, where skeletons dance with the living, is a late invention. So is the Capuchin cemetery in Rome, where every scrap of decoration is some good friar's bone. *Memento mori*. Remember thou shalt die. Small chance of forgetting it here.

The centrepiece of the macabre display in the Capuchin cemetery is a complete skeleton carrying scythe and hourglass (these also being composed of fragments of long-forgotten friars). It is this same skeletal figure of death with his scythe which reappears each year in the Good Friday pageant at Verges. But here

death is only the prelude to the central performance of the evening — an ancient Passion play in which a villager plays Christ, as he stumbles along the street burdened down by a massive cross and by the blows of the crowd of extras. The emphasis is all on the suffering, the blood, the thorns forced deep into the flesh, the weals of the scourging — leading up to the ultimate torment of the Crucifixion itself. The suffering of Jesus for mankind is the central theme of Christianity, but the medieval fascination with every last detail gave a gory emphasis to the 'Passion' of Jesus, which it never had in the earlier centuries. To the villagers of Verges, watching their annual spectacle, it must almost seem as if the pain is the point of it.

Naturally the possibilities of this theme were seized on by painters, and as art moved in the later Middle Ages towards greater realism, so the earlier formality in representations of the Crucifixion gave way to the most detailed accounts of Christ's torment. Matthias Grünewald painted in the Renaissance, but he has been called the last great artist of the Middle Ages. In his Isenheim altar, the flesh of the crucified Christ seems almost to be rotting, as if those dark medieval obsessions could putrefy even Jesus himself, corrupting the incorruptible. Yet in this moment of horror lay the one and only hope. For Christ, so everyone believed, had risen even from this. Death, thou shalt die.

The only way of avoiding the devil and his cauldron was to do penance for one's sins whilst still on earth. But there were more pleasant ways of doing penance than wearing a hair shirt or saying a thousand Hail Marys, and the most pleasant of all was to go on pilgrimage. It was a serious business, travelling from shrine to shrine, but it was also a very good outing — this was the tourism of the Middle Ages. A party of pilgrims set out with just as much excitement as a package tour today, and they would be just as varied a group of people. Chaucer's Wife of Bath would be good value on any tour. She knew almost as much about pilgrimage as about love. Three times to Jerusalem, five husbands — a fair balance. And she had been on all the obvious shorter trips. She had been to Rome. She had visited the relics of St James at Santiago in Spain. She had inspected the remains of the Three Wise Men at Cologne. And if Chaucer had been writing a hundred years earlier, he might well have sent her to Vézelay — a small town in the centre of France, dominated still by its abbey church, which in the twelfth and thirteenth centuries was one of Europe's most popular places of pilgrimage.

Nowadays a place becomes a tourist resort if it has a good beach, or famous buildings and works of art. In the Middle Ages, when every tourist was a pilgrim, what mattered was relics — fragments of saints, which could range from a tiny splinter of bone to a whole skeleton. It was Mary Magdalene who brought the pilgrims to Vézelay. The abbey claimed to have her entire skeleton, and that was a powerful attraction. Pilgrims praying to a relic hoped that the saint, in heaven, would put in a good word for them; and who better than Mary Magdalene? She had herself been a sinner, it was believed even a prostitute, and yet she was a special friend of Jesus. She would understand; she could explain.

But there was a commercial value to relics too. A good relic would bring

The great entrance to the nave in the pilgrimage church of Mary Magdalene at Vézelay,
twelfth century.

people from miles around, and the clergy were quite ruthless in coming by these precious commodities. Saints were cut up, they were sold, they were even stolen. A bishop of Lincoln was much admired — in Lincoln — for the way he had brought a relic back to his cathedral. He had been abroad on pilgrimage, and had knelt down to kiss what was said to be another bone of Mary Magdalene — not at Vézelay, somewhere else. When no one was looking the good bishop managed to bite off the end of the bone, and he got his precious fragment safely home to Lincoln. That was a modest affront by the standards of the Middle Ages. When St Elizabeth of Hungary was lying in state in 1231, the mourners cut off her hair, her nails, and even her nipples. Each tiny portion would later inspire the faithful in some local church.

At Vézelay pilgrims are little more than a memory, and local Protestants long ago burned the remains of Mary Magdalene. At Chartres they still have relics and pilgrims. When the annual pilgrimage of students arrives from Paris, the look of the whole event may seem very different from the Middle Ages — with the modern paraphernalia of slogans held aloft and a brass band. The fear of hell and of God's wrath on the Day of Judgment are no longer the motive for pilgrimage in the twentieth century. But the feeling of the occasion must have been very much the same. Sheer enjoyment of the outing, a strong sense of celebration, and now, as in the past, at the end of the journey a solemn moment of wonder as the procession enters the great cavern of the cathedral, lit now with a thousand candles, and music swells up in greeting. If there is near darkness at ground level in the cathedral, above all is light, in glowing reds and blues. To a modern pilgrim the stained glass of Chartres comes as a revelation. In the thirteenth century, when the cathedral was built, it must have seemed even more amazing, for such a vast expanse of colour was something entirely new.

But it was the Virgin Mary who brought the medieval pilgrim to Chartres. She had become at that time the best-loved figure in the entire Christian hierarchy. For she combined, more than anyone else, both approachability and influence — as St Bernard explained:

> If you fear the Father, there is Christ the Mediator. If you fear Him, there is His Mother. She will listen to thee, the Son will listen to her, the Father to Him.[10]

The relic which more than any other brought the pilgrims to Chartres was *La Sainte Chemise*, the Holy Tunic. It was believed in the Middle Ages to have been the Virgin's undergarment when she was giving birth to Jesus. A most intimate relic, you might think, but not by medieval standards. One small reliquary at Chartres suggests very well how naïve, or how literal, the whole business of relics had become. It was designed to hold a relic of Jesus himself. As he had ascended into heaven, you could not have his skull or his bones as with an ordinary saint; you had to make do with parts of his body which he had shed before his death. This meant his milk teeth, various tears that he had wept, drops of blood. Most awe-inspiring of all, it meant the relic of the circumcision, and that was what the Chartres reliquary was designed to hold — what the French call *Le Saint Prépuce*, or in English the Holy Foreskin. At the height of the Middle Ages there were no less than fifteen foreskins of Jesus being worshipped in various churches around Europe. The best known of them all had been given to Charlemagne as an engagement present by the Empress Irene, but this one at

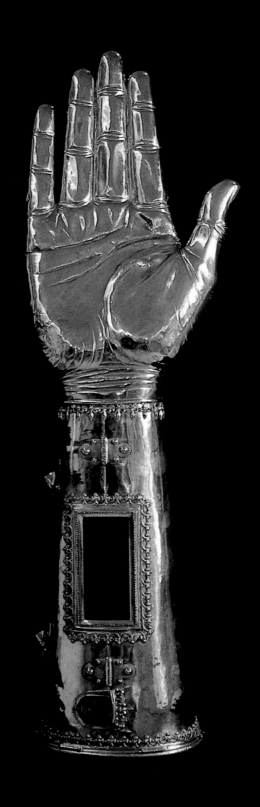

Chartres was a good second best. It was originally at Coulombs, and was extremely popular as it was believed to save women from pain in childbirth. Henry V of England stole it in 1422 to help his French wife, and the monks had great difficulty in getting it back. I am sorry to say it has long since vanished again, leaving us only with its precious casket.

Every great church had by now a vast number of relics (you could hardly go any earlier than at Canterbury, where they showed the pilgrims some of the clay which had been left over after God had fashioned Adam), and the reliquaries made to contain them were growing more ornate with each new century. These were the treasures of the church — literally so, for in a crisis the jewels from them would be sold. Rich men and rich churches were keen collectors.

One of the most delicately jewelled of all reliquaries was commissioned by our Croesus of Bourges, the duke of Berry, as a present for his brother, the king of France. It was designed to house one thorn from the Crown of Thorns. The long and treacherous-looking spine sits in a glass compartment, rather out of place at the centre of this lavish structure — of a type which Fabergé might have produced if asked for a small memorial of Prince Albert. But within the delicate context of precious metals and stones, the old themes still hold their own. Below the thorn the dead can still be seen clambering from their tombs on the Day of Judgment, but they are now tiny gold figures rising from a green-enamelled ground in place of the uncompromising weather-beaten stone above the west doorway at Bourges.

The most impressive reliquary of all was an entire chapel, the Sainte Chapelle in Paris, the biggest casket in the world. It was built by Louis IX, later St Louis, to house the Crown of Thorns itself, which he had bought in Constantinople. The king walked barefoot through the streets of Paris, bringing the precious relic to its exquisite Gothic home. The scene was an intriguing mixture of humility and pride. The walk through the streets echoed the suffering and humiliation of Christ; but the superb stained-glass windows in the Sainte Chapelle use the Crown of Thorns to add lustre to the crown of France. Later Louis spent another 20,000 marks on further treasures for his chapel, adding the swaddling clothes of Jesus, the lance, the sponge and the chain of the Passion, a portion of the True Cross, the rod of Moses, and part of the skull of John the Baptist.

There were always some who rejected the grandeur and wealth of the medieval church. Most of them Rome branded as heretics and persecuted. But one she wisely adopted as her own, and allowed him to found his own order of friars. He was born in 1182 in Assisi, the son of a rich cloth merchant. In his twenties he suddenly rejected his wealth — even to the point of taking off his clothes in the street to return them to his father. From then on he saw himself as married to Lady Poverty. He led a life of utter simplicity, working with his own hands to restore small churches and chapels. He was St Francis, founder of the Franciscans. The Poor Clares, a similar order for women, were established by his close friend and follower, St Clare (who miraculously saw events that were happening far away on the other side of the town and so is now the patron saint of television).

The spirit introduced by St Francis was something new in the medieval church. It was humble, but without a neurotic sense of self-mortification. His was a sunny, open-air kind of saintliness, responding to God and to nature with a

Opposite: *The treasures of the Church: a golden reliquary designed in the fifteenth century to house fragments of Charlemagne's arm (Cathedral Treasury, Aachen).*

carefree acceptance. His famous 'Canticle of the Sun' expresses it perfectly. In 1225 he was lying ill in the garden of San Damiano. It was a small church which he himself had restored and had given as a convent to Clare. Clare built a rush hut in the garden for him to rest in, and he wrote the verses which he taught his friars to sing when they preached:

> Praise to thee, my Lord, for all Thy creatures,
> Above all Brother Sun
> Who brings us the day and lends us his light.

The little chapel of St Francis encased in the later church of Santa Maria degli Angeli.

> Praise to Thee, my Lord, for Brother Wind,
> For air and cloud, for calm and all weather,
> By which Thou supportest life in all Thy creatures.
>
> Praise to Thee, my Lord, for Sister Water,
> Who is so useful and humble,
> Precious and pure.
>
> Praise to Thee, my Lord, for our sister Mother Earth,
> Who sustains and directs us,
> And brings forth varied fruits, and coloured flowers, and plants.

The following year, when he knew he was dying, he added another verse:

> Praise to Thee, my Lord, for our Sister bodily Death,
> From whom no man living may escape:
> Woe to those who die in mortal sin. [11]

They had to give him an armed guard on his death-bed, to prevent people making off with him, prematurely, as a relic. And knowing the ways of the world, he left a final instruction to his friars:

> Let all the brethren beware of accepting churches, houses, or anything else provided for them unless they conform to Holy Poverty, to which we are vowed in our Rule, always lodging as strangers and pilgrims. [12]

It was a vain hope. As soon as he was dead, his friars began to collect funds for a massive basilica at Assisi in his memory. It is a staggering achievement, and our gain, for its frescoes make it one of the great buildings of the Middle Ages. Yet it is precisely what Francis had forbidden, and it split his followers into two camps. One of the disenchanted, who would soon pointedly call themselves the Observant Franciscans, was said to have visited the new buildings at Assisi and made only a brief comment: 'Now all you lack is women.' Five miles away, at Santa Maria degli Angeli, the contrast is even more striking. A massive church has been built around St Francis's favourite chapel. It was the last that he rebuilt with his own hands, and it sits today like a mouse in a palace.

It is the eternal dilemma. The way of St Francis was the way of the gospel: the opulence of Assisi has more often been the way of the church. Francis died in 1226. By 1247 a Franciscan, Odo Rigaud, was Archbishop of Rouen and had three palaces with massive estates on both sides of the English Channel. When he was on his way to Rome with a retinue of eighty horsemen, an Italian bishop offered to pay his expenses. Odo replied that half his income was sufficient for him to live in splendid style, so he had no need of charity. In 1318 four Franciscans were burnt as heretics, for adhering too strictly to Francis's ideals of poverty, and in 1322 the pope condemned as heretical the doctrine of the poverty of Christ. The early lives of St Francis were edited to tone down his unfortunate views on this matter.

Like the major part of the cathedrals of Siena, Lincoln, Chartres and Bourges, the basilica at Assisi was built in the thirteenth century. In the following century the darker side of the Middle Ages prevailed. There was more superstition, more hysteria. Above all, death stalked the world as never before. For this was the century of Europe's most disastrous plague — the Black Death. Like the Day of Judgment, its approach had an inexorable quality — and yet it was predictable too, as it moved relentlessly westwards. In 1346 news arrived of a great plague devastating China. That same year the disease itself had reached the Middle East. By late 1347 it was in Sicily, by early 1348 in northern Italy and in the summer of that year in England. Such a disaster prompted many hysterical responses, including the traditional Christian one of anti-Semitism. Word got around that the Jews had caused the plague. More were killed in reprisal for the Black Death than in any persecution up to the twentieth century.

The plague hit Siena harder than almost any other city of Europe. Today it remains medieval in its appearance, much as the Black Death left it. In that dreadful summer of 1348, the sun rising over Siena revealed every day new horrors. More corpses pitched into the streets, more houses boarded up. Six out of every ten people died. It was the climax of a series of catastrophes in the 1340s. First, many banks in Florence and Siena had failed. Then 1346 and 1347 brought disastrous harvests, and in 1348 came the Black Death. Nowadays we would talk of depression, famine, disaster. In the Middle Ages the hand of God was sufficient explanation. In an orgy of guilt and repentance bands of flagellants wandered the countryside, whipping themselves to appease the Almighty.

Just before the Black Death the people of Siena had decided to build themselves a massive new cathedral, something so huge that it would put to shame for ever their old rivals, Florence. They were going to use the existing cathedral as nothing more than the transept. But then the Black Death came, half the masons died, and they wondered whether God had meant them to build anything quite so ambitious. Some of the arches they pulled down, others they bricked up and yet others they left standing quite empty against the sky — as they remain today, gaunt reminders of Siena's moment of pride. Instead of their great cathedral the people of Siena built themselves just a tiny chapel at the foot of the civic tower, a plague chapel thanking God that at last the Black Death had ended.

Siena cathedral has kept a record of another new development of the fourteenth century. The more intolerable life on earth becomes, the more people turn to the promises of heaven. Pilgrimage was the pleasant way to heaven, and a Latin inscription over the door commemorates the first Holy Year — the great pilgrimage to Rome in 1300. In translation it reads:

> At Rome each hundredth year
> Occurs the Jubilee:
> Sins are washed clear, the penitent set free.
> Pope Boniface made this decree.[13]

The official decree had announced:

> Boniface, Bishop, Servant of the Servants of God. We grant to all who, being truly penitent, and confessing their sins, shall reverently visit these basilicas of St Peter and St Paul in the present year 1300 not only a full and copious but the most full pardon of all their sins, given at St Peters Rome February 22nd 1300.[14]

Six and three-quarter centuries later, Pope Paul echoed those words in announcing that 1975 would be another Holy Year:

> Paul, Servant of the Servants of God, to all the faithful. We impart the gift of the Plenary Indulgence to all the faithful who are properly disposed, after confessing their sins and receiving Holy Communion, if they undertake a sacred pilgrimage to

the Basilica of St Peter's in the Vatican, St Paul's Outside-the-Walls, the Lateran Archbasilica of the Most Holy Saviour, or Saint Mary Major's. Given in Rome, at St Peter's.[15]

A plenary indulgence means the escape from whatever punishment in purgatory is due for all the sins so far laid to the sinner's account. The debt is held to be paid. The language of commerce is not sacrilegious in this context. It was considered from the start to be appropriate to the bargain of indulgences. Purgatory was a concept which had developed in Christian thought to explain what lay ahead for the great mass of people who are neither saints (destined for immediate heaven) nor among the damned (condemned to eternal hell). In purgatory the souls would suffer punishment for their sins, until they were free to enter heaven. It

The crowd in St Peter's Square, on Easter morning of Holy Year, 1975.

was not until the Middle Ages that the doctrine became clearly formulated, and hard on its heels followed the idea of indulgences — special tokens for the remission of sins and therefore the avoidance of purgatory. The debt was not wiped out: it was specifically stated by St Thomas Aquinas (the conclusive umpire on such medieval matters) that the debt was paid, by means of the indulgence, from the inexhaustible treasury of merits and good works stored up by Jesus, the Virgin Mary and the saints.

A bargain with heaven hardly seemed out of keeping with a bargain on earth, and it was not long before indulgences were offered for sale — to avoid the trouble of earning them by pious acts such as pilgrimage. Pope Boniface VIII, founder of the Holy Years, (whose papal crown is described in an inventory of 1295 as containing 48 rubies, 72 sapphires, 45 emeralds, and 66 large pearls) used the phrase 'this happy commerce' in a Bull about the sale of indulgences. But like more mortal forms of currency, indulgences were prone to severe devaluation. Holy Years were originally planned to happen once a century but the interval rapidly slid through fifty, forty and thirty-three years until it became stabilized (from 1450) at the present level of four times a century. In 1300 it had been necessary to come to Rome to win the plenary indulgence; by 1390 the indulgence was on offer throughout Europe for the price of the return trip to Rome, and by 1500 it could be bought for one-fifth of the fare. The happy commerce was capable of infinite refinement. Exemptions proved almost as profitable as indulgences, and one pope raised money by allowing people not to go on a non-existent crusade. At the lower end of the scale, ten days off purgatory was at one time on offer for anyone who would remain in church until the end of mass.

All the Christian churches would in later centuries condemn the traffic in indulgences. Nevertheless, the effectiveness of an indulgence — if properly earned — remains a part of present-day Roman Catholic dogma, though less and less emphasis is placed on it. Pope Paul VI announced that the theme of his Holy Year was reconciliation, and this was uppermost in the minds of pilgrims to Rome in 1975. No one that I spoke to in the great Easter morning crowd in front of St Peter's seemed to have given much thought to the escape from purgatory which their visit was earning them.

Even so, there are other details of a present-day pilgrimage to Rome which hardly seem part of the twentieth century. There is no piece of devotion more humble than to climb on one's knees the Scala Santa, the Holy Staircase. Tradition says that these are the very steps of the house of Pontius Pilate, the steps that Jesus, bleeding, walked down to begin his Passion. They were brought three centuries later to Rome for safe keeping, and since then millions have climbed them on their knees — including on one occasion a young monk, Martin Luther. Luther decided that such rituals were nothing but medieval superstition, but it is clear that even today for many people to climb each one of these twenty-eight steps, meditating at each on the suffering of Jesus, can remain an act of deeply felt faith. It does also add at the bottom that climbing them may save you nine years in purgatory.

And so the contrasts of the Middle Ages remain — as in the bell, that beautiful and very medieval sound, the public voice of the church. The bell that tolls for

death, for plague, for famine, is also the bell that peals for birth, for marriage, for

Easter morning. Striking dread into every heart? Or hope and joy? It depends, like so much else from the Middle Ages, on how you look at it.

When the bell tolled for a rich man and he presented himself to St Peter at the gates of heaven, the gospels were uncompromising — no chance. But our rich man of Bourges, the duke of Berry, had an answer even to this. Before he died he had given away all his precious treasures and manuscripts (to the church, of course), and during his life he had spent so much money that there was nothing left at the end even to pay for his funeral. The clamour of creditors round his deathbed must have seemed like a passport to heaven. He had already commissioned an artist to paint that future scene for him. St Peter, standing at the gate of heaven, seems to welcome the good duke. And the duke, wearing simpler clothes than ever in his lifetime and keeping only one beautiful jewel on his coat, approaches and shows the jewel to St Peter, seeming to say: 'Surely one is all right? Just one.'

At the top of the Scala Santa pilgrims kiss a spot where a drop of Jesus's blood is said to have fallen.

CHAPTER FIVE

People of the Book

I N about the year 615, the archangel Gabriel spoke to a merchant from Mecca:

> Allah has made plain to you the religion which He enjoined upon Noah . . . and upon Abraham, and Moses, and Jesus. To establish religion, and not to be divided therein.[1]

The merchant was the prophet Muhammad. And the list of names — Abraham, Moses, Jesus — gives the family link between the three great Middle Eastern religions. Jews, Christians, Muslims; all worship one god, whose instructions to man — they all believe — began on Mount Sinai. For it was here that he first gave the law to Moses. Each of the three religions, since then, has recorded in writing further words of God to man. They are all, in the powerful phrase of the Koran, 'people of the book'.

At the foot of Mount Sinai is a Christian monastery, St Catherine's, founded fourteen hundred years ago by the emperor Justinian. For most of those fourteen centuries it has been in Muslim territory, and its massive walls make it look like a Christian fortress — under attack from Islam. The very opposite has been the case. The local Bedouin have for centuries guarded the monastery. Inside it they have their mosque. Christians in medieval Europe were amazed to hear that Muslim caliphs had actually subsidized these monks in the desert. They also gave money to the Jewish academy at Jerusalem. Clearly the people of the book are capable of living together, however much their books may differ. Yet for much

Previous pages: *A pilgrim on the top of Mount Sinai.*

St Catherine's monastery, sheltering below Mount Sinai.

of history they have slaughtered each other — each claiming to please God by doing so.

Islam, meaning submission to the will of God, began among merchants. Muhammad was one himself. He had married a wealthy widow and was looking after her business affairs, when Gabriel first spoke to him. The theme of the message was simple, very similar to that preached by Jesus and countless other religious reformers. Repent: for the Day of Judgment is at hand.

But Gabriel also dictated a set of rules, which would enable the faithful to survive that judgment. Clearly defined rules — on questions of morals, of law, of worship — and rules simple enough to be adapted to any circumstances. When Islam began to spread from the cities to the desert tribesmen, the Koran provided them with a code well suited to their way of life. Instead of the complicated mysteries of Christian worship, a Muslim needs only his prayer mat to carry out his devotions. Instead of a hierarchy of priests, he relies for advice on individual holy men whose influence comes only from their knowledge of the Koran, or from a blameless life. And in place of that most mysterious of mysteries, the Trinity, here there really is only one god — without equivocation. The greater simplicity of Islam was to prove one of its advantages. When Mongol tribesmen later conquered both Christian and Muslim territories, Islam was the religion they chose. It was said that they found it easier to practise, and easier to believe.

The Muslim armies moved with astonishing speed. Within fifteen years of the death of the Prophet they had conquered Egypt, Palestine, Libya, Tunisia, Syria, Iraq and Iran. Another sixty years, and they were in Pakistan and Spain.

The earliest Muslim building to survive is in Jerusalem, the Dome of the Rock. It was built in imitation of a Christian church, and on the site of the Jewish Temple. It rises today high above the Wailing Wall, or Western Wall, those massive blocks of masonry which for centuries were all that remained visible of the Temple. The Temple itself had been on top of the great platform which was partly supported by this wall.

One of the chief causes of friction between the people of the book has been that so many of their holy places are the same. Even in the 1970s riots have been caused by the fact that Jews, as well as Muslims, want to pray on the Temple Mount. The last Jewish Temple was demolished by the Romans in the year 70, and only one part of it remains on the Mount itself. But that one surviving detail was the holiest part of all — a bare patch of rock on which, it was believed, Abraham had offered his son Isaac as a sacrifice to God, and which David had chosen as the site for the first Temple. So it became the inner sanctuary, the Holy of Holies. The reason it survives today is simple. The Muslims also venerated Abraham. And for good measure, with the economy typical of religious legend, they decided that Muhammad had ascended to Heaven from the same piece of rock.

When the Arabs captured Jerusalem in 638 this whole temple platform was a derelict site in the middle of a Christian city, much as the Romans had left it six centuries before. The documents say that the Jews eagerly helped the Arabs to clear away the ancient rubble. No doubt they were less enthusiastic when a superb Muslim shrine began to rise above the sacred rock — the Dome of the Rock. Muslims coming to worship here were reminded that Christianity was partially right — or not wholly wrong. One of the earliest mosaics included a   107

text from the Koran praising Jesus; but praising him as one of the prophets, in line with Moses and Muhammad, no more and no less:

> O People of the Book, speak nothing about God but the truth. The Messiah, Jesus, Son of Mary, was only the Messenger of God. So believe in God and his Messengers, and say not Three-in-One. God is only one God.[2]

A few years after the Dome of the Rock, the caliphs built the great mosque at Damascus. And a Muslim praying there demonstrates even more precisely the early link between Christianity and Islam. He prays at the shrine of John the Baptist, who is described in the Koran as 'one of the righteous'. The reason is that this mosque was built, in the eighth century, inside the walls which had previously contained an orthodox church in honour of John the Baptist — and before that a temple to a Roman god, and before that a temple to a Babylonian god. Throughout history new religions have moved, like hermit crabs, into the shells left by their predecessors.

Opposite: *A Muslim says his prayers inside St Catherine's.*

Islam and Judaism in Jerusalem: the Dome of the Rock rising above the Western Wall of the Temple enclosure.

The change-over in Damascus from Christianity to Islam was reasonably peaceful. Christian craftsmen provided mosaics for the mosque, just as they would have done for a Byzantine church, except that here there were no living figures. And we know that Christian officials, trained to administer the Byzantine empire, stayed on to work for the Muslims. The Arabs had conquered a more highly developed civilization; very sensibly they took advantage of it.

Among the Christians are men versed in speculative theology, medicine and astronomy. They are in our estimation philosophers and men of learning.[3]

Opposite: *Byzantine mosaics in the courtyard of the mosque at Damascus.*

Praying at the shrine of John the Baptist, inside the Umayyad mosque at Damascus.

Precisely the reasons for which Christians, in later centuries, would come to admire the Arabs. And oddly, the Christians were now doing just those jobs which they would later think of as Jewish:

> The Christians are secretaries, servants to kings, money changers; whereas the Jews are but dyers, tanners, cuppers, butchers and cobblers. [4]

There have been many reversals among the people of the book.

It may seem strange that a conquering people, who in Christian tradition are thought of as bloodthirsty and very partial to the Holy War, should have received such co-operation from those they conquered. Part of the reason can be seen in the countryside north of Damascus, at the little Syrian village of Sadad.

Sadad was Christian before the Muslims conquered Syria in the seventh century. It has remained Christian ever since. But the significant detail is that even before the Muslim invasion these Christians were regarded as heretics by the orthodox establishment in Constantinople: they were considered to hold incorrect ideas about the divinity of Christ, and they hold them still. But they disliked being called heretics. And they also disliked being governed by an imperial bureaucracy thousands of miles away. There were many Christians like them in the Middle East, and later in North Africa, who thought that Muslim rule might even be preferable to Byzantine rule. Provincial dissatisfaction: a powerful force at all times, and one that certainly helped the spread of Islam. And in a way the Christians of Sadad chose right. In what other culture has a tiny village like this survived intact, keeping to its own ways, entirely surrounded by a rival religion for some 1,200 years? It was the Koran which made it possible, specifying that people of the book — Christians and Jews — must be allowed to worship God in their own manner. When the crusaders reached Syria, they were horrified to find Christians living peacefully under the Muslims. By that time, four centuries after the beginning of Islam, the Muslims had long been more civilized than any western Christian. In Cordoba, the Muslim capital of Spain, a Christian had long ago complained:

> My fellow Christians delight in the poems and romances of the Arabs. They study the works of Muslim theologians and philosophers, *not* in order to refute them; but to acquire a correct and elegant Arabic style. The pity of it. Christians have forgotten their own tongue. Scarcely one in a thousand is able to compose in fair Latin a letter to a friend! [5]

The ancient Muslim tradition of learning continues today in the Al Az'har mosque in Cairo, the world's oldest surviving university. Western Europe is rightly proud of its early universities. Bologna was founded in about 1100; Paris in about 1160; Oxford a few years later. But the university mosque in Cairo had been founded two centuries before Oxford, in 970. Teaching has been going on here for over a thousand years.

When the Al Az'har mosque in Cairo was founded, the west was illiterate and violent. The Franks, the Germans, the Normans — these were people of restless energy, always looking for new horizons. And the Muslim world was soon to feel the cutting edge of that energy. In 1096, and throughout the next century, heavily armed men streamed eastwards in a mood of high enthusiasm. The crusades were based on a powerful combination: idealism and greed. Both

Opposite: *Inside the abbey church of Vézelay, which was the rallying point for the Second Crusade.*

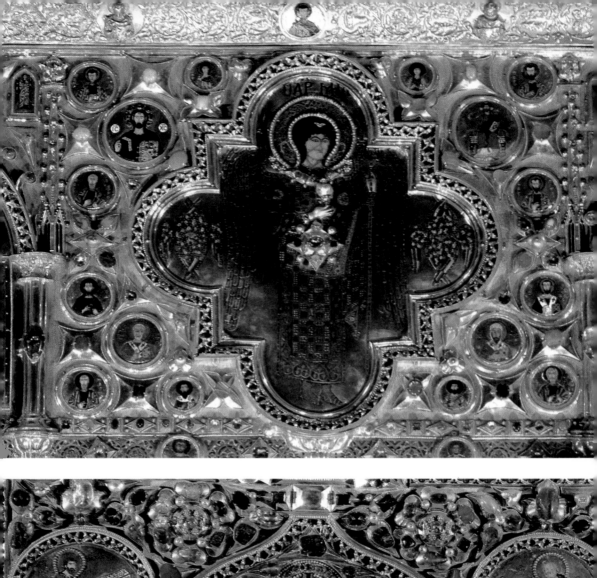

inspired violent feelings. 'We shall slay', said one popular slogan, 'for God's love.' Every death, on either side, would please God. Religious minds are adept at seeing totally opposing events as equal evidence of God's perfect intentions, and St Bernard applied the principle neatly to the crusades:

> A Christian glories in the death of a Muslim because Christ is glorified. The liberality of God is revealed in the death of a Christian, because he is led out to his reward.[6]

So powerful was the saving grace of going on crusade that St Bernard urged 'murderers, rapists, adulterers, perjurers, and all other criminals' to join the expedition. However holy the motive, it sounded much like an invitation to violence.

Christians who died would go to heaven — the pope had promised that. Christians who lived could hope for a new life in the east. Perhaps a manor, with Muslim slaves, for the knight; freedom for the European peasant or serf. The peasants were even more fired by crusading zeal than the knights. They began with zest on their own doorsteps. No Muslims here, but plenty of other unbelievers:

> We have set out to march a long way to fight the enemies of God in the East, and behold, before our very eyes are his worst foes, the Jews. They must be dealt with first.[7]

They were. The First Crusade was launched with a massacre of thousands of Jews, particularly in the towns of Germany, in what was to become almost a traditional beginning to every expedition eastwards.

The knights, in that first crusade, restrained themselves until they reached their goal: Jerusalem. The city fell to them on July 15th, 1099.

> With drawn swords our people ran through the city; nor did they spare anyone, not even those pleading for mercy. If you had been there, your feet would have been stained up to the ankles with blood. What more shall I tell? Not one of them was allowed to live. They did not spare the women or children.

> The horses waded in blood up to their knees, nay up to the bridle. It was a just and wonderful judgement of God.[8]

It was not quite true that no one was allowed to live. The Muslim governor of the city and his bodyguard paid enough to buy their escape, but they were the only exceptions. The Jews, whose reaction had been to take shelter in their synagogue, were burnt alive.

An occupying army needed castles, and the famous crusader castles are now almost the only visible trace of what was called the Latin Kingdom of Jerusalem. One of the most romantic is in the north of Syria. Now known as Saladin's Castle, it reflects the changing fortunes of this area. It was originally a Byzantine fortress, high on a rocky mountain. It was taken from them by the Muslims, and from the Muslims by the crusaders — whose remarkable energies can still be judged by the needle-like column of rock, 160 feet high, which used to support their drawbridge. It was formed by cutting an artificial ravine down into the hillside, to improve the defences on the weaker side of the castle, and by leaving this narrow pillar of rock untouched. Even so, the castle fell to Saladin, Richard

Opposite: *Treasures of the Pala d'Oro in St Mark's, Venice: the Virgin, looted from Constantinople by the Fourth Crusade; and Christ, bought there earlier.*

I's great rival, who recaptured Jerusalem from the Christians in 1187 and who gave a much-needed example in his merciful treatment of the Christian inhabitants. But the most spectacular of all crusader castles, also in Syria, is the one described by a Muslim writer of the time as 'a bone in the throat of the Muslims'. Even Saladin skirted around it, apparently considering it too strong to attack. It is Krak des Chevaliers, the Castle of the Knights.

Looking down from the top of Krak, the military confidence of the place is unmistakable. This is a giant, in a perfect suit of armour, expecting a fight and certain of winning it. But if you look down inside the castle, you sense a different atmosphere. If the colleges of Oxford and Cambridge ever fall into ruins, then some quiet corner will look a little like the courtyard at the heart of Krak. The delicate Gothic arches along one side were a cloister. Monks of a sort walked here in the thirteenth century. Sometimes, I suppose, they must have been reading a sacred text — as a good monk should — and there's a Latin jingle carved in the stone which warned them against pride. It is a warning they may have needed. They were just as likely, when walking here, to have been planning a raid on the

Saladin's castle: the needle cut from the rock to support the crusaders' drawbridge.

Krak des Chevaliers, watching over the valleys.

Muslims. They would clap on armour over their robes — black robes with a white cross — and ride out to battle.

All the important crusader castles belonged to two great military orders, the Templars and the Hospitallers. They had been founded soon after the First Crusade captured Jerusalem, and their members swore the same vows as a monk — poverty, chastity, obedience — but their function was to fight, and they were known as Knights Templar, or Knights Hospitaller. Krak belonged to the Hospitallers. Originally their order had done work a little closer to monkish charity — they had run a hospital in Jerusalem — but they lost the hospital when Saladin captured the city. As fighting was the most important business in the Latin Kingdom, the Hospitallers soon became quite unashamedly military monks. Krak, which even in times of peace held 2,000 fighting men, was a monastery and a garrison and still shows traces of both, from its cloister to the ring of fortified towers.

The knights came to seem almost a symbol of the crusading movement. But their fortunes reflect its slow end. The Hospitallers lost Krak des Chevaliers to the Muslims in 1271. Twenty years later they had been pushed from the mainland entirely. They became the Knights of Rhodes: and finally, farther west still, just the Knights of tiny Malta. The crusades were over. They had created 115

little except a misleading fund of romantic stories, and a new legacy of bitterness between the people of the book.

The crusades had been expeditions across and around the Mediterranean. That meant there was another side to them: trade with the east. And it was this, rather than Christianity, which interested Venice. Today Venice seems a tired old city; beautiful, worldly-wise, decked out in the finery that comes from centuries of power. In the twelfth century Constantinople was all those things. Venice was by comparison an upstart, with more of a future than a past. But she was ready now to expand her trade into areas where she would clash with Constantinople. She believed herself to have long-standing links with the east. Her patron saint, St Mark, was thought to have died in Alexandria — and a popular legend told how Venetian merchants had smuggled his bones out of Egypt, hiding them in a barrel of salt pork which the Muslim officials would be too fastidious to pry into. A mosaic above the entrance to St Mark's shows the relics arriving, and it is typical that the church named after him is entirely Byzantine in style — perhaps even directly modelled on one at Constantinople. The older city had taught Venice her architecture, and much else besides. But the pupil was about to replace the teacher in what became the most shameful crusade of all.

Opposite: *The cloisters at the heart of Krak des Chevaliers.*

The faded charms of medieval Venice.

In 1202 Venice devised a sinister plan. She provided the ships to carry the Fourth Crusade to attack Egypt, and she provided them on credit; the crusaders could pay with the wealth they would win in the east. They can't have known that the Venetian Doge had recently signed a trading agreement with Egypt; and they accepted his suggestion of calling in at Constantinople on the way. The Doge managed to delay the crusaders there for ten months, and the result was predictable. The uncouth western knights were allowed into the city as allies. They wandered round as tourists, staring wide-eyed at the treasures of the richest city in the world. There were political and religious differences between the over-civilized hosts and their rough guests; there was the mounting debt to Venice; there was the frustration of a crusade that had set off in high spirits and had got nowhere. When the violence began, it turned into three days of indiscriminate looting. Mounted men rode into the great church of Santa Sophia and smashed the altar for its gold and silver ornaments. A prostitute was placed on the patriarch's throne, and obligingly sang a bawdy song in Norman French. When they gradually came to their senses, they settled down to share things out on a more orderly basis. One share for each foot soldier; two shares for a priest; and of course the lion's share for Venice. The acquisitions of the Fourth Crusade still grace the city.

The fourth-century porphyry sculpture of four emperors: loot. Ancient

Mosaic above the doorway of St Mark's, showing the relics of the saint arriving at the church.

Loot: on a corner of St Mark's, two of the fourth-century porphyry emperors.

reliefs, dotted like postage stamps over the walls of St Mark's: loot. Even the great bronze horses, almost by now a symbol of Venice: loot. They had stood in the hippodrome of Constantine's city. Many of the most beautiful objects in the treasury of St Mark's were brought back from the crusade. Their arrival proved a great inspiration to European craftsmen, and their quiet perfection makes an odd contrast to the event which brought them here. In the words of the pope himself, in a rebuke to his own crusaders in that same year of 1204:

> It was not against the Infidel but against Christians that you drew your swords. It was not Jerusalem that you captured, but Constantinople. It was not heavenly riches upon which your minds were set, but earthly ones. Nothing has been sacred to you. You have violated married women, widows, even nuns. You have despoiled the very sanctuaries of God's Church, stolen the sacred objects of altars, pillaged innumerable images and relics of saints. It is hardly surprising that the Greek church sees in you the works of the Devil.[9]

So Venice grew richer, but Constantinople never fully recovered. Somehow the ancient city staggered on for another two and a half centuries, until the day in 1453 when she fell to a twenty-one-year-old sultan, Muhammad II. In later life his features reminded people of a parrot about to eat ripe cherries. This particular ripe cherry was all too well aware of his intentions, but the citizens of Constantinople placed their hope in the Christian God, and in the famous barrier across the harbour entrance which prevented ships from reaching the only weak side of the city. They were in for a shock. At dawn one Sunday morning the sultan hauled his ships over a 200-foot hill. To the encouragement of drums and fifes they were dragged on wheeled carriages, running on a wooden tramway, and were launched into the harbour.

The city was surrounded. The weight of the Turkish army was outside the great western walls. At sunset on the evening of May 28th, 1453, cannon were moved up and the attack began. The Byzantine emperor and his soldiers were on the walls, dazzled by the setting sun. In front of them, the threatening fife and drum. At their backs, every bell in the Christian city was sounding the alarm. The churches were full. *Kyrie Eleison* they were singing in Santa Sophia, as they prayed to the icons; to Jesus; above all to Mary, Mother of God, patron of the city, to protect them in their hour of need.

All night the battle went on, but by dawn the Turks were inside. After eleven centuries of Christianity, Constantinople was a Muslim city. The cathedral of Santa Sophia was a mosque. The conqueror had gone straight there to hear a proclamation from the pulpit — that there is no God but Allah, and Muhammad is his Prophet. As soon as the masons could get to work, the old church grew minarets.

Places shared by the people of the book. Opposite: *Mosque and church inside St Catherine's monastery, Sinai.* Overleaf: *Greek Orthodox priests and Orthodox Jews in Jerusalem.* Overleaf right: *The domes of Christianity and of Islam in Jerusalem.*

The fifth-century walls of Constantinople, on which the last Byzantine emperor fought at the fall of the city.

A parrot about to eat ripe cherries: the features of Sultan Muhammad II (Topkapi, Istanbul).

In obedience to the Koran, Muhammad allowed the Christians to keep some of their churches and to worship freely. It was a civilized attitude which later sultans would not always live up to, and which the first crusaders had all too plainly lacked.

When the military effort in the east began to fail, certain Christians conceived the possibility of approaching Muslims other than with drawn swords. The crusades had caused a developing interest in the details of Islam. The twelfth century saw the first European translation of the Koran and the first European biographies of the Prophet Muhammad (one of the biographers, Guibert of Nogent, admitted that he had no written sources for the black picture he painted of the Prophet, but added disarmingly 'it is safe to speak evil of one whose malignity exceeds whatever ill can be spoken').[10] The basis for a different

Opposite: *The Lion Courtyard in the Alhambra, Granada (see page 123).*

approach to crusading was well expressed considerably later, in about 1300, by Ramon Lull:

> I see the knights going overseas to the Holy Land thinking to take it by force of arms and in the end exhausting themselves without achieving their aim. Then I think that this conquest should be made as Thou madest it, Lord, with Thine apostles: that is by love, by prayer, and by shedding of tears. Then let the holy knights of religion set forth, let them arm themselves with the sign of the cross, let them be filled with the grace of the Holy Ghost, let them preach to the heathen the truths of the Passion.[11]

One of the strangest events in the whole remarkable story of the crusades had happened in 1219, fifteen years after the knights of the Fourth Crusade ransacked Constantinople. The Fifth Crusade was besieging the town of Damietta in Egypt, when a scruffy-looking friar surrendered himself to the Muslim soldiers and asked them to take him to their leader. He was St Francis of Assisi, and he had travelled out from Italy to convert the sultan. Amazingly, the guards took him into the royal presence and he was politely received — perhaps because anyone so poor, so dirty, and so full of conviction will be listened to in the east as being touched with holiness. Francis explained to the sultan the merits of Christianity, then asked for a bonfire which he could step into to demonstrate his faith. The sultan was a considerate man, and he said no to this display of zeal. But he listened, and sent the saint safely on his way.

That much was fact. Legend added another chapter. When Francis arrived back in Italy, he was sent for by someone as free-thinking as himself. He was sent for, so the story goes, by the emperor Frederick II, a man of insatiable curiosity, who promptly locked him up in a room with a beautiful girl, and settled down to watch the encounter through the key-hole. St Francis — who emerges from these stories as something of a pyromaniac — had a neat solution. He would lie with the lady, he told her, if she would join him on a bed of coals which he had raked from the fire on to the hearth. The emperor was so impressed that he dismissed the girl, and spent all night in earnest discussion with the saint.

If Francis told him that one should reason with Muslims, he was preaching to the converted — for Frederick had grown up in Sicily. The island had long been a meeting place between east and west, as well as between Africa and Europe. It was an important part of the ancient Greek empire, then of the Carthaginian empire, of the Roman empire, and of the Byzantine empire. It was conquered by Arabs from North Africa in the tenth century, and by Normans from France in the eleventh. The buildings reveal the mixture — and none more so than the chapel which Frederick's grandfather, Roger II, built in his palace at Palermo in about 1140. The mosaics are Byzantine, and some of them were certainly done by Greek artists. The shape of the nave is Norman, with its rounded arches — even though the pillars are distinctly classical. But the ceiling is the sort of thing you would normally find in a mosque or a Muslim palace. The three separate traditions of medieval Sicily — eastern Christianity, western Christianity, and Islam — come together in a delightful compromise. The same mixture can be seen in many lesser Sicilian details. One of the many small paintings on the ceiling of the chapel at Palermo shows Roger II sitting cross-legged as a sultan, with slave-girls in attendance, while a mosaic in another of his churches in the city, La Martorana, presents him as a Byzantine emperor being crowned by Christ.

They were broad-minded in more than just their artistic tastes, these kings of Sicily. Frederick II loved talking with theologians of all three religions, and it is said that he enjoyed telling them that the world has seen three great imposters — Moses, Jesus and Muhammad. He did himself take a leaf from the notebook of Muhammad. He kept a harem, and by doing so got one of his popular names, that of 'the baptised sultan'. When it came to crusading, Frederick was clearly not the man to go rampaging eastwards with the simple faith of any ordinary Christian knight. Instead he achieved the remarkable feat of capturing Jerusalem without even drawing his sword, and he did so by visiting the sultan who had received St Francis (it was only ten years later), and by making with him a treaty whereby the Christians received Jerusalem, but would continue to allow the Muslims and the Jews to worship there. In fact, Frederick called it the city of three religions. Europe was scandalized. The pope, who had already excommunicated Frederick, now preached a new crusade — this time against Sicily.

Crusades were no new thing inside Europe, though usually they were not sent against Christian monarchs. The longest-running of all had been against the Muslims of Spain. The Muslims had been driven back from the northern part of the peninsula, but they were still firmly in control of the south. While Frederick was crowning himself king of Jerusalem, or relaxing with his harem at Palermo, the last and perhaps greatest achievement of Muslim Spain was starting to be built: the Alhambra at Granada.

The courtyards of the Alhambra, with the permanent sound of water, are like those which the Muslim rulers of India would later build in Agra or Delhi. And they are like what the Koran promises in Paradise:

> Paradise is watered by rivers. There is perpetual fruit. There shall be rivers of wine, and rivers of honey clarified. There shall be shade. And reclining on couches with clear-eyed houris. [12]

But this was too much even for the broad-minded Ramon Lull:

> What will their Paradise be, but a tavern of unwearied gorging and a brothel of perpetual turpitude? [13]

In these lovely courtyards I incline to the Muslim view.

By the time the Alhambra was built, Christians and Muslims had lived side by side in Spain for five centuries. They had fought each other, but they had also learnt from each other. In particular it was the Christians who learnt from the Muslims. The most striking of medieval Spanish paintings were done by Christians living under Muslim rule — in what is now known as the Mozarabic style, much influenced by eastern and perhaps North African art. But it was in the field of scholarship that the Christians had most to learn from the Muslims. The scholarly traditions of the university mosque at Cairo — or, closer to hand, of the great mosque at Cordoba — made much of translating, copying and commenting on ancient manuscripts. Books by classical Greek authors, long forgotten in the west, had been carefully preserved in Arabic manuscripts. In Spain, in the twelfth and thirteenth centuries, these in their turn were translated into Latin. It

View from the walls of the Alhambra, Granada.

came as a revelation to discover the Greek attitude to the world and to science, so much more inquisitive about nature than any tradition Europe had inherited from Rome.

The emperor Frederick, as usual, had been up to date. He wrote a highly technical work about falconry, *De Arte Venandi*. His artist was still trapped in the stylistic awkwardness of medieval painting, but tried desperately hard to show the real differences between the various birds. The emperor's opening chapter had sternly given him the clue: 'Our work is to present things that are, *as* they are.'[14]

The Greek philosopher who best represented this down-to-earth scientific approach was Aristotle, whose work had been only partially known in the west until it was translated from Arabic. In an altar painting in St Catherine's at Pisa, Aristotle shows his work to St Thomas Aquinas, the theologian who was first to reconcile Aristotelian methods with the existing Christian traditions (which had long been influenced by the more other-worldly approach of Plato). Being beamed into St Thomas's head (presented with some justification as the medieval church's computer) the ideas of the two Greek philosophers are joined by the more traditional strands of Christian truth, from God himself, from Moses, from the evangelists, and from St Paul. And at the feet of Aquinas lies the distinguished Arabic philosopher who had worked at Cordoba — Averroës. He is shown as having been defeated by Aquinas, but in fact it was his commentaries on Aristotle which had greatly stimulated Aquinas and so had led, indirectly, to much of the new intellectual excitement of the later Middle Ages.

124

Thomas Aquinas was a Dominican, a black friar. The order had been founded in 1216 by a Spaniard, St Dominic, who was a contemporary of St Francis. Francis brought a much needed simplicity back into Christianity, Dominic a new intellectual energy. Soon the most distinguished teachers at Oxford or Paris were nearly all Dominicans. But there was a darker side to the intellectual energies of the black friars. Dominic's first interest had been in preaching against heresy. The Inquisition was officially established soon after Dominic's death, and his wandering friars were a natural choice as inquisitors. The most notorious Grand Inquisitor of all, Torquemada, came from Dominic's order; and their shared country, Spain, was to prove the richest hunting-ground for heresy. Here, more than anywhere in Christian Europe, there were infidels to convert: not only the Muslims, but also Europe's largest and most prosperous community of Jews.

In the thirteenth century — the century of St Francis, St Dominic and Frederick II — there had been kings in Spain who called themselves 'Kings of Three Religions', acknowledging their Jewish and Muslim subjects alongside the

The fountain which gave its name to the Lion Courtyard in the Alhambra.

Christians. Three centuries later the situation was very different. And Granada, more than anywhere, saw the change.

Granada was the last Spanish city in Muslim hands, and the district known as the Albaicin — running up the hillside opposite the Alhambra — is still the best preserved of the old Muslim quarters of Spain. In a typical house the small rooms have wooden ceilings painted in elaborate arabesques, and they give on to a little garden courtyard. In the middle of the courtyard there is a pool for ritual washing. But anyone using such a pool in a Muslim fashion after 1502 did so at grave risk from the prying eyes of the Spanish Inquisition, because by then, by

Forced baptism of the Muslims: relief beside the altar of the royal chapel, Granada.

royal decree, it was illegal for any Jew or any Muslim to practise his religion. The final act in the long Spanish crusade had happened in Granada in 1492. In that year, on January 2nd, a Christian flag flew for the first time over the Alhambra: the flag of Ferdinand and Isabella.

In the marriage of Ferdinand and Isabella, Christian Spain found a new unity. Ferdinand brought his kingdom of Aragon, Isabella brought Castile. Together they conquered Granada, and it was there that they chose to be buried. In their royal chapel they lie side by side on their monument, and it is often said that anyone can tell which of the two had the harder head by the dent in Isabella's pillow. I am not so sure. Isabella was the more bigoted, Ferdinand the more unscrupulous. They were a match for each other, and together they were certainly more than a match for anyone else. Maybe she just had the softer pillow.

'Their Most Catholic Majesties': that was their joint title, and they made the most of their Christian zeal. Their adviser on religious matters was none other than the dreaded Torquemada. With shrewd common sense, and no doubt with Torquemada's hearty approval, they used money that they had seized from the Jews to finance their attack on the Muslims of Granada. A relief to one side of the altar shows the Muslims handing over the keys of the city, while Ferdinand and Isabella ride in in triumph. On the other side there is seen an event which happened ten years later, when the Muslims of the city were given a simple choice: burn the Koran, become a baptized Christian, or leave.

It was a choice which the Jews of Spain had already faced in that year of 1492. Granada had fallen in January. In March Ferdinand and Isabella took Torquemada's advice and signed a decree that all Jews must leave the country by the end of July. Almost 200,000 of them left, many of them oddly enough to Constantinople, where the official policy was to welcome them. Those who stayed, by pretending to be converted to Christianity, would keep the Inquisition busy for many years to come. The country which had been the most tolerant in medieval Europe became notorious as the most intolerant of all.

It was the end of a long story. But it was also the beginning of another. Two days after the deadline for the Jews, on August 2nd, this year of 1492 saw yet another momentous event. On that day, Columbus set sail westwards in the service of Ferdinand and Isabella, not only to find a shorter trade route to the Far East or lands rich in gold, but to convert more infidels for Christ. He recorded in his log-book:

> Your Highnesses decided to send me, Christopher Columbus, to the princes and peoples of India to consider the best means for their conversion. For Your Highnesses have always been enemies of the sect of Mahomet and of all idolatries and heresies.[15]

It would be a new crusade, along the same old lines — with that well-tried and powerful blend of courage, cruelty, idealism and greed.

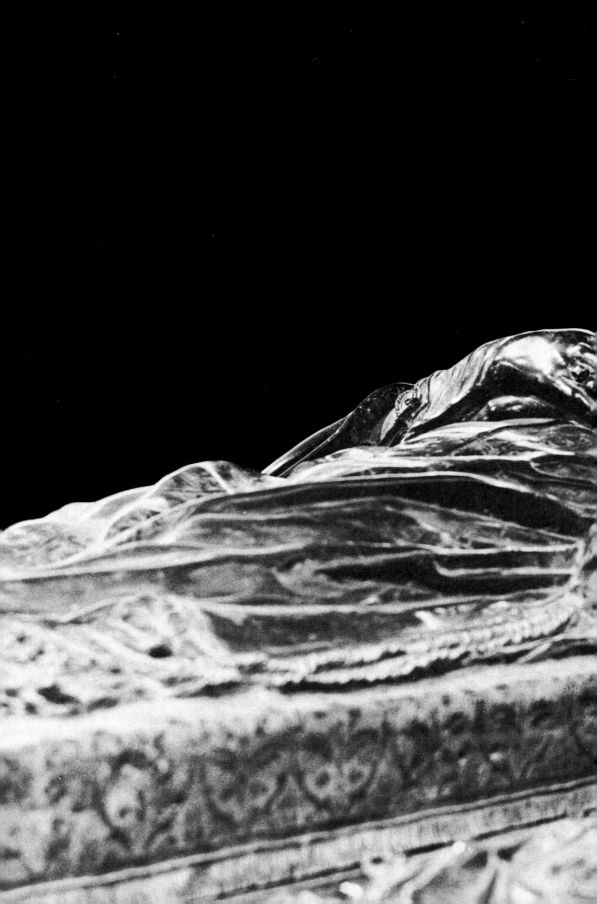

CHAPTER SIX

Princes and Prelates

I N the fourteenth century, seven popes in succession were Frenchmen. It seemed as natural in northern Europe then that the pope should be French as it has seemed in recent times that he should be Italian.

The French popes have left a striking memorial of themselves on the soil of France — the Palace of the Popes at Avignon. And if it looks more like the castle of some prince, that is not entirely inappropriate. The popes lived there in a worldly style which shocked many of their contemporaries. But then they were in France for worldly reasons. France was dominant in the European politics of the time. It suited the papacy to be there for the same reason that it suited the cardinals to elect Frenchmen as pope: reasons of state.

The prestige of the papacy had been declining fast since its great days in the twelfth century. Just before the popes moved to Avignon, a French king had sent troops to arrest an Italian pope whom he accused of blasphemy, simony, heresy, fornication and the murder of the previous pope. Such scandalous charges would have been unthinkable a hundred years earlier, but were almost commonplace — as the material of idle gossip — two centuries later. The papacy was moving towards a high tide of temporal splendour and the lowest ebb of its spiritual authority.

While the popes were still at Avignon, their most outspoken critic was an Englishman, John Wycliffe. He attacked their abuse of indulgences, and argued that the popes had lost all authority now that they behaved like princes — adding, for good measure, that the present pope was Antichrist himself. He argued that the Bible should be in the language of the people, and even went so far as to doubt whether the body and blood of Jesus were literally present in the bread and wine of the mass. Amazingly, after such observations, Wycliffe died peacefully of a stroke while worshipping in his own parish church at Lutterworth. It was abroad, and some thirty years after his death, that his ideas were to take fire, carrying into the flames with them several other reformers — most notably John Hus of Czechoslovakia.

Books by Wycliffe were first brought to Prague by a Czech scholar, Jerome, who had copied them out in Oxford. Hus was teaching at the university of Prague when Jerome arrived, and it was there that the furore over Wycliffe broke out. Soon there were student riots for and against Wycliffe, much as today there might be for and against Karl Marx. Hus and his friends already shared many of Wycliffe's ideas. The Bethlehem Chapel, close to the university, was the centre of their reform movement. It would have greatly impressed Wycliffe. It had been founded in 1391 specifically for the preaching of sermons in Czech. The central feature was not the altar but a pulpit, from which Hus and Jerome preached. On the walls there were Czech texts from the Bible, with a tune to sing them to (hymnbooks for the congregation), alongside paintings which compared the behaviour of the popes with the example of Christ. The pope was seen riding on a horse near a picture of Jesus walking barefoot. Jesus was shown washing the feet of his disciples, while the pope preferred to have his own feet kissed. And when Jesus ascended to heaven, the pope of course was pitched in full regalia into the other place.

Previous pages: *The nepotistical pope Sixtus IV, on his tomb by Pollaiuolo (St Peter's, Rome).*

Pulpit and wall paintings in the largely reconstructed Bethlehem Chapel, Prague.

The popes had recently been giving renewed cause for such satire. They had returned from Avignon only to land in the even deeper trouble of the Great Schism. For most of Hus's life there had been two rival popes: from 1409 there were three. Three popes at a time is too many by almost anyone's standards, and things became worse when one of the popes preached a crusade against another and started selling indulgences in Prague to pay for it. Czech protest reached a climax. Hus himself was excommunicated — by only one of the three popes, admittedly — and the whole ecclesiastical system seemed to be drifting into chaos.

To solve the situation a general Council was called in 1414 by Sigismund, king of Hungary and Germany and soon to become Holy Roman Emperor. The Council was to tackle two main problems: a surfeit of popes, and the Czech unrest. Hus was offered a safe conduct by Sigismund to put his case to the Council. Jerome urged him to go, and with considerable courage he set off.

Sigismund insisted on the Council being held outside Italy. His choice was the lakeside city of Constance, in the very south of Germany. People came there in 1414 from all over Europe, as many as 70,000 of them. It was the last great medieval gathering. There were tournaments to amuse the ladies, and you could make your confession in the cathedral in any one of twelve languages.

Luckily for us, one local citizen, Ulrich Richenthal, recorded the remarkable events that had happened in his city between 1414 and 1418, and later in the century his chronicle was profusely illustrated. In it one can see the city getting ready for its greatest occasion. The local bakers, for example, were unable to cope with the numbers of people, so portable ovens were brought in. Exotic foods were on sale to suit foreign tastes, including snails and frogs (for the Italians, oddly enough, not for the French). One of the popes arrived with due ceremony. The other two declined to come, and the one who arrived was soon deposed under accusations of simony, fornication, sodomy and murder: little, it would seem, had changed in papal affairs. The emperor turned up in time for Christmas, and at last the Council was ready to discuss its many problems. Eventually it deposed two popes and accepted the resignation of the third. The way was open for a new conclave. The cardinal who was elected, and who took the name of Martin V, was not even a priest — a circumstance far less surprising then than it would seem now. On almost successive days he was rushed through the necessary stages, ordained deacon and then priest, consecrated as bishop, enthroned as pope.

Christendom was respectable again. And on that other matter of heresy, here too there had been satisfactory progress. John Hus had arrived in Constance in

Martin V is rushed through the stages of deacon, priest, bishop and pope
(Richenthal Chronicle, Rosgarten Museum, Constance).

November 1414. He found lodging with a friendly widow in St Paul's Street, but within a month the Council betrayed his safe conduct. He was arrested and thrown into a cell in a tower on the lake shore (his cell is now part of a bedroom in Constance's best hotel). The Council tried to trap him into admitting he was a heretic. They accused him of sharing the more extreme views of Wycliffe, which in fact he did not — such as that the bread of the sacrament remains bread even after it is consecrated. They invented fantastic charges (even that he had claimed to be the Fourth Person of the Trinity). But behind it all lay the inescapable clash: that Hus did not accept the authority of unworthy popes, or corrupt priests, or of a church which, he believed, had become more interested in politics than in Christ.

To add to his troubles, Hus knew that his faithful disciple Jerome had promised to come to Constance to help him. Jerome never reached Hus, but was himself captured and imprisoned. It was only a matter of time before they were both burnt. Hus was ceremonially disrobed of his priest's garments. A paper crown was put on his head, decorated with three devils and the caption 'This is a heretic'. And he went singing into the flames. Ten months later Jerome was burnt on the same spot. Hus's ashes were thrown into the Rhine, for fear that they might be kept as relics to inspire the Czechs. And the Council ordered a similar indignity, far away to the north-west, for the remains of Wycliffe. He was dug up and thrown into the river at Lutterworth, in a ceremony which

perhaps was less unpleasant for him than for the pious people carrying it out.

The new pope, Martin V, travelled slowly southwards from Constance to Rome. He took three years on the journey: there was little enough at the other end to entice him. After a century of neglect Rome was largely in ruins. Grass was growing and goats were grazing on the steps of St Peter's. The Colosseum was occupied by a tribe of bandits. A contemporary, anticipating a major theme of the Renaissance, wrote:

> The beauty of Rome is what lies in ruins. The men of the present day, who call themselves Romans, are very different in bearing and conduct from the ancient inhabitants. To put it bluntly, they all look like cowherds.[1]

The city was at present held by the army of the queen of Naples. Time and diplomacy were necessary to persuade her to withdraw, and Martin carried on the negotiations from Florence. It was an apt choice. The pope who was expected to lead the church into a new age could see here, better than anywhere else, what that new age held in store.

Over the past two centuries Florence had been establishing herself as a centre both of culture and commerce. The city of Dante and of Giotto was also the city whose gold coin, the florin, had become the first stable international currency. When Martin V arrived, a building was nearing completion which fulfilled both sides of Florence's genius. Orsanmichele is a unique combination of market-place and church. It stands on the site of a medieval market which had grown up around a miraculous image of the Virgin. In the fourteenth century the guilds decided to build for themselves and the Virgin a splendid new home. She would still preside over the market activities on the ground floor: upstairs would be two floors to serve as warehouses; and to embellish the outside each guild was invited to provide a sculpture of its patron saint. In the bankers' niche there stands, naturally, the saintly tax-collector, St Matthew. But there was an element of contradiction for the bankers in all this commercial piety, because the Church held usury to be a sin. In the popular mind lending money on interest was like encouraging money to breed — a perversion of God's natural arrangements for procreation. The Elizabethan playwright Thomas Dekker explained it very effectively. 'A usurer', he wrote, 'is like a bawd to his own money bags, taking a fee that they may engender together.'

By 1420 there were some seventy-two separate banks in Florence. One of the most important was run by Cosimo de' Medici, with foreign branches as far afield as Geneva, Bruges, London and Avignon — the latter a survival from the days when the popes were there. It was said that even Cosimo de' Medici felt guilty that his family had made so much money by usury, so he consulted the bank's best customer — who happened to be the pope — about what he should do. The pope said God might look more leniently on the family fortune if Cosimo built a monastery. It was an arrangement to suit both sides. And when Pope Eugenius IV moved a convent of Dominican friars into Florence, Cosimo built for them the monastery of San Marco.

It seems typical of Florence at the time that even among the friars there was a painter of the stature of Fra Angelico. He and his pupils worked their way through the convent, illustrating each brother's cell with a fresco. Nowhere in the world is there a more beautiful or moving expiation of the sin of usury. At

Cosimo's cell in the monastery of San Marco, Florence.

the end of the corridor a cell was reserved for Cosimo himself, who would sometimes retreat here from the cares of the world. His cell is exactly the same as that of any ordinary friar, except that it is twice the size. Humility has its limits.

While San Marco was being built, Cosimo was also playing impresario in another event of the greatest interest to Florence. The pope had called a Council, inviting to it the Byzantine emperor and his bishops from Constantinople. By offering to pay the living expenses of the Greeks, Cosimo enticed the entire clerical circus to Florence in 1439. The Council itself achieved very little (for five months the theologians of both sides argued about one word in the Latin creed, the famous *filioque*, without reaching a conclusion), but its effect on Florence was enormous. The latest enthusiasm in the city was for the classics of ancient Greece and Rome. Florentine scholars, under Cosimo's patronage, had been hunting through old libraries to find forgotten texts. And suddenly here were a large number of real live Greeks, learned men, the living tradition. Cosimo founded his famous Platonic Academy because of what he had learnt from the Greeks in

The right hand of the Creator touches Adam into life (Michelangelo, Sistine Chapel).

Opposite: *The right hand of Michelangelo's David (Accademia, Florence).*

1439. Fourteen years later the city of Constantinople finally fell to the Turks, and a Florentine was able to write, 'Greece has not perished, but has migrated to Italy'.[2]

To walk up the steps of the Biblioteca Laurenziana in Florence is like going into church. It is the library which Michelangelo designed to house the Medici collection of manuscripts, and the activity inside it must have had something of the high seriousness of church-going. We think of burrowing in the classics as a slightly dusty occupation, but at that time it was a matter of the greatest excitement. Ancient Rome was thought of as the land of heroes. Greek was the language of philosophy, but also of early Christianity — of Plato, the gospels, St Paul. Studying the original texts was like rediscovering humanity before the clutter of the Middle Ages.

A manuscript in the Biblioteca Laurenziana makes the point. Medieval churches had been in the shape of a cross — nave and transept — and in those days that signified the pain of the crucifixion. But now a Renaissance scholar-artist, Francesco di Giorgio, draws the same shape in his work on architecture, but fits into it a superb young man — arms outstretched, as if in the full joy of life. It is typical that Francesco was working out the ideas of an architect from ancient Rome, Vitruvius, who had said the human body represented perfect proportion and that architecture should be based upon it. It was an idea certain to appeal to humanists in the Renaissance, and — like so much else — it was developed by Leonardo da Vinci. In one of his most famous drawings he demonstrates how a man in different positions fits perfectly into a circle and a square — the two shapes which make up the characteristically domed pattern of many Renaissance churches.

So God could be honoured in the beauty of his most superb creation: man. In a book written when Michelangelo was a child, God says to man:

136

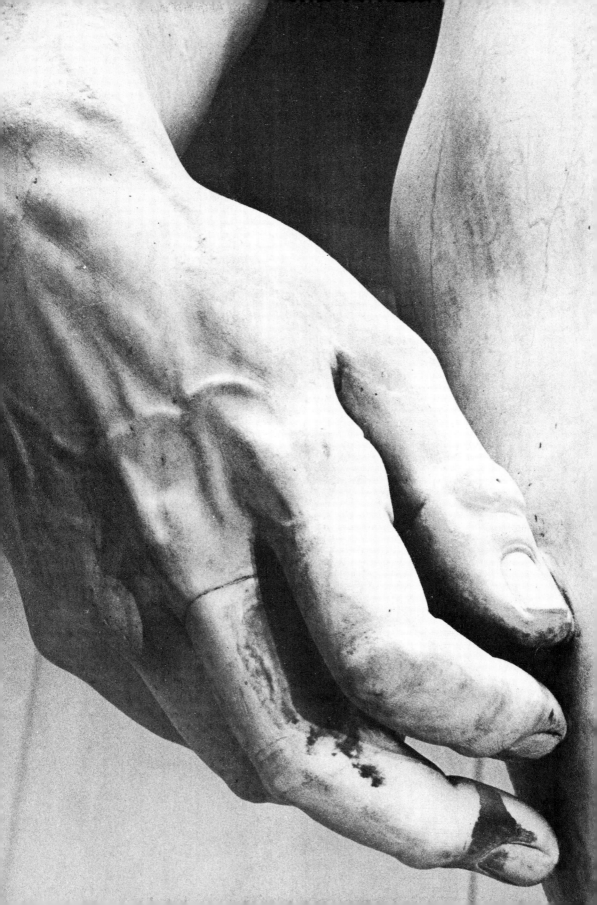

Virgin and Child *by Luca della Robbia on the exterior of Orsanmichele, Florence.*

We have made you neither of heaven nor of earth, so that with freedom of choice and with honour you may fashion yourself in whatever shape you prefer.[3]

In Michelangelo's series of sculptures known as the Captives, the human form seems to struggle to free itself, to emerge into its full perfection, as if to justify the words of Hamlet:

What a piece of work is a man! . . . in form, in moving, how express and admirable! in action how like an angel! in apprehension how like a god![4]

Michelangelo is at the heroic end of Renaissance humanism. Others, freed from the old medieval guilt about earthly desires, were able to take more playful delight in human beauty — none more enchantingly than Luca della Robbia, in the gallery of singing boys which he carved to hold the choir in Florence's cathedral.

Naturally the idea of the Holy Family was also affected by the new mood. The Virgin Mary gradually acquired the enchanting appeal of any beautiful girl. One of the stories recorded by Vasari tells how Filippo Lippi was painting a Virgin for a convent when he asked if a particular young nun could sit as his model. She did. He made off with her, had children, and perhaps — to judge by the similarity of his Virgins — went on being inspired by her lovely face.

But intelligence as well as beauty was a Renaissance passion. Piero della Francesca's *Resurrection* shows the highest ideal of Renaissance humanism. Here is a Christ who will redeem not by medieval suffering, not by Byzantine authority,

The Resurrected Christ *by Piero della Francesca (Pinacoteca Comunale, Sansepolcro).*

but through the virtues which make man most fully himself, most nearly a god.

In October 1405 an Italian family clambered down the steep lane to the village church of Corsignano, not far from Siena. They were coming to baptize their latest infant. There was nothing special about the occasion. The child was one of eighteen, of whom only he and two sisters survived into adult life. The family was poor. But they christened him, in true classical fashion, Aeneas. He was to become the most famous humanist of his day, because he also became pope, as Pius II.

Aeneas grew up working the land on his father's few acres; but the village priest taught him Latin and the family saved to send him to the local university, Siena. As a student, he was much impressed by the preaching of a local saint, St Bernardino, who violently attacked the frivolity of an age which had so recently seen the scandal of three popes at a time. Bernardino persuaded people to burn their playing cards, their lottery tickets, their false hair, and even their musical instruments. He preached a new morality, based on a renewed papacy. Vain hope, as it turned out.

Aeneas wrote later that he had been deeply moved, but for the moment the attractions of the world proved stronger. His intelligence, and his ready pen, won him a place in the glittering retinue of various powerful men. He was sent as ambassador on confidential missions, even on one occasion making the arduous journey to Scotland — to the court of James V, whom Aeneas described as 'small, fat and hot-tempered'. Outside the halls of diplomacy, Cupid was waiting. Aeneas records that Scottish girls were eager to entice a young Italian into their beds. At least one succeeded. Aeneas was sad to hear, later, that his infant son had died soon after birth.

His most powerful patron was the emperor, Frederick III, who made him his poet laureate. In true humanist fashion, Aeneas amused his friends by writing a saucy classical play and a novel about two lovers. But his life was about to take a more serious turn. Perhaps the demands of St Bernardino at last coincided with the demands of his career. The church could satisfy both piety and ambition.

When Aeneas stage-managed a meeting between the emperor and his Portuguese bride, he was already bishop of Siena — but a bishop who had written:

> He who has never truly felt the flames of love is but a stone, or a beast. It is no
> secret that into the very marrow-bones of the Gods has crept the fiery particle. [5]

Aeneas had been ordained a priest in 1446; he became a bishop in 1447; and a cardinal in 1456. His clerical career was progressing as smoothly as his secular one. And in 1458 he became pope. He chose the name Pius. Again a classical gesture: Virgil's favourite phrase for Aeneas had been *pius Aeneas*.

When Aeneas became pope, he tried to suppress his novel, *The Tale of Two Lovers*. I read it to find out what was so shocking, and it provides a fascinating glimpse of a humanist obsessed with the classics. Like *Lady Chatterley's Lover*, it takes a great many pages to get going. And then, at last, the big love-scene:

> They went into her room where they passed so sweet a night that both said: Mars
> and Venus could not have been better together.
>   'You are my Ganymede, my Hippolytus, my Diomedes,' said Lucretia.
>   'And you my Polixena,' he replied, 'my Aemilia, Venus herself.'
>   And sometimes, raising the blankets, he gazed at those secret parts he had not

seen before, and cried: 'Thus, when she bathed in the spring, must Diana have appeared to Actaeon.'[6]

That would hardly have cut much ice with the girls in Scotland. But it does suggest that classical literature was not quite so liberating for the writers as classical sculpture for the artists.

Knowing Aeneas's background, many people expected a gay time in Rome with him as pope. They were disappointed (they would have to wait a while yet for that). Pius devoted himself mainly to the most pressing problem of his time: a crusade against the Turks, who only five years earlier had captured the great Christian city of Constantinople. In 1464, when he was ill and in constant pain, Pius decided to lead the crusade eastwards himself. At the port of Ancona, waiting to embark, he died.

The crusade had been one over-riding passion of his six years as pope. The other was the transformation of his place of birth. As a boy he had gone out into the world from a country village, Corsignano. By the time he died he had turned that village into a perfect little Renaissance town. He called it after himself: Pienza, the town of Pius.

Pienza stands today completely unspoilt, like a preview in miniature of what the later Renaissance popes would do for Rome herself. In other ways too Pius's successors were about to go to extremes, where he had been comparatively modest. Pius made only one of his nephews a cardinal: ten years later a pope did the same for no less than seven nephews. Pius had two bastard children, both of whom were dead before he became a priest: Alexander VI was to be seen in public with his mistress even after he became pope, and was happy to leave his daughter, Lucrezia Borgia, in charge of the Vatican when he was out of Rome. Pius died leading a crusade against the Muslims: Julius II would ride out to assault Italian cities. The popes were about to become the most wordly of princes, turning Rome into the most spectacular of capital cities. Martin V had found the city overgrown by weeds. A century later Michelangelo and Raphael were only the two leaders among a galaxy of talent working to glorify Rome and the papacy. The final touches would be contributed another century after that with the work of Bernini.

Rome was being restored to her ancient greatness, and every time the builders sunk foundations for a new palace they were likely to find souvenirs of that greatness. The *Apollo Belvedere* was dug up in the Renaissance, so was the *Vatican Venus*; the *Laocoön* was found in seven separate pieces. These discoveries were eagerly bought by the popes, and as eagerly studied by the artists. Later generations would be shocked by this Renaissance friendship between Christianity and pagan antiquity. In the late sixteenth century all the classical sculptures in the Vatican were issued with the fig-leaves which they still wear (decencies unknown in the ancient world), and the great nineteenth-century historian of the papacy, Ludwig Pastor, saw the bronze doors of St Peter's as typical of the 'evil influence' of the Renaissance.

In this work, destined for the principal entrance of the noblest church in the world, the artist had — to use the mildest term — the bad taste to place together with the figures of Our Saviour and His Virgin Mother not only busts of the Roman Emperors, but also the forms of Mars and Roma, of Jupiter and Ganymede, Hero

and Leander, of a Centaur leading a nymph through the sea, and even of Leda and the swan.[7]

A tomb inside St Peter's sums up everything Pastor most disliked about the Renaissance. It is the tomb of Sixtus IV, famous for building the Sistine chapel. Around the edge, pretty girls in various stages of undress represent the Liberal Arts. On top, the sculptor has caught with brutal realism the raddled old pope of whom Machiavelli wrote:

> He was the first who began to show how far a pope might go, and how much which was previously regarded as sinful lost its iniquity when committed by a pontiff.[8]

This was the pope who made seven of his nephews cardinals. But if he made the most of his own chances, he could also sympathize with the problems of others. The young Caesar Borgia had difficulties in becoming a priest because he was illegitimate. When the case was presented to Sixtus, he decided that the normal rules need not apply — because at least Caesar's mother had been a married woman, and his father was a cardinal.

The cardinal who was Caesar's father also became pope, as Alexander VI. He

Opposite: *Laocoön by Agesander, first century* B.C. *(Cortile del Belvedere, Vatican).*

Leda and the Swan, by Filarete, on the bronze doors of St Peter's.

Naked Theology gazes at the man in the sun; detail from Pollaiuolo's tomb of Sixtus IV (St Peter's, Rome).

had at least four children before he became pope — and possibly as many as three more after receiving the papal crown. In his apartments he had himself painted in attendance at the Crucifixion: but even on that occasion his mind seems to be on other things. A contemporary wrote: 'The pope has no care for aught but exalting his children by hook or by crook.'[9] The hook and the crook were more often for his own good than theirs. His daughter Lucrezia owes her ill fame largely to the succession of marriages forced upon her by the pope to suit his own political ends. But the popes were not alone in making much of their children. A Council of 1512 ordered that priests should at least refrain from turning up at the marriages of their sons and daughters.

Naturally there was a puritan reaction. It surfaced when Florence, during the papacy of Alexander VI, was mesmerized by the sermons of a Dominican friar, Savonarola. Like St Bernardino before him, he arranged bonfires on which people must throw what he called their 'vanities':

> Oh Florence, the time of singing and dancing is over; now is the time to weep for your sins with torrents of tears.[10]

Savonarola preached against many of the more particular characteristics of the age. Against classical learning:

> Plato and Aristotle are fast in Hell. Any old woman knows more about Faith than Plato. It would be good for the Faith if many of these seemingly precious books could be destroyed.[11]

Against contemporary art:

> Ye trick out the Mother of God in the frippery of a courtesan, ye give her the features of your paramours.[12]

Against the clergy in Rome:

> With courtiers and grooms, horses and dogs, with mansions full of tapestries and silks, perfumes and lackeys, would you hold them to be pillars of the church or temporal lords?[13]

But in the end the anger of the pope and the pleasure-loving instincts of Florence coincided. The last bonfire of Savonarola's life was his own.

Meanwhile the papacy had more surprises in store. There was a contemporary joke about the change from Alexander VI to Julius II: 'First Venus ruled, then came the God of War.' Julius had been one of the seven nephews whom Sixtus made into cardinals. When he came into his papal inheritance, he set about enlarging and glorifying it. He was the first pope to employ Michelangelo and Raphael. He laid the foundation stone for the new St Peter's. He established the famous Swiss Guards, who still wear the uniform which Michelangelo designed for them. In those days the Swiss were Europe's best mercenary soldiers, and Julius employed not the odd one or two to stand at gateways, but 6,000 of them. They were a serious army. When they set out to capture cities for the papacy, Julius marched with them — more like a victorious general than a pope.

Behind this grandiose and unscrupulous Renaissance, an easy prey for satirists then and ever since, there lay the quieter Renaissance of the scholars. Deriving from fifteenth-century Florence, it reached its fullest expression in the following century and in northern Europe. Its most distinguished representative was

Opposite: *A Swiss Guard in Bernini's Bronze Doorway, the main entrance to the Vatican.*

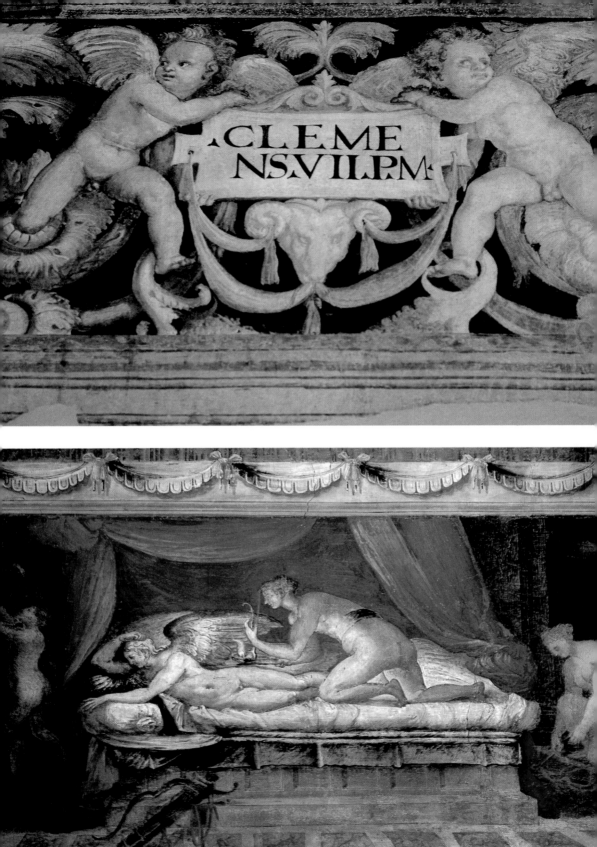

Anonymous portrait of Savonarola (San Marco, Florence).

Erasmus, and the two traditions clashed in their extreme forms when Erasmus first visited Italy in 1506. He came in high hopes to the birth-place of the Renaissance — and what did he find? Pope Julius II entering in triumph the city of Bologna, which he had just conquered. Erasmus was appalled. 'The high priest Julius', he wrote, 'wages war, conquers, triumphs, and in effect plays the part of that other Julius, Julius Caesar.'[14]

Erasmus had grown up in a background very different from the Rome of the Renaissance popes. He had been educated in a convent of the Brethren of the Common Life. The order, founded in about 1380, was part of a wider movement in the Low Countries which emphasized the value of a life of quiet devotion and of a close personal relationship with God. It was a form of practical religion open to laymen as well as priests. The most evocative traces of it today are the peaceful courtyards of the *béguinages* in Holland and Belgium, in which lay women or *béguines* used to live together practising a life of prayer and charity. The name given to the movement was 'Devotio Moderna', the modern form of devotion: its most influential book was *The Imitation of Christ* by Thomas à

Opposite: *Papal frescoes in Rome, of a type to reduce Savonarola to apoplexy: in the apartments of Clement VII and Paul III in the Castel Sant' Angelo.*

Madonna of the Cherries, *by Joos van Cleve (Suermondt Museum, Aachen).*

Kempis. This impulse towards a more personal religion can be seen now as a reform movement within the Roman Catholic church which anticipates by many years the final explosion of the Reformation. It is reflected, too, in the religious painting of northern Europe. In Italian art, donors kneel at a respectful distance from the Holy Family, remaining well outside the painted scene they have paid for: the Virgin Mary acquires the friendly face of the painter's mistress, but she remains in a formal or architectural framework, well removed from the everyday world of Renaissance Italy. In the north, Jan van Eyck painted Canon van der Paele being personally introduced to the Virgin and Child by a well-disposed saint, and even showed Chancellor Rolin alone in a room with the Holy Family. In the same way the Virgin Mary herself became increasingly natural, even bourgeois, moving into a series of delightful living-rooms with spotless but functional furniture, and the bustle of any Flemish street visible through the window. At her most enchanting she can be seen in Joos van Cleve's *Madonna of the Cherries*. There is no place for anything so unbourgeois as a halo — though a hint of it may be allowed to remain in the circular bonnet, or in such natural-istic sleight-of-hand as the fire-screen behind Robert Campin's Virgin in the National Gallery (to me, I must confess, a hideous lady, but then if Virgins are to be convincingly human they can't *all* be beautiful).

Virgin and Child, *by Robert Campin (National Gallery, London).*

The type of intellectual life which appealed to Erasmus lay between the two extremes of the monastic and the courtly. It was essentially domestic, and he found it above all in England — in the family circle of Sir Thomas More, in the friendship of John Fisher and John Colet. He shared with them the exciting Renaissance rediscovery of the classics. The group of friends put their new enthusiasm to more purely practical and Christian ends than had been the case in the earlier Italian Renaissance. Erasmus's chief reason for mastering Greek was so as to edit the Greek New Testament and the works of the early fathers. And the experience of a visit to Italy inspired Colet to found a school, St Paul's, for the creation of Christian humanist gentlemen through solid grounding in the classics and the Greek New Testament — an ideal which lasted for four centuries as the basis of the English public school.

The solemn side of this northern circle was offset by a famous playfulness. More's *Utopia* and Erasmus's *In Praise of Folly* were best-sellers in their own day and have remained so ever since. Less well known is the scurrilous Latin play which Erasmus wrote (though he never acknowledged it) after his visit to Italy. It was his satirical response to the sight of Julius II waging war. It is called *Julius Exclusus* (Julius excluded), and it tells of what happens when Julius reaches the gates of heaven. He finds them closed and locked. A translation of a brief extract will give the flavour.

JULIUS. What the devil is going on here? Doors won't open. Looks as if the lock has been changed, or tampered with anyway. Open this door right away, somebody.

ST PETER. Immortal God, what a sewer I smell here! Who are you? And what do you want?

JULIUS. I trust you recognise this key. And do you see the triple crown, as well as this robe shining all over with jewels and gold?

ST PETER. Why are you in armour?

JULIUS. Do you expect me to wage war naked?

ST PETER. You are bristling with weapons. To say nothing of the fact that you are all belches and smell of brothels, booze and gunpowder. In fact you appear to me to have just finished vomiting.

JULIUS. Thanks to me the Christian church, once starving and poor, is flourishing now with all sorts of adornments. Royal palaces, beautiful houses, plenty of servants, well trained troops.

ST PETER. In poverty, sweat, fasting, thirst and hunger Christ passed His life: and in the end He died by the most humiliating of deaths.

JULIUS. Well, perhaps He will find someone to praise Him for that — but no one to imitate Him. Not these days, at any rate.[15]

In 1527 the popes were finally paid out for playing at soldiers. In that year the pope found himself besieged for a month in his own castle in Rome by one of the armies of the emperor Charles V. It was the bitter end of many years of shifting alliances in the papacy's game of power politics.

The pope, Clement VII (an illegitimate son of one of the Medici) was praying in what is now the Vatican when the imperial army broke through the city walls and entered Rome. 'Had he tarried for three creeds more,' wrote a contemporary, 'he would have been taken prisoner within his own palace.'[16] But he hurried to safety along a raised way into the Castel Sant' Angelo. At almost exactly the same moment history's leading braggart, the goldsmith Benvenuto

The raised way that leads from St Peter's to safety, seen from the Castel Sant' Angelo.

Cellini, claims to have reached safety in the castle after fighting to the very last moment, with incredible courage, on the city walls. He found the pope's gunners in a state of panic, but vastly relieved to see him. They put him on the highest point of the castle, up by the angel, with five cannon. From there he dealt out death and destruction, accompanied by the cheers of a group of cardinals standing below. 'Anyhow,' Cellini writes, 'all I need say is that it was through me that the castle was saved that morning.'[17]

To critics of Rome, the fall of the city seemed like a prophesy fulfilled. It was a hundred years now since Czech insurgents, crying vengeance for Hus, had defeated five papal armies, and had sworn that Rome would be destroyed. It was ten years since Luther had begun predicting disaster for Rome. And there were Lutheran soldiers in the imperial army who had been deliberately encouraged by the prospect of slaughtering Roman priests. The whore-mongering Rome of the Renaissance popes had long been identified with the Bible's scarlet woman, the Whore of Babylon. Some felt she was only getting what she deserved.

The sack of Rome was much like the sack of any other rich city by an indisciplined army. Hardly a church or mansion escaped looting. Rich citizens were seized for ransom, and there were stories of nuns offered for sale on the streets. The patients of the Hospital of the Holy Spirit, just below the walls of the Castel Sant' Angelo, were thrown screaming into the waters of the Tiber. Surrounded by this turmoil, Clement VII sheltered in the rather grand papal apartments of the castle. His delightful painted bathroom is still one of the sights shown to tourists, and a frieze of cherubs enlivens his state reception room. 149

The bathroom of Clement VII in the Castel Sant' Angelo.

Opposite: *The colossal angel at the top of Castel Sant' Angelo (a later replacement of the one beneath which Cellini fired his cannon).*

Cellini says that he was himself summoned there for the pope to congratulate him on a particularly brilliant piece of marksmanship. He took the opportunity to clear his account with heaven:

> Falling on my knees, I begged the pope to absolve me of the deaths I had caused while serving the Church in the castle. He gave me his blessing and forgave me all the deaths I had ever caused and all that I ever would cause in the service of the Apostolic Church.[18]

After a few weeks of violence the city of Rome, so recently rebuilt, was largely in ruins again. But politics and diplomacy rise above such matters. Negotiations led to the army being removed from Rome, and soon pope and emperor found grounds for a new alliance. The emperor would prop up the pope's family, the Medici, in Florence: the pope would show his good will by formally crowning

Charles emperor. A seedy sub-plot later cemented the link. It was arranged that the emperor's illegitimate daughter should marry the pope's son.

By then a new fresco was going up in the building which housed Michelangelo's confident image of the birth of man — one more in keeping with the times. Clement VII commissioned Michelangelo to paint the *Last Judgment* in the Sistine Chapel as a solemn warning after the Sack of Rome. Here are still the naked realistic human bodies of the Renaissance. But not the languid nakedness of Michelangelo's Adam. Not the heroic nakedness of his David. Instead the massive nakedness of the avenging Christ. The tense nakedness of even the blessed. And the utter nakedness of the damned. Hamlet has continued with his speech:

> What a piece of work is a man! . . . in form, in moving, how express and admirable! in action how like an angel! in apprehension how like a god! . . . and yet, to me, what is this quintessence of dust? man delights not me.

One of the damned in Michelangelo's Last Judgment *(Sistine Chapel).*

CHAPTER SEVEN

Protest and Reform

I N 1517 some citizens of Wittenberg travelled to the near-by town of Jüterbog to buy future ease for their souls. They went to hear the skilful preaching of Johann Tetzel, one of the leading practitioners in the art of selling indulgences. He was selling for a good cause, the rebuilding of St Peter's in Rome, and he had an effective knack of reducing theology to jingles. His best line was provided by a rather recent doctrine, that payment could instantly benefit even the souls of the dead:

> As soon as the coin in the coffer rings,
> The soul from Purgatory springs.

At a local level the trade in indulgences was open to many abuses. Three years later a Florentine historian was complaining: 'In Germany many of the pope's ministers were seen selling at a cheap price or gambling away in the taverns the power of delivering the souls of the dead out of Purgatory.'[1] But self-indulgent friars, in the Chaucerian vein, had long been a familiar feature of Europe and would have surprised few people at Jüterbog. What would have shocked them, had they known the details, was the seedy scenario among the princes of the church which also lay behind Tetzel's indulgences.

The local prelate, Albert of Mainz, had become archbishop of two dioceses and bishop of a third, all by the age of twenty four. Such plurality was against canon law, but Pope Leo X agreed to overlook it in return for a handsome contribution to St Peter's. Albert borrowed the money from the Augsburg banking house of Fugger. To enable him to pay it back, Leo farmed out to him the sale of indulgences in Germany. Those listening to Tetzel in Jüterbog were under the impression that all their money was going to St Peter's: half of it was, but the rest would reduce Albert's debt to the Fuggers. It was the type of ecclesiastical transaction which had led many in recent years to cry out for reform in the church.

The people of Wittenberg had to travel elsewhere to hear Tetzel because his sale of indulgences had been banned in their own town by the local prince, Frederick the Wise. The reason was not that Frederick disapproved of such medieval superstition: precisely the opposite, it was a case of commercial and professional jealousy. Frederick had one of the best collections of relics in Germany, many of them brought back by himself from Jerusalem, and he wanted people to buy the indulgences attached to his own treasures. When Lucas Cranach had made an illustrated catalogue for him in 1509, the collection had already consisted of 5,005 items. The prize piece was a thorn guaranteed to have been on the inside of the Crown of Thorns, and therefore to have pierced Christ's brow, but there were also six fragments of St Bernard, four of St Augustine, a twig from the Burning Bush and a crumb from the Last Supper. By 1520 the total would rise to over 19,000 items, including no less than 204 separate portions of the children massacred by Herod. Anyone who saw all these relics on the correct day of the year, and made the necessary gifts of money, could be excused nearly two million years in purgatory.

All Saints' Day was the occasion when Frederick's indulgences were on offer, and at this same season in 1517 people were returning to Wittenberg with Tetzel's — having apparently been told they were so powerful that they could save even someone who had raped the Virgin Mary. The combination of events

Previous pages: Much Wenlock: beneath the ruins of the abbey church, the old priory has been in use since the sixteenth century as a pleasant country house.

Silver image of the child Jesus, designed to hold one particle of the town where he was born, one particle of his swaddling clothes, and so on: woodcut by Cranach the Elder for the catalogue of Frederick's relics.

stirred the leading theologian of Wittenberg university into a gesture of protest. It was largely academic, but it turned out to be the spark which ignited the Reformation. On the eve of All Saints' Day Martin Luther nailed a list of ninety-five theses or propositions to the door of the castle church at Wittenberg. The document criticized many aspects of current church practice, of which the sale of indulgences was only one, and nailing it to the door was a conventional way of inviting the town and university to public discussion of the matter. No doubt Luther was as surprised as anyone else by the explosive results.

The speed of Europe's reaction was made possible by the spread of printing. The technology was already sixty years old, but the first printed books had been expensive rarities, cheaper than manuscripts but nevertheless luxuries. Only recently had the craft become equipped for rapid production of pamphlets, with all the exciting potential of a gutter press. Someone in Wittenberg printed the ninety-five theses. It was said that in two weeks all Germany had read them, and in four the whole of Europe. Soon there was a full-scale pamphlet war between those who supported Luther and those who opposed him. More pamphlets were

157

published between 1521 and 1524 in Germany than in any other four years in history, and by 1523 there had been 1,300 different editions of tracts by Luther alone. Scurrilous cartoons were on sale to rival the violence of the language in which the debate was conducted. Luther wrote about 'the cardinals and the pope and the whole swarm of Roman Sodom, who corrupt youth and the Church of God'.[2] The pope described Luther as 'that child of Satan, son of perdition, scrofulous sheep, and tare in the vineyard'.[3]

For the argument to catch fire so quickly there had to be a large number of people already in agreement with Luther. On the negative side his criticism of the ways of Rome was by now part of a long tradition, which was increasingly reinforced by each new wave of nationalism. It was essentially *Roman* Sodom that he was attacking, and he made much of the fact that very few Germans could travel as far as St Peter's: would the pope soon be expecting Germans to pay for the palaces and bridges of Rome as well as its churches? But on a deeper level too his voice was part of a chorus, deriving from the 'Devotio Moderna' and the long-standing demand for a more personal religion than Rome had provided.

Whatever his qualities as a theologian, it is the character of Luther himself which stands out so powerfully from the pages of history and makes him — for me — the most attractive of all those who have diverted the course of Christianity. Brash, obstinate, hasty, unreasonable, he lived life with a ferocious warmth and openness. The cloister at Wittenberg which housed him as a tormented young monk remained his home as a middle-aged pastor with an ex-nun for a wife, six children, four orphans, and at every meal a table-full

Martin Luther, by Cranach the Elder (Uffizi, Florence).

of students. His life was as remarkable as his character.

As a young man, Luther had been obsessed with guilt. Not many sins are available to a serious-minded monk, but on one occasion Luther confessed for six hours on end and still, a few minutes later, remembered something he had omitted. He felt that he could never survive the judgment of God, a conviction which seemed to drag him towards the fatal blasphemy of hating God. His peace of mind was saved through lecturing on St Paul (his monastic superiors had guided him into academic paths, and he had become professor of biblical theology at Wittenberg). Feeling himself so sinful that he despaired of having the merit to be saved, he suddenly found in Paul that idea reversed. Man was so sinful, said Paul, that only through God's mercy could he be saved. Therefore his only merit was to have faith in that mercy; 'we hold that a man is justified by faith, apart from works of law.'[4] Justification by faith was to become the central theme of Luther's teaching. It undercut the entire code of discipline of the medieval church, which was much like that of an old-fashioned school — with a recording angel awarding bad marks for sin and good ones for merit, until on the last day of term each pupil must settle his account with God. Worst of all, and frowned upon in any school, bad marks could be erased for cash in the system of indulgences. The abuse which prompted the ninety-five theses touched upon the very essence of Luther's thought.

Luther disregarded every order from Rome that he should recant, and he would certainly have been burnt as a heretic if Frederick had handed him over. It is one of the most remarkable details of the whole story that Frederick did not do so, particularly since Luther's attack had touched so precisely on his own beloved collection of relics. No doubt he felt something of the power of Luther, even though he met him only once, and certainly regional independence played its part. Frederick had founded the university of Wittenberg in 1502 and was intensely proud of his creation. Luther, its most distinguished member, had suddenly become famous throughout Europe. Frederick was in no hurry to deliver such a man to certain death at the hands of an Italian pope.

Frederick's protection of Luther was soon to go far beyond diplomatic inaction. In 1521 the emperor, Charles V, summoned Luther to justify himself at the Diet of Worms. Nobody knows whether Luther actually spoke those famous words 'Here I stand: I can do no other,' but that was certainly the essence of his case. Scripture, he said, had given him his idea of Christianity. If anyone could prove *from Holy Scripture* that he was mistaken, then he would immediately recant. But Charles V was interested in being obeyed, not in being debated with. He declared Luther an outlaw, and his pronouncement followed the current fashion for strong language:

> This devil in the habit of a monk has brought together ancient errors into one stinking puddle, and has invented new ones. His teaching makes for rebellion, division, war, murder, robbery, arson, and the collapse of Christendom. He lives the life of a beast.[5]

Luther gave his own version of the affair in a letter to Cranach:

> I expected that His Majesty the Emperor would have collected fifty doctors of divinity to confute the monk in argument. But all they said was: 'Are these books yours?' 'Yes.' 'Will you recant?' 'No.' 'Then get out.'[6]

Luther left Worms under a safe conduct guaranteed for a few days by the emperor. Once the safe conduct expired, it was the duty of any loyal subject to seize him as an outlaw. He was bumping along in his wagon, through some woods, when armed men appeared and dragged him off. For almost a year he was not seen in public, and many assumed he was dead. But the armed men had been servants of Frederick the Wise. They took Luther to one of Frederick's strongest castles, the Wartburg, where he was given new clothes and a new identity — that of a minor nobleman, who became known to the local people as Junker George.

Junker George was far from idle in his unusually grand accommodation (though he did blame the rich food for his constipation and his piles suddenly becoming worse). Being Luther, he immediately launched into a string of polemical pamphlets; and he began one of his greatest undertakings, the translation of the Bible into German. He completed a first draft of the New Testament in less than three months, and it was published by Cranach in September 1522 — with a series of powerful woodcuts from Cranach's studio to illustrate Revelation (the book which provided by far the best opportunities for anti-papal satire). There had been earlier German Bibles, but they had offered only pedestrian and confused texts. Luther was the first writer of genius to apply himself to the task, and his translation came at a time when a great number of Germans were ready for it. Books were still expensive (the New Testament cost about the weekly wage of a carpenter), but in fifty years one firm in Wittenberg alone printed 100,000 copies of the entire Bible. In Protestant countries today, where the Bible has long been listed as the world's best-selling book and can be found free in every hotel bedroom, it is hard for us to imagine the excitement of being among the first generation of ordinary Christians able to read it for themselves.

While Luther was in hiding, his followers at Wittenberg were eagerly taking reform into their own hands. Monks and nuns were being urged to marry each other. Mass was being said in new forms, with all mention of sacrifice removed and with the wine as well as the bread given to the congregation. Priests who kept to the old ways were attacked, altars and paintings were smashed. The violence predicted in the Edict of Worms was becoming a reality. The town council of Wittenberg urged Luther to return. He did so (relying for safety now on the strength of his own following, for Frederick would not guarantee him protection outside the Wartburg), and he was soon able to restrain the leading hotheads in his own city. But his own rejection of established authority in the church was now having a side-effect — releasing, if only by example, other long-standing pressures which had built up within Germany. For over a century there had been peasant unrest against intolerable feudal conditions, but it was no accident that the final eruption came in the early years of the Reformation or that the influence of Luther could be seen in some of the peasants' demands. Luther's first reaction to the Peasants' War of 1524–5 was a liberal one (he sat on the fence, explaining that he could see merits and weaknesses in both sides of the argument), but as the violence escalated he penned a hasty tract *Against the Murderous and Thieving Hordes of Peasants* which included the words:

Let everyone who can smite, slay and stab, remembering that nothing can be more devilish than a rebel. It is just as when one must kill a mad dog.[7]

The heritage of Renaissance Italy, against which Luther reacted. Opposite: *Luca della Robbia's Singing Gallery (Museo dell Opera dell Duomo, Florence) (see page 138).* Overleaf: *The miraculous Virgin of Orsanmichele (see page 134).* Overleaf right: *The power of the keys, a colossal statue of St Peter in front of St Peter's, Rome.*

The scarlet woman of Rome; woodcut from Cranach's studio, illustrating Luther's New Testament.

By the time his pamphlet was in circulation the peasants had been defeated, and in the usual pattern of such events the ruling classes were exacting a revenge far more brutal than the original offence. Some said that as many as 100,000 peasants were butchered in a frenzy of aristocratic reprisal. Luther's hasty words were

Opposite: *Cambridge, where Lutheran ideas first took hold in England; and the Reformers' Monument in Geneva, capturing the severity of Farel, Calvin, Beza and Knox.*

never forgotten, and by many never forgiven, but the whole gruesome episode left him with a determination to stand aside from politics. A somewhat passive acceptance of political overlords became a characteristic of his church, even — in many cases — when those overlords were the Nazis.

In 1525 the Lutherans had not yet achieved any settlement with the imperial authorities. Germany was ruled by many independent princes, some of whom had allowed their local churches to adopt Luther's reforms while others remained faithful to Rome. Charles V had outlawed Luther at Worms and regarded his ideas as heretical, but he needed a united Germany to support him in defending the east of the empire against the Turks. He therefore called a diet at Augsburg, in 1530, in which he would hear both Lutheran and Catholic princes and attempt to settle their argument. Instead of the single monk nine years before at Worms, the emperor was now confronted by a powerful and well-organized faction who would use the occasion to present their articles of faith. The obvious man to argue the case was that single monk from Worms (by now himself married to a nun), but Luther was still an excommunicated outlaw. The task fell to his more diplomatic and more scholarly lieutenant, the young professor of Greek at Wittenberg university — Philip Melanchthon, who alone, among all Cranach's portraits of the healthy and square-jawed leaders of the Reformation, has the scraggy look of an intellectual. It was he who drafted the Confession of Augsburg, tracing the Protestant ideals back to the early days of Christianity (a pattern repeated by almost every new Christian sect in history), and presenting Protestantism as a movement for reform from within an apostolic church betrayed by more recent developments in Rome.

The emperor turned out to be no more inclined to conciliation at Augsburg than he had been at Worms. He rejected the Confession outright, and gave the Protestant princes nine months to retract — after which he would bring them to heel by force. In fact he was in no position to do so, and the unresolved situation dragged on for a quarter of a century until the Peace of Augsburg in 1555. The treaty established the principle which would later be defined in the phrase *cuius regio eius religio*: whoever has the kingdom chooses the religion. Each prince or duke could decide whether to be Catholic or Lutheran, but everyone in his territory must either follow suit or move elsewhere. It was hardly freedom of conscience, but only a few dangerous radicals regarded that as desirable in the sixteenth century.

By the time of the Peace of Augsburg Luther himself was dead. His later years had provided a quite new image in western Christianity — that of life in the vicarage, with a married pastor living like any other man among his own family. Luther's marriage to Catherine von Bora had hardly started out on a high note of romance. Twelve nuns, inspired by his teaching, wanted to leave a convent near Wittenberg and Luther helped them do so. Three returned to their homes, but the other nine had nowhere to go. A student described their arrival in Wittenberg: 'A wagon load of vestal virgins has just come to town, all more eager for marriage than for life. God grant them husbands lest worse befall.'[8] Luther was able to find homes and husbands for all but one, Catherine: so he took her in himself. 'There is a lot to get used to in the first year of marriage,' he said later. 'One wakes up in the morning and finds a pair of pigtails on the pillow which were not there before.'[9] But soon he was able to write to friends: 'My Catherine

Philip Melanchthon, by Cranach the Younger (Städ. Kunstinstitut, Frankfurt-a.-M.).

is fulfilling Genesis 1:28. There is about to be born a child of a monk and a nun.'[10] In the end they had six children, and adopted four orphans as well. After the initial shock Luther came to see the raising of children as enhancing a priest's spiritual life. With his usual pungency of phrase and observation he expressed the clash in a work entitled *Concerning Married Life*. Reason is arguing with Christian Faith. Reasons says:

> Why must I rock the baby, wash its nappies, change its bed, smell its odour, heal its rash? It is better to remain single and live a quiet and carefree life. I will become a priest or a nun and tell my children to do the same.

Christian Faith replies:

> The father opens his eyes, looks at these lowly, distasteful and despised things and knows that they are adorned with divine approval as with the most precious gold

163

Luther and his wife Catherine: portraits, possibly for their wedding, by Cranach the Elder (Kunstmuseum, Basel).

and silver. God, with his angels and creatures, will smile — not because nappies are washed, but because it is done in faith.[11]

That has both the satirical edge and the down–to–earth warmth which were two of Luther's most powerful qualities. And his life with Catherine and the nappies was to establish the pattern of parsonage life which has lasted in Protestant communities ever since.

The Peace of Augsburg had only recognized one Protestant church, the Lutheran, but from the earliest years of the Reformation there had been several varieties of reformed Christianity arguing almost as much with each other as with Rome. It was the beginning of the growth of sects, which became inevitable once truth was agreed to be in the Bible and the Bible made available to everyone. The process was seen in dramatic form at a conference in the castle of Marburg in 1530. A young ruler, Philip of Hesse, had adopted Lutheran views when he was only twenty and had established the first Protestant university at Marburg, but he became disturbed by the already differing Protestant interpretations of the Christian sacrament. So he invited the most distinguished Protestant clergy to discuss the problem in his presence. The chief adversaries were Luther and Huldreich Zwingli, the founder of the Reformation in Zurich. The two men agreed in dismissing the Catholic doctrine of transubstantiation, according to which the bread and wine are transformed entirely at the moment of consecration into the body and blood of Jesus (the appearance of bread and wine remaining, but no trace of their original substance). Zwingli believed that the bread and wine merely represented the body and blood of Christ, in a sacred metaphor. Luther had devised a middle way, often loosely referred to as consubstantiation, according to which the sacrament received by a communicant was both things at once, the body and blood of Christ existing 'in, with and under' the bread and wine. Both men came to the debate armed only with a Bible. Luther began by warning that no one would shift him from the irrefutable certainty of Mark 14:22, where Jesus says, 'Take, eat, this is my body.' He produced a piece of chalk, drew a circle on the table, wrote in it THIS IS MY BODY

164

and sat back as though there were no more to be said. Zwingli was equally dogmatic in his insistence on John 6 : 63: 'The spirit alone gives life; the flesh is of no avail.' Agreement proved impossible. All truth was in the scriptures, but the scriptures were capable of almost infinitely varied interpretation. Marburg provided a vivid glimpse of the Protestant future.

Certain city states of Switzerland, with no princes to dictate their religious policy, rapidly achieved more radical changes than were possible in Germany. By 1523 Zwingli had brought Zurich over to reformed ways, but a few years later he himself died on the field of battle against neighbouring cantons loyal to Rome. By mid-century it was another city, Geneva, which had become the dynamic centre of the Reformation. The year 1536 had been a momentous one for Geneva. In that year the city won its freedom from Savoy, adopted the tenets of the reformed faith, and welcomed a refugee from France — John Calvin.

Calvin was both the clearest thinker and the most able administrator among the leaders of the Reformation. As a result he was able to create in Geneva what many of his contemporaries regarded as a perfect working model of a godly city, run according to the precepts of the Bible. It would not have suited most of us today. Portraits of Calvin show him with an inordinately long nose — for poking into other people's affairs, his enemies might with some justice have said. Pastors and magistrates joined forces to supervise every detail of the citizens' lives. Annual visits were made to each home to ensure there was no moral laxity. Adultery was punishable by death (in keeping with Leviticus 20:10), and on one occasion a young man was beheaded for striking his parents (Exodus 21:15). Admittedly other cities were accustomed to similar supervision by bishops or princes, and discipline at the university of Paris, where Calvin had studied, was

The Protestant sense of intimacy with God: various reformers sharing in the Last Supper, Melanchthon on Jesus's left, Luther two to his right (Cranach the Younger, Marienkirche, Dessau).

based on a system of organized snooping very like the methods of Geneva. It was largely the joylessness of the reformed legislation that was new — the attitude which opponents would later define as Puritan. Dancing was banned, together with taverns and lewd songs (though many of these regulations proved predictably difficult to enforce). On the credit side there was a more democratic approach to church affairs. The presbyterian system, which Calvin believed to be a return to the ways of the early church as described in the New Testament, puts power jointly in the hands of pastors and lay elders; but neither group has any authority until elected by the congregation. A sense of civic responsibility, combined with a nagging concern for other people's morals, encouraged a new orderliness and honesty in everyday life — virtues which would cause Calvinist communities to be particularly well suited to the making of money. But there was also, in Calvin himself, that self-righteousness which would be one of the least attractive Puritan qualities. A maker of playing-cards, whose business was affected by the new legislation, was overheard criticizing Calvin. The council ordered him to kneel and apologize to Calvin in their presence, but Calvin insisted that this was not enough. In the end the man had to walk all round the town, dressed only in a shirt and crying to God for mercy.

Geneva had in a sense been taken over by outsiders. In 1546 not one of the thirteen pastors was a native of the city. Calvin had been among the earliest of a string of distinguished refugees, one of whom, John Knox, has left us with the best-known definition of Calvin's city: 'the most perfect school of Christ that

Opposite: John Knox preaching; detail from the Reformers' Monument in Geneva.

The new form of worship, centred on the pulpit; a service in the Calvinist church at Lyons in 1564 (Bibliothèque Publique et Universitaire, Geneva).

BVCHA

LE RÉFORMATEVR DE L'ESCOSSE

ever was in the earth since the days of the Apostles'.[12] It was a school from which pupils would return to their own countries taking the principles of Geneva, so that Calvinism rapidly became more international than either of the other Protestant churches of the Reformation, the Lutheran or the Anglican. By the end of the sixteenth century there were Calvinist churches in parts of Germany, in the Netherlands and in Scotland, as well as the powerful Huguenot minority in France.

In the Netherlands Calvinism became the rallying point for opposition to the oppressive rule of Catholic Spain. Calvinist ministers had been among the earliest leaders of a small group which we would describe today as guerrillas or freedom fighters, from whom there developed a national party of the northern provinces. The princely leader of the fight for independence, William the Silent, joined the reformed church in 1573 and during the next decade a Dutch republic gradually emerged. The song written for the followers of William the Silent, the 'Song of the Prince', is today the national anthem of the Netherlands. Calvinism had been the driving force in creating a new country, free from foreign domination.

In Scotland the Calvinists went one stage further, in a political programme which was even more radical in its implications. At precisely the same period as the Lutherans in Germany were establishing the principle of *cuius regio eius religio*, the Scots were asserting the very opposite — that the people had the right to choose their own religion, regardless of the will of the monarch. In 1560 the Scottish parliament abolished papal authority and decreed a form of Calvinism as the religion of the country. Scotland became something unique in the Europe of the day: a land of one religion with a monarch of another. Admittedly there were, as always, political as well as religious causes for this state of affairs. The monarch, Mary Queen of Scots, was an eighteen-year-old girl living abroad, and English troops were underwriting Scottish independence for fear that Mary might deliver Scotland into the hands of her husband, the king of France. But the notion that the people could assert themselves against their ruler was a triumph for the ideas of one man, John Knox. 'God help us', wrote the archbishop of Canterbury, 'from such visitation as Knox has attempted in Scotland, the people to be orderers of things.'[13]

The most formative event in the life of Knox had been the accession of Henry VIII's Catholic daughter, Mary I, to the throne of England in 1553. Knox had been preaching in England during the previous reign, indeed had been a leading figure among those who were trying to hurry the cautious English into the Calvinist fold, but then almost overnight the country was a Catholic one again, with all the work apparently undone and clergy of Knox's complexion now likely candidates for the stake. Knox escaped to the continent, where he developed the theory that people practising the true Protestant faith had the right to resist, if necessary by force, any Roman Catholic ruler who tried to prevent them. Calvin disagreed with Knox on this point, recommending a patient acceptance of persecution, but it was a theory greatly attractive to many of the nobles of Scotland — who had their own political reasons for resisting the French-orientated royal family.

Knox returned to Scotland when civil war broke out in 1559; by the summer of 1560 the Protestants were in control of Edinburgh, where he drafted the articles of religion passed by the parliament; and in 1561 Mary Queen of Scots, still only nineteen but by now a widow, decided to return to her kingdom. Over the next few years the ferocious man of God and the young queen came to symbolize the two sides of the argument: not only Protestant against Catholic, but also the democratic claims of Calvinism — with elected elders of the church running their own affairs — against the establishment hierarchy of a monarch with the power to appoint bishops. Events were to favour Knox. Scotland followed his path rather than Mary's. And even though Mary's descendants later fought back, foisting bishops for a while upon the Church of Scotland, the country has remained more thoroughly Calvinist than almost any other. Mary's present-day descendant, Queen Elizabeth, is head of an episcopal church south of the border and of a presbyterian one north of it. It is an arrangement which would have horrified Elizabeth I.

The Church of England was the last of the three great Protestant groups of the Reformation to find its own identity, and — in true English fashion — it found it in a compromise between the many different pressures of the century. Henry VIII, its ostensible founder, had intended to do little more than replace the pope with himself: he wanted an English Catholic church instead of a Roman Catholic one. But during his reign the various influences of the continental Reformation were surreptitiously circulating and competing for favour among the people of England. Once the tyrannical Defender of the Faith died, the struggle was on to define that faith — and it was to be carried through to its conclusion by his three children in what was almost the Hegelian pattern of thesis, antithesis and synthesis. The thesis was the newest available, the reformed faith of Calvin, which was urged upon the nation by the ministers of Edward VI. The antithesis was the full-scale return to the opposite extreme, the ways of Rome, under Mary. And the synthesis was achieved by the reconciling genius of Elizabeth, who enabled the Anglican church to settle into its characteristic pattern. It was a pattern capable of lurching, in later centuries, towards either of the extremes which had gone into its formation. The churches and services of the eighteenth century were plain enough for a Puritan, but in more recent years one section of the Anglican church has swung far enough in the opposite direction to acquire the name of Anglo-Catholic.

The mingling of influences which went to make up Anglicanism seem personified in the life of Thomas Cranmer, the new church's first archbishop and the author of its Prayer Book. The earliest stirrings of Lutheranism in England were at his own university, Cambridge, where secret meetings were held to discuss the new ideas at the White Horse Inn, and where the authorities reacted with a public bonfire of Luther's books outside Great St Mary's. That was in 1520, when Cranmer was thirty-one and a university preacher. He seems to have played no part in the White Horse circle, and he remained in safe but respectable obscurity until he was commanded by Henry VIII, in 1529, to write a treatise on the royal divorce. Henry had been trying to persuade the pope that his marriage to Catherine of Aragon was against canon law because she had been the widow of his elder brother. Cranmer's task was to choose between two verses of the Old Testament: between the pope's favourite ('If brethren dwell together, and one of them die, and have no child, the wife of the dead shall not marry without unto a stranger: her husband's brother shall go in unto her, and take her to him to wife, 169

Henry VIII, by Hans Holbein the Younger (Galleria Nazionale, Rome).

Thomas Cranmer, by G. Flicke (National Portrait Gallery, London).

and perform the duty of an husband's brother unto her', Deuteronomy, 25:5), and the one preferred by Henry ('If a man shall take his brother's wife, it is an unclean thing: he hath uncovered his brother's nakedness; they shall be childless', Leviticus, 20:21). It was a dramatic example of the new sixteenth-century fashion of each man interpreting the Bible for himself. Cranmer chose Leviticus and a successful career. Four years later, as archbishop of Canterbury, he formally pronounced the marriage to Catherine invalid. It was only the first of four marriages which he would help Henry to unscramble.

With the Act of Supremacy, in 1534, Henry repudiated the authority of the pope and declared himself head of the Church of England. Now king and archbishop were free to guide the new church in whichever direction they might please: but, while Cranmer was steadily becoming a more convinced Protestant (moving into broad agreement with Luther and then on towards a more Calvinist position), Henry had no interest in reform for its own sake. In 1539 the king even decreed the death penalty for anyone denying the Catholic doctrine of transubstantiation. This was no idle threat, but it did complicate matters that the archbishop of Canterbury had himself by then ceased to believe in transubstantiation. Cranmer wisely bided his time. His opportunity as a reformer came under Edward VI, when the two successive protectors of England (the dukes of Somerset and Northumberland) were committed reformers. It was now that Cranmer wrote his two versions of the Prayer Book, which show a careful and far from bigoted selection from the available models. The 1549 version follows Luther's example in keeping as much as possible of the Roman Catholic service, while strictly eliminating any hint of the mass as a sacrifice. In the following years Cranmer came under increasingly Calvinist influences, and the 1552 version is correspondingly more radical.

The slowly developing Church of England was proving itself anything but dogmatic, but it was about to be swamped by a brief return of the old dogmas. In the reign of Mary, Cranmer was tried for treason and then for heresy. His famous death-scene was as much hedged about with ambiguities as his life. He had been tormented and tricked into recanting his past beliefs, but when he finally approached the flames, after months of delay, his courage returned. In a gesture which was to provide lasting inspiration to the young Anglican church, Cranmer publicly withdrew his recantation and held in the flames the hand which had betrayed him by signing it. His entire life had had a bumbling and very human quality markedly different from the strong certainties of Knox or Calvin, and the churches south and north of the border were to reflect that difference.

It must have come as a profound shock in the villages of England to hear that an archbishop of Canterbury was being burnt as a heretic. It was only one of many such jolts. Probably no two generations have had to adjust to so many religious surprises as the people of England between 1521 and 1571. It provides an intriguing glimpse of a turbulent period to imagine the changes as they affected an ordinary English community.

The half century began with a gratifying token of England's orthodoxy. It was in 1521 that Henry VIII sent a book he had written, *Defence of the Seven Sacraments*, for presentation in Rome to Pope Leo X. It consisted of a violent attack on what Henry called that 'scabby and incurable sheep', Martin Luther. The average Englishman would have heard with pride how the pope had rewarded Henry, giving him the title 'Defender of the Faith' — a title mysteriously carried ever since by his successors, who so soon were to be busy defending another faith.

Thirteen years later came the announcement that Henry had himself replaced the pope. Changes followed in profusion. Every Englishman lived near some monastery or priory (it has been calculated that the income of the religious houses was more than three times that of the crown, a fact which provided Henry's real motive for closing them down), and during the second half of the 1530s government officials were to be seen arriving to assess the wealth of each foundation. Soon the monks or nuns were moved out and some rich man arrived to take possession of his new purchase. The monks were given a reasonable pension, but the nuns were less well provided for. They were expected to have a family to return to, and Henry decreed that they should not be allowed to marry even though they now found themselves back in the world.

Another local excitement at much the same time was the arrival of the Great Bible, the first authorized English translation, which was ordered to be placed in every church. As in other countries, the sudden access to the scriptures caused the greatest excitement — so much so that Henry became alarmed by the possibly radical influence of Holy Writ. New regulations arrived in 1543. From now on only noblemen and gentlemen were to be allowed to read the scriptures to their families. Richer merchants and the wives of the aristocracy were to be trusted to study the Bible in the privacy of their own rooms. Nobody else was to have access to it at all.

The Protestant view of the power of the Bible: the four evangelists stone the pope (Girolamo da Treviso, c. 1536, Royal Collection, Windsor).

Developments were fast and furious after the accession of Edward VI. The mass was now to be celebrated in English instead of Latin (a profound shock, as the experience of Roman Catholics in our own time has proved: ten years later an old woman complained that Satan still wouldn't let her pray in English, but kept thrusting the Latin words into her mind). It was announced that priests could marry. To add to the excitement the archbishop of Canterbury, Thomas Cranmer himself, began appearing in public with a wife, and it turned out that he had been secretly married to her for the last twenty-five years. The ex-nuns were told that they too could now marry. And word arrived, to the considerable annoyance of most congregations, that there were to be no more candles at Candlemas, no more ashes on Ash Wednesday, no more palms on Palm Sunday, and no more use of images in the church.

People were still grumbling at the more kill-joy of these changes when the pendulum swung back again with the reign of Mary, immediately killing the joy of at least a few of those who had benefited under Edward. The ex-nuns were informed that it had been a mortal sin in them to marry. They were ordered to separate from their husbands and to hurry straight back into nuns' costume. That was all that remained for them to hurry back into. The recent purchasers of the convents and monasteries were sufficiently powerful to extract a promise from the queen, before they consented to a cardinal setting foot in England again, that there should be no returning of monastic lands. Now the Latin mass was back, and from 1555 to 1558 there came regular news of the burning of Protestant martyrs — nearly 300 in the three years. The number was not great compared to those who lost their lives for religion in other European countries — but it exceeded all the executions for heresy under Henry VIII or Elizabeth. Those three years laid the basis for the long-lasting and hysterical strain of anti-Catholicism in English life.

When Elizabeth came to the throne, some of these local stories had a happy ending. Records survive of at least one nun whose convent was dissolved under Henry, who married under Edward, who was separated from her husband under Mary, and who rejoined him under Elizabeth. The mass was in English once more, but from the start Elizabeth was determined to rule for all her people. Catholics were informed that they would not be punished for their religion, but only for any actions harmful to the realm. Such tolerance, unusual for the time, was threatened by two developments. The excommunication of Elizabeth by Pius V made it difficult for any English Catholic to proclaim himself a loyal subject. And soon the threat of invasion from Spain made Protestants suspect him of being a disloyal one. In 1571, the last year of this topsy-turvy half century, Foxe's *Book of Martyrs* appeared. It enshrined the suffering of all the Protestants who had gone to their deaths (their last moments being depicted in vivid woodcuts), and it was soon to win a cherished place in every Anglican home second only to the Bible.

Two years after Elizabeth's death came the Catholic attempt at treason which finally gave Protestant bigotry its chance. After the gunpowder plot had been discovered, and the king and parliament saved from death by explosion, November 5th was decreed an annual day of thanksgiving. In a few places it remains, even today, an opportunity for anti-Catholic propaganda as much as for fireworks. It was to be more than two centuries before Catholics recovered a normal role in English life.

In the 1970s Britain is the only European country to suffer what seems the most outrageous anachronism — a religious war, more in keeping with the sixteenth or seventeenth centuries. The obscene horrors of Ulster are certainly more political than religious (Protestant settlers were moved there for political reasons, and the modern resentment of the Catholics has economic and political causes), but this is in keeping with those earlier and equally violent struggles. It was equally true in Reformation Germany, Switzerland, Holland, Scotland or England that politics and religion were inseparable.

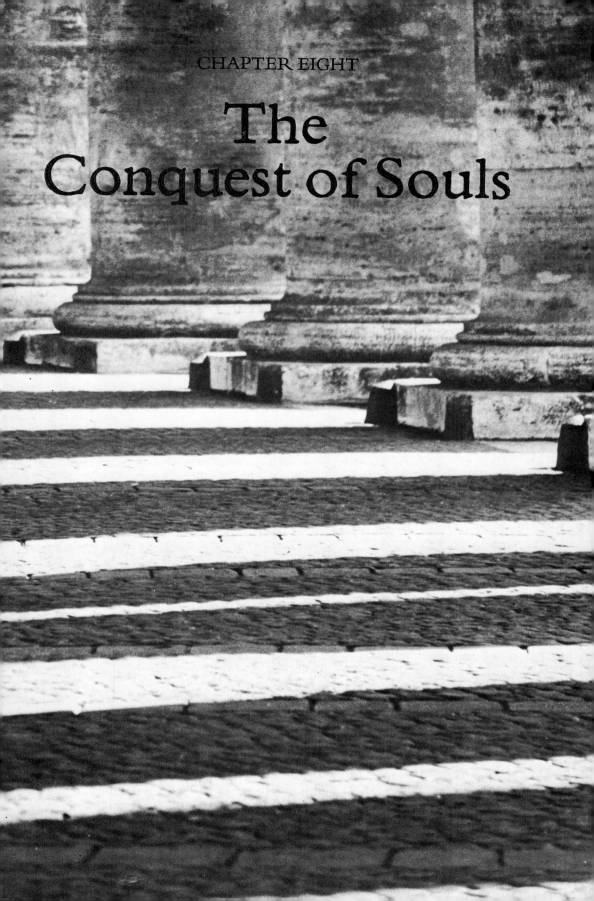

CHAPTER EIGHT

The
Conquest of Souls

ANYONE alive in Europe around 1490 heard two pieces of news, in rapid succession, which were as startling to them as the first landing on the moon was to us. In 1488 a Portuguese ship sailed round the southern tip of Africa and discovered the ocean stretching on to the east. Four years later a Spanish ship found America to the west. The pattern was set for the next century: Portugal going east, Spain west, and both of them offering Christianity in return for spices and gold. Priests eager to convert Indians had sailed with the first Portuguese ships looking for a cheap route to the spices of the east (ground pepper and gold dust had almost the same value in those days), and when Columbus came back with news of gold and the West Indies, the reaction of someone present at his home-coming was: 'Behold how posterity will see the Christian religion extended.'[1]

Within ten years of the Portuguese first rounding the Cape, their ships had explored up the east coast of Africa and Vasco de Gama had reached India. The king of Portugal, Manuel I, was now cheerfully calling himself 'Lord of the Conquest, Navigation and Commerce of Ethiopia, Arabia, Persia and India'. When he visited Rome he gave a present to the pope which was a huge success — an elephant from India. Rome was amazed at the king's procession, which included other exotic details from the east: Persian horses, Indian poultry, parrots, leopards, a panther.

It was a display designed to please and impress the pope — a necessary piece of diplomacy, because if Spain and Portugal were to sail the globe converting natives to Christianity they needed a licence from Rome. The very year that Columbus returned from America, in 1493, Pope Alexander VI had drawn an arbitrary line down the Atlantic. He decreed that everything to the west would belong to Spain, and everything to the east to Portugal. The following year the Portuguese persuaded him to shift the line 370 leagues farther west. Nobody knew it at the time, but the line now nicked the coast of Brazil (which was discovered six years later). Today huge Brazil is still the odd one out in South America, the only country speaking Portuguese instead of Spanish. It was important to keep in with the pope.

The Portuguese, sailing eastwards, were opening up rich new areas for trade: India, the Spice Islands, even Japan and China. But these were civilized countries with long-established and sophisticated religions. The merchants and the priests would come alike as suppliants. The Spaniards, on the other hand, were discovering lands in the west which could be conquered — both for Christ and for the Spanish king. The glamour and the real wealth, throughout the sixteenth century, was with Spain. The harbour of Seville was a constant bustle of ships setting off for the islands of the West Indies, for Cuba, and above all for Mexico.

Mexico was the most important of Spain's conquests in the New World. It became the administrative centre for all her American territories, and was also the first place where the Spaniards found, and annihilated, a culture older than their own. The huge temple-city of Teotihuacan is a measure of Mexico's cultural past. This was a busy place in the century before Christ. And it was here that nearly all the traditions of ancient Mexico had their beginning.

The largest monument is the Temple of the Sun. The gods had created the sun,

Previous pages: *Under Bernini's colonnade in St Peter's Square, Rome.*

Opposite: *The Holy Spirit, in Bernini's stained-glass window for St Peter's, Rome.*

The harbour at Seville, attributed to Sanchez Coello (Museo de America, Madrid).

it was later believed, in Teotihuacan. But the sun that they made was stationary. They found that it needed blood if it was to move through the heavens, so the gods sacrificed themselves to set it going. It was a legend which was to have gruesome consequences in Mexican history, when men came to feel that it was up to them — and to human blood — to keep the sun on its course.

But that was later. Teotihuacan itself seems to have been a gentle place, run by priests rather than warriors, and with gods who made no extravagant demands. There was the owlish, bespectacled rain god; and Quetzalcoatl, the plumed serpent, who may look fierce but who was the god of craftsmen and artists. Perhaps in the long run Teotihuacan was too gentle. It was destroyed by a more warlike tribe, the Toltecs, in the seventh century.

The Toltecs built themselves a city of pyramid-temples to the east of Teotihuacan, at Tula. Here began the Mexico which the Spaniards discovered — a society of warrior kings and of gods insatiable for blood, which was developed by the Toltecs and later carried to its furthest extreme by the Aztecs. By the time the Spaniards arrived, the ceremonial year had become a grisly round of human sacrifices. Children were drowned to please the rain-god. Women danced in the temple, knowing that their heads would be slashed off as they did so. Prisoners were flayed so that the priests could dress up in their skins. And above all there was the insatiable thirst of the sun.

The most important sacrifice of all took place once every fifty-two years. It was the end of a cycle in the Mexican calendar, the time when the sun was most likely to die unless human blood refreshed him. His rebirth was encouraged, and

177

Opposite: *A fountain in the form of a galleon, in the gardens of the Vatican.*

Quetzalcoatl, the plumed serpent, on one of the pyramids at Teotihuacan.

then celebrated, in the ceremony of the New Fire. A fifty-two-year cycle came to an end in 1507; it was to be the last time that the New Fire was lit because by then the Aztec ruler was Moctezuma, the man who would later lose his empire to Cortes and the Spaniards.

The ceremony took place in the middle of the night, and it must have been highly dramatic. All fires had been put out throughout the empire — the perfect image of death. Huge crowds gathered round the base of a hill, watching and waiting in the darkness. On top of the hill stood the emperor, his priests and the chosen victim. The priests were following the movement of the stars. If a certain moment passed, the sun might rise again. Suddenly they gave the sign. The victim was slit open, his heart was torn out, in the cavity a fire-stick was twirled; and a flame sprang up, life from death. Torches were lit at this single flame to carry the precious fire to altars and hearths.

It was a ceremony with uncanny echoes for a Christian. It is like a gruesome parody of the ritual of the Holy Fire performed each Easter at Jerusalem, where the patriarch goes into the darkened tomb of Christ and brings out a miraculous flame which is carried off by runners to light other altars. There is no more basic human symbolism — spring from winter, life from death. But in the Christian version the death, as well as the life, is symbolic.

178   When Moctezuma celebrated the New Fire in 1507, nobody in Mexico knew

that strangers had already landed on Caribbean islands not far from the east coast. And no Spaniard was aware that the vast, rich and exotic empire of the Aztecs was only a short sea-journey ahead. It was one of those dramatic pauses in history, a lull before a very brief and violent storm.

The storm broke in 1519, when Hernan Cortes landed with 500 soldiers and sixteen horses. Amazingly, it was only two years before they had captured Moctezuma's capital city at Tenochtitlan (now the site of Mexico City) and had gained control of his empire. They had been helped by one of the most improbable coincidences in history. A Mexican legend said that a certain Toltec king would one day return in the form of the god Quetzalcoatl to reclaim his empire. He would come from the east, he would be fair-skinned, and he would come in a particular year of the fifty-two-year cycle. That year was 1519. There is evidence that Moctezuma suspected Cortes might be the returning god-king.

Tula, with its great stone warriors still dominating the main pyramid.

Instead of crushing the tiny Spanish force, Moctezuma on several occasions tried to buy Cortes off with presents. They were of a type carefully chosen to please Quetzalcoatl.

Even so, the Spanish achievement required an astonishing mixture of courage and bluff, made possible perhaps by the fact that these were fortune-hunters with a difference. They were in the happy position of serving both God and Mammon, and certainly for Cortes himself God came first. Often when he had carefully built up an alliance with a tribe hostile to Moctezuma, he would jeopardize the new friendship by insisting that they must now destroy all their idols. His companion, Bernal Diaz, who left the most lively account of the conquest, summed up in a famous phrase the mixed motives of the conquistadors: 'to serve God and His Majesty, to give light to those who were in darkness, and to grow rich, as all men desire to do'.[2]

Those who were in darkness were soon being shown the light in startling numbers, and at a not entirely convincing speed. Hard on the heels of the soldiers came the friars and priests, and they moved just as quickly. Within ten years of Cortes's landing a Franciscan friar calculated that he personally had baptized more than 200,000 Indians — sometimes as many as 14,000 in one day. Often the friars must have baffled the Indians. One, who spoke no Indian language, travelled from village to village carrying large paintings showing heaven, hell and purgatory. To add to the cautionary effects of hell he had a portable oven in which he roasted live cats and dogs. Their cries he believed, had a very moral effect: and no doubt the Indians were riveted.

But many friars did make a great effort to adapt to Indian ways, to learn Indian languages and even to teach Indians the best of European learning: some Indian children, it was claimed, were soon writing Latin as fluently as Cicero himself. Above all, the friars pandered to the Indian love of ceremony, celebration, display. They tried to introduce Christian and Spanish festivities which would be lively enough to replace the many Indian festivals. None was more successful

Opposite: A small boy, resting from the dance of the Christians and Moors, with the Spanish St James embroidered on his cloak.

A strip cartoon by the friars to teach the Indians Christianity: detail from a sixteenth-century illustrated catechism (private collection).

than the Spanish dance of the Christians and the Moors. It was an old favourite in Spain, celebrating victory over the Muslims, and was performed by Spaniards in Mexico City in 1538. Soon after that the friars took it to the villages. It swept Mexico, and has been performed ever since throughout the country. In an ironic parallel to the Spanish conquest of Mexico, the Mexicans joyfully enact Spanish conquistadors subduing and converting another group of unbelievers.

The friars were particularly keen to impress upon the Indians that Christianity was a peaceful religion, but here they ran into one immediate problem. Spanish Christianity was the most gory in all Europe. It positively indulged in the more lurid aspects of Christ's ordeal on the cross. How were the friars to present this version of Christ to a people so recently inclined to human sacrifice? Very wisely, they decided not to.

A remarkable form of cross, characteristic of early Mexican Christianity, was the friars' excellent solution. One of them stands today outside the sixteenth-century fortified church at Acolman, not far from Mexico City. There is no blood, no gore, no body even. In place of the Spanish Christ wracked by pain, the cross itself has here become an abstract body of the god, arms outstretched as

A crucifix in the gory tradition, now at Acolman.

if in blessing or welcome. A very wise and peaceful god, rightly mourned — or so it seems — by a patient and long-suffering Indian peasant who sits in stone below. She says a lot about what many of the friars increasingly came to feel was their real vocation in Mexico — to protect the innocent new Christians, the Indians, from the Christians who had conquered them. After the conquest each Spaniard had been given a grant of land, and a number of Indians to work it. But the conquistadors were tough adventurers. They treated their Indians as slaves.

The leader of those who protested was a Dominican, Bartolomé de las Casas. Fourteen times he crossed the Atlantic, travelling between New and Old Spain to demand protection for the Indians. Madrid was extremely sympathetic to his case. So was Rome. But it was the familiar colonial situation of the government at home passing liberal laws to which the colonists pay little attention. Admittedly the laws were sometimes laughable. One required the Spaniards not to fire on any hostile tribe of Indians until they had read them an official document. It explained that God was of the Christian variety and that the pope, his representative on earth, had given this part of the world to Spain: it was the duty of the Indians to obey the Church and the Spanish king. If this document had no effect,

The almost abstract stone crucifix at Acolman.

183

the Spaniards were allowed to open fire. Las Casas said he didn't know whether to laugh or cry.

More serious were the laws stipulating death or excommunication for any Spaniard who enslaved an Indian. But in Mexico, as Las Casas discovered, these were merely disregarded. He himself refused the mass to anyone who kept Indian slaves — so hardly any Spaniard in the district came to his church. He also wrote an account of the Spanish atrocities, which was later illustrated with lurid engravings. His book became part of the standard Protestant ammunition against the Spanish, but there were other Spaniards willing to support his allegations. One wrote:

> Spaniards have committed such cruelties that the Indians, far from believing us to be Christians and children of God, as we boasted, could not even believe that we were born on this earth or sired by a man and born of a woman: so fierce an animal, they concluded, must be the offspring of the sea.[3]

Las Casas's efforts to protect the Indians had a much publicized finale, in a great debate. It was held not in Mexico, but back in Old Spain — at Valladolid.

In the year of the debate, 1550, the emperor Charles V had suspended all further expeditions of conquest until it could be decided whether they were just. In implication, therefore, the debate was far from academic. In form it could hardly have been more so, for both Las Casas and his opponent, Sepulveda, based their arguments on the opinion of Aristotle. On behalf of the colonial lobby, Sepulveda argued that certain people were so inferior that they were intended by God to be slaves. He relied on a passage where Aristotle was himself trying to justify the Athenian use of slaves, so naturally the argument fitted. Indians, he explained,

> are as inferior as children are to adults, as women are to men. Indians are as different from Spaniards as cruel people are from mild people. Compare those blessings enjoyed by Spaniards of prudence, genius, magnanimity, temperance, humanity and religion with those of the Indians, in whom you will scarcely find even vestiges of humanity. Neither do they have written laws, but barbaric institutions and customs. They do not even have private property.[4]

Sepulveda found a willing audience. It was commonly held in Spain at the time that the Indians were human in appearance only. But Las Casas was uncompromising:

> All the races of the world are men. The entire human race is one. When some very rustic peoples are found in the world, they are like untilled land, which easily produces weeds and thorns, but has within itself so much actual power that when it is ploughed it gives useful and wholesome fruits.[5]

Las Casas even managed to find proof in Aristotle that human sacrifices were in some circumstances justifiable. The rivers of blood in the temples have always spoilt the argument that brutality entered Mexico with the Spaniards, but in true debating style Las Casas described the Aztecs and their subjects as little worse than lambs:

> Among these gentle sheep the Spaniards entered like wolves, tigers and lions, and for forty years they have done nothing else. Nor do they otherwise at the present day, than outrage, slay, afflict, torment and destroy them.[6]

184

The attempt to conquer souls east and west. Opposite: A Moghul emperor with Jesus Christ, c. 1620 (Chester Beatty Library, Dublin). Overleaf: A Mexican Indian in the role of the Spanish crusading saint, St James of Compostela, in the village dance of the Christians and the Moors. Overleaf right: Awaiting the Aztec Virgin of Guadalupe, on her brief journey from old to new basilica (the pattern on the ground is composed entirely of coloured sand).

The debate dragged on. The commission appointed to weigh the evidence was soon floundering. Nothing was decided, nothing proved. But it was on record that an enlightened section of Spanish opinion, led by the religious orders, disapproved of Spanish colonial methods.

The Spain in which this debate took place was deeply moral, deeply serious, and had recently seen the romantic buccaneering spirit of the conquistadors turned to a more purely Christian end. St Ignatius, who was born in 1491 at the castle of Loyola in the Basque country to the north of Spain, could well have become a conquistador: except perhaps that he was rich enough not to bother. He grew up as a swaggering young nobleman, a soldier. His leg was shattered by a cannon ball in a siege, and he was lying ill in his castle when he found there were none of his favourite books to hand. Heroic romances were what he liked. Instead there was a Bible, and the lives of some saints. As he read, he seems virtually to have decided to become a saint himself, a new sort of romantic hero. 'St Dominic did this, therefore I have to do it. St Francis did this, therefore I have to do it.'[7]

His method of training himself for sainthood was military in its precision. Known as the *Spiritual Exercises*, it remains the basic routine of self-discipline in the order which Ignatius founded, the Jesuits. It is, literally, a four-week programme of exercises, a spiritual assault-course for the soldiers of Jesus, aiming to detach the mind from this world by concentrating on the horrors of hell, the saving truth of the gospel story, and the example of Christ. As with a modern diet, there was even a chart for recording progress, comparing each day's spiritual self-examination with the previous results. Much of the technique seems medieval in its combination of the literal and the obsessive, though perhaps this is a timeless quality in religious asceticism. An early exercise is designed to induce physical self-disgust:

> Let me look at the foulness and ugliness of my body. Let me see myself as an ulcerous sore running with every horrible and disgusting poison.[8]

In similar vein are the instructions to imagine hell:

> Hear in imagination the shrieks and groans and blasphemous shouts against Christ our Lord and all the saints. Smell in imagination the fumes of sulphur and the stench of filth and corruption. Taste in imagination all the bitterness of tears and melancholy and a gnawing conscience. Feel in imagination the heat of the flames that play on and burn the souls.[9]

To happier scenes the same literalness lends a mood closer to nineteenth-century naturalism. Of the Nativity:

> Represent to yourself in imagination the road from Bethlehem, in its length and breadth. Is it level or through valleys or over hillsides? In the same way, study the place of the Nativity. Is the cave spacious or cramped, high or low? How is it furnished?[10]

The exercises had a powerful effect on several of Ignatius's contemporaries: initially perhaps because a month of rigorous self-discipline has a certain attraction if it is also guaranteed to be good for you (much like the appeal of yoga today), but first acquaintance rapidly led to a deeper involvement. Ignatius went

Opposite: A Mexican Indian arriving to worship in the new church built for the Aztec Virgin of Guadalupe.

at the age of thirty three to study at Barcelona university, two years later moved to Alcala, and finally went to Paris — still as a mere student. A small group of friends developed around him, sharing his exercises, and at Paris they took a vow together to dedicate their lives to Christ. Later they offered themselves to Pope Paul III in Rome, promising complete obedience to him and to his successors. Their first draft charter announced that their chief purpose would be the propagation of the faith, particularly by the 'instruction in Christianity of children and the uneducated'. They promised they would go wherever the pope might send them, 'whether to the Turks or to the New World or to the Lutherans or to others, be they infidel or faithful'.[11]

The Rome in which the new Jesuit order established itself was making a very rapid change from the immoralities of the old days under Alexander VI to a puritanical city which would almost have impressed Calvin. One of the young men joining the order in Rome did so when he discovered, to his horror, that he was the son of a priest, the grandson of a bishop, and that both his mother and grandmother had been nuns. And the third general of the Jesuits, St Francis Borgia, was himself the great-grandson of Pope Alexander VI.

The new puritanism was not purely in response to the Protestant example: there had been the beginnings of moral reform, particularly in Spain, long before Luther. But the sense of crisis in the church did push Rome to extremes. The pope who established the Jesuits, Paul III, was also the one to set up the Roman Inquisition. Soon this was followed by the first Index of prohibited books — works which any Catholic risked damnation by reading. For a long time merely to possess one of them was punishable in Spain by death. The list was kept up to date until 1959, and was finally abolished by Pope Paul VI.

The first Inquisitor-General became pope as Paul IV. It was he who put fig-leaves on the Vatican's famous collection of antique sculptures. It was he who employed a painter, Daniele da Volterra, known for ever after as 'the breeches-maker', to clothe some of the more striking bits of nudity in Michelangelo's *Last Judgment*. A notorious libertine, Pietro Aretino, reformed by advancing years and the spirit of the times, now declared that the *Last Judgment* was fit only for the wall of a brothel. Even Michelangelo's gentle *Pietà* was considered too sensuous. It prompted a Florentine to write: 'That inventor of obscenities, Michelangelo Buonarotti, is concerned only with art, not with piety.'[12]

Soon another Grand Inquisitor, even more puritanical, had become pope: Pius V. Calvin was known as the pope of Geneva, but Pius certainly proved himself the Calvin of Rome. He set himself the remarkable task of clearing all the prostitutes out of the city within a week. He failed in that, as also in his plan to make adultery punishable by death. But his serious reforms were positive ones, concerned chiefly with improvement of the clergy. He tried to put an end to the buying and selling of church appointments, and to train more effective priests — men who would be educated enough to preach an effective sermon, and self-disciplined enough to practise what they preached. For centuries celibacy had seemed an impossible ideal for the average priest to live up to. The Protestant Reformation solved the matter by announcing that celibacy was unnecessary: the Catholic Reformation set about proving it possible.

Pius V was largely putting into effect the decisions of the Council of Trent, 186 which had sat, on and off, from 1545 to 1560. Many hoped the Council would find some compromise with the Protestants. Instead it rejected outright their theology, and dismissed all claims for the people to receive both the bread and the wine in the mass or to hear the service in their own language. The Council standardized Roman Catholic worship throughout the world. The mass which bears its name (the Tridentine mass or the mass of Trent) is the service which for four centuries has been familiar to every Catholic wherever he may travel. It has only been abandoned, to the regret of many, in the last few years — in the reforms initiated by Pope John XXIII.

The strong position taken by the Council of Trent established the battle lines for the future, between Catholics and Protestants. The struggle against the break-away sects was seen as a holy war. The duke of Alva, who unleashed a reign of terror to hold down the Netherlands for Spain, had his portrait done as a crusader. In the Vatican, Vasari was commissioned to paint frescoes of two events of the 1570s as if they were equally important Catholic victories: the Battle of Lepanto, where the Turkish navy was defeated; and the Massacre of St Bartholomew's Day, in which thousands of Protestants were hauled from their beds and killed in the streets of Paris. To celebrate the massacre a triumphal mass was held, and a commemorative medal was struck showing Huguenots being butchered.

The lasting success of the Catholic Reformation was not the military but the

St Peter's and the residence built for Pius IV, who concluded the Council of Trent.

The ceiling in the church of St Ignatius, Rome.

spiritual battle. And here the church had found, at just the right moment, its elite corps of soldiers for Christ — the Jesuits. Ignatius of Loyola died in 1556. By then the Jesuit church, the Gesu, had already been established in Rome. It was Europe's first baroque church, and the baroque style increasingly came to express the almost operatic self-confidence of the Catholic Reformation: that joyful indulgence in the maximum number of gilded saints in every conceivable posture of sentimental ecstasy, as if in deliberate contrast to the severity insisted on by the Protestants.

The ceiling in the church of St Ignatius, in Rome, was commissioned in 1622 in honour of the new saint. High in the centre Christ soars towards heaven with his cross. Close behind him is Ignatius. Between us and them there is an astounding swarm (it is the only word) of flying saints. There could hardly be a more pointed denial of the Protestant claim that no intermediary is necessary between an ordinary worshipper and God.

The tomb of St Ignatius in the Gesu is itself a striking piece of baroque propaganda, and it has, to either side of it, sculptures which glorify the Jesuit effort in propagating the faith. To the right, religion triumphs over heresy: to the left, barbarians adore the faith (a dusky king bows the knee to a lady with the lamp of Catholic Truth). On the opposite side of the church there is a memorial to the man who launched the Jesuit mission to the east — Ignatius's fellow-student from university days in Paris, St Francis Xavier.

Xavier blazed the trail which was to be followed with great courage but little long-term success by later generations of Jesuits. He was the peaceful Cortes of the Catholic thrust eastwards and was known as the 'conquistador das animas', the conquistador of souls. In 1542 he was at Goa, the island off the west coast of India which the Portuguese had captured and were using as the capital of their Indian empire. A year later he was converting thousands of pearl-fishers in the south of India, by 1545 he was in Malaya and the Spice Islands, from 1549 to 1551 in Japan, and in 1552 he died while waiting to enter the great closed empire of China. Understandably, he is now the patron saint of all Catholic missions.

Xavier's success gave the Jesuits the hope that the east might be won for Christ. Within Europe they specialized in educating the aristocracy, and their policy for Asia was the very sensible one of trying to convert the rulers — who, like

Religion triumphs over heresy, on the tomb of St Ignatius in the Gesu in Rome.

Constantine, might formally bring their empires into the fold. There were encouraging signs. The Indian emperor Akbar, himself a Muslim, sent to Goa for some learned men who could expound the truths of Christianity at his court. Three Jesuits arrived in 1580, and were immediately brought before the emperor to engage in learned controversy with Muslim divines. The Jesuits ridiculed everything about Islam, with the courage of men courting martyrdom, but Akbar allowed them to set up a chapel and even to teach his son. The fathers were unaware that the emperor collected religions the way another man might collect exotic books — out of fascinated curiosity. Two years after the Jesuits arrived he announced a new religion of his own. It must have shocked the Christians as

St Francis Xavier is shown a tempting map of the east: print by Giovanni Gavignani (Museo della Xilografia Italiana, Carpi).

190

Two Jesuits debating with Muslims in the presence of Akbar (Chester Beatty Library, Dublin).

much as the Muslims. Its central feature was an apparently deliberate confusion between Akbar and God.

In China the Jesuits eventually won the confidence of the emperors, not through theology but through science. When they at last reached Peking, after years of patiently applying for permission, their best gifts to the emperor were a statue of the Virgin and a clock which struck the hours. He kept the clock for himself, and rarely let it out of his sight, but sent the Virgin Mary straight on to his aged mother. For nearly two centuries there were to be Jesuits in Peking, impressing everyone by their skill in astronomy and mathematics but making few converts. If anything the conversion appeared to be in the other direction. The Jesuits found so much to admire in Chinese society that they decided to proselytize from a middle position. Soon they were wearing the clothes of mandarins and even attending Confucian ceremonies of ancestor worship. The Chinese were delighted, Rome rather less so. The resulting quarrel within

the Catholic ranks disenchanted everyone. 'In this Catholic religion', wrote a
Chinese emperor in the early eighteenth century,

> the Society of Peter quarrels with the Jesuits, and among the Jesuits the Portuguese
> want only their own nationals in the Church while the French want only French in
> theirs. This violates the principles of religion.[13]

Japan seemed for a while the most hopeful of the territories visited by Xavier.
He left behind him a community of about 1,000 converts in 1551. Soon the
Jesuits were claiming 150,000 and the numbers may eventually have risen as high
as 300,000. The warrior class or *samurai* were particularly susceptible, perhaps
because they felt a kinship with many of the Jesuits who also had aristocratic or
military backgrounds. But Christianity became an element in the internal
struggles of the Japanese ruling class, and from about 1614 there was a mounting
campaign of persecution which was to prove one of the goriest in Christian
history. A Japanese Inquisition hunted down suspected Christians as relentlessly
as the Spanish version pursued Crypto-Jews or Muslims, although when it came
to refinements of torture Japan had the edge — at Yedo, for example, seventy
Japanese Christians were crucified upside down on the beach, to be drowned by

Etching of a Jesuit in the dress of a mandarin, with one of his Chinese converts.

In the graveyard of a village church in Mexico.

the incoming tide. The most likely of the eastern empires had proved the most disastrous.

Four centuries after the great missionary effort of the Catholic Reformation, both east and west, the balance sheet seems to show a total contrast. Utter failure in the east, where a handful of Roman Catholics in Goa and Macao are all that remain from the heroic endeavours of Francis Xavier and those who followed him. Complete success in the west, with the Christians of Latin America now forming the largest single group in the Church of Rome. 193

But how complete, in reality, was that success? The extremely rapid conversion of the Indians in Mexico had been accompanied by the herding of large groups of them into specially built villages (where the friars could keep an eye on them), and by often brutal punishments for anyone suspected of backsliding into idolatry. With a new god forced upon them, of whose powers they were still uncertain, many Mexicans took the elementary precaution of hiding a trusted idol or two behind the Christian altar — so that they could at least pray to everyone at once. When early Mexican crosses are taken to pieces, Aztec cult objects are often found inside them. The process of merging the two religions, hoping for benefits from each, has continued in more subtle ways ever since. The resulting confusion is painfully clear in a ceremony which took place in Mexico in 1557. Inside the church at Sotuta a native priest presided over the crucifixion of two little girls with the words: 'Let these girls die crucified as did Jesus Christ, who they say was Our Lord but we do not know if this is so.'[14]

A major difficulty in accepting Jesus Christ was his identification as the god of the alien and white race of Europeans, the conquerors. As recently as the 1860s a cult developed in the Mayan districts of Mexico, following a leader who argued that Indians need not worship images representing non-Indian saints. He proposed to crucify an Indian boy, so that the local people would have a Lord of their own to worship. The crucifixion took place in 1868.

In the central or Aztec part of Mexico, the problem of race seemed to have been solved by an early miracle. There is a hill near Mexico City which in pre-conquest days had been sacred to the Aztec goddess Tonantzin, who was held to be the virgin mother of several other gods. In 1531 a beautiful Indian lady, dressed in rich clothes, appeared to a Mexican, Juan Diego, who was a convert to Christianity. She spoke to him in his own language, Nahuatl, and told him that she was the Mother of God and 'one of his kind'.

When Juan Diego asked how he could prove to the Spanish bishop that he had seen her, she told him to gather the flowers on the hill top. He carried them in his cloak. When he opened it, to give the bishop the flowers, a miraculous image of the Virgin was found to be imprinted on the inside of the garment. The Aztec Virgin of Guadalupe rapidly became, and has ever since remained, the most popular saint in Mexico. Naturally a church was built on top of the hill to house the sacred piece of cloth with its full-length image of what Juan Diego saw. (In our own photographic age the faithful take the image with a desperate literalness: there are devotees in dark-rooms working on massive enlargements of the Virgin's eyeball, because the outline of Juan Diego is now believed to be reflected in it.) Later the Virgin was moved to a larger basilica below the hill, but over the years that building has subsided alarmingly. In 1976 she was moved to a modern church, specially built for her, about a hundred yards from the old one. It was the first time she had been seen in the open air for nearly three centuries — a most solemn and joyful occasion, celebrated by vast crowds ranging from Spanish grandees to the poorest of Indians. It was also the nearest that I have ever come to a miracle. For a week there had been heavy rain each day. The morning was grey and overcast. It seemed likely that the Virgin's rare walkabout would be a disaster. But when the loudspeakers announced that she was about to emerge

The Aztec Virgin of Guadalupe above the altar of the old basilica.

from the old basilica, the clouds parted and she made her slow journey in the first patch of sunshine for days. Hardly anyone else seemed to notice the fact until the radio made much of it. Presumably the faithful had expected no less.

By the same process of adaptation that lies behind the original miracle, the Indians have always known this Virgin affectionately as Tonantzin. But the Aztec Tonantzin was a terrifying goddess who wore a necklace of human hands and hearts and who, like all her cronies, was addicted to blood. The Christian Virgin of Guadalupe has the same qualities as other Madonnas throughout the world: beauty, gentleness, understanding. Instead of human sacrifice, she asks from her devotees only pilgrimage, offerings, good behaviour. By any standards Tonantzin has been improved through the process known, in current academic jargon, as syncretism.

On the other hand it is difficult to maintain that the average peasant of Latin America has been converted, even today, to what is considered in more sophisticated circles to be the Roman Catholic faith. In the small Mexican village of San Francisco Tecospa, the most venerated of the local deities is the Virgin of Guadalupe, or Tonantzin. She is more powerful even than God, because God has acquired the Aztec characteristic of being the Destroyer as well as the Creator — and it is only Tonantzin who prevents him putting an end to his Creation. St Francis of Assisi, to whom the village is dedicated, has among his many functions the bringing of rain. But he is helped in this task by a team of Aztec rain dwarfs.

Examples can be multiplied throughout Latin America. One of the most famous is Chichicastenango, a shrine as popular with the Indians of Guatemala as Guadalupe is in Mexico. Here the local Christians sacrifice a chicken to a stone god at the top of the hill, and sprinkle his lips with its blood, before descending to worship in the church below. The parish is still administered — even today — by a priest from Spain who is almost as perplexed as any of his sixteenth-century predecessors by the agile compromises of the Indian mind. His parishioners, in a ritual entirely their own, scatter the floor of his church each Sunday with petals of white and red roses. He knows that each red petal wishes good health for a friend, each white one some disaster for an enemy. He does his best to discourage the white petals. Yet, within the walls of his church, the ritual lives on.

The Indians of Chichicastenango may not seem fully Christian by the standards of today; but then neither would the average European peasant in that most fervently Christian of all periods, the Middle Ages. One of the great strengths of a religion as intrinsically mysterious as Christianity is its ability to adapt, to be most things to most men. And one of the paradoxes of the Catholic Reformation is that the same energy which put an end to so many of the abuses of medieval Christianity in Europe was fostering something remarkably similar in a new continent. A seventeenth-century observer of priest-ridden, superstitious Latin America might well have concluded that the Middle Ages — by some mysterious alchemy of time and the turning world — had merely moved west.

Waiting for the Virgin to emerge from the old basilica at Guadalupe, for the brief journey to her new home.

NOS PIDES UN TEMPLO, TE CONSAGRAMOS EL CORAZON

IZTAPALAPA OT. 12-1976

CHAPTER NINE

In Search of Tolerance

THE Mennonites of Pennsylvania or Ohio are best known to the outer world for their determined rearguard action against such modern conveniences as electricity, the motor car and even the button, not to mention the zip. A bearded farmer — solemnly joining the hooks and eyes on his clothes by lamplight at crack of dawn before climbing into his horse-drawn buggy — can be made to seem a figure of fun in modern America. But an afternoon in the rolling landscape of Lancaster County, in Pennsylvania, left me with a different impression. Every few hundred yards there is a neat white farm, surrounded by perfectly kept and unfenced fields. The animals in the farmyard (geese walking purposefully among the cattle and sheep) contribute to the look of a child's model farm, just as the occasional horse and buggy, turning out of the forecourt to trot away over the hill, complete the nostalgic photograph. A few years ago such a response would have seemed the purest sentimentality: and no doubt, in the real world of poverty and overpopulation, it still is. But this Mennonite world is precisely the Utopia which ecologists now preach. The wheel has come full circle. It is the reactionary Mennonites who find themselves most up to date.

In fact it is only one section of the Mennonite community, the Old Order Amish, which keeps to these ways. The majority of Mennonites look like any other American. What identifies them as one group with the Amish is a shared

Previous pages: *In Lancaster County, Pennsylvania.*

A service in the Mennonite church at Paradise, Pennsylvania.

Preaching in sign language for the deaf.

system of values and beliefs which dates back to the beginnings of Anabaptism in the 1520s: a strong sense of community (capable of strikingly modern innovations, such as a church in Pennsylvania which holds services entirely in sign language for the deaf); an insistence on the right of the individual to resist unacceptable demands by the state, such as conscription to carry arms; and an emphasis on personal religion, centred on the family and on study of the Bible. The Mennonites are split into many independent sects (seen at their most comic in certain practical results, as in the difference between those who will use a car, those who only ride in buggies, and, in between, the 'black-bumper Mennonites' who will own a car so long as all the frivolous chrome is painted black), but even this type of fragmentation dates right back to the beginnings of the movement. The community takes its name from Menno Simons, who became its minister in 1536. That was only eleven years after the beginnings of Anabaptism, but already Menno's was just one among several Anabaptist sects.

During the sixteenth century three Protestant groups won for themselves the position of established churches in different parts of Europe: the Lutherans, the Calvinists, and the Anglicans. From the start the Anabaptists were the outsiders, the radical wing of the Reformation, persecuted by Catholics and Protestants alike. For them, as for other Protestant minority groups — the Huguenots in France, and later the Dissenters or Nonconformists in England — the sixteenth and seventeenth centuries represented one long and frequently blood-stained search for tolerance.

Anabaptism had its origin in Zurich, in 1525, when a group of ordinary people studying the Bible decided to baptize each other. The conventional baptism of a dribbling baby, they said, was meaningless. Entry into the church must be a solemn moment of acceptance by a responsible adult. It terrified the existing churches, Protestant as well as Catholic, that people should take religion in 201 this way into their own hands. Protestant Zurich reacted sharply. Anyone even attending an Anabaptist ceremony was to be drowned, said the council with macabre irony; if they want water, they shall have it. Even so, the movement spread rapidly.

The first of many places of refuge was Mikulov in Czechoslovakia. For two exciting years, from 1526, Anabaptists came to shelter beneath the castle there. Its owner, Leonhard von Liechtenstein, was a Lutheran (and that in itself was a notion that was still less than ten years old), but already he felt inclined to go further. So he offered the Anabaptists his protection. Soon there was a thriving colony: Liechtenstein welcomed their skilled labour on his estates as well as sympathizing with their religious convictions. But one colony turned rapidly into two. As the Catholics have always known, nothing leads to such a variety of opinion as reading the Bible. Half the Anabaptists at Mikulov understood the gospels to say that one could use force to defend oneself: the rest saw only a message of complete pacifism and even of communism, the sharing of worldly goods like the early Christians. Even in Mikulov it was persecution, from outside, which put an end to argument. The leader of one group was burnt, and his wife thrown into the Danube with a stone around her neck. The eventual leader of the communist group, Jakob Hutter, ended by being whipped and having brandy poured into his wounds, after which he was set alight.

A larger proportion of Anabaptists were martyred for their faith than any other Christian group in history — including even the early Christians on whom they modelled themselves. In the seventeenth century their stories were gathered together into an anthology, known as *The Martyrs' Mirror*. To their contemporaries they appeared a threat to the very fabric of society. To us they seem to have made a more simple demand: a man's right to his own beliefs. In their quiet pursuit of that right a voice was heard which had been silent in recent centuries: the voice of ordinary men and women, prepared to assert themselves against all authority for conscience's sake. It is heard at its most moving in a letter which a young Anabaptist woman wrote in 1573, in Antwerp gaol, to her daughter of a few days old. The father had already been executed as an Anabaptist: the mother had been reprieved only long enough to give birth to her child. Her voice might be that of any good townswoman in a Flemish painting of the period, as she writes to tell her daughter not to grow up ashamed that both her parents were burnt:

My dearest child, the true love of God strengthen you in virtue, you who are yet so young, and whom I must leave in this wicked, evil, perverse world.

Oh that it had pleased the Lord that I might have brought you up, but it seems that it is not the Lord's will. Even so it has now gone with your father and myself. We were so well joined that we would not have forsaken each other for the whole world, and yet we had to leave each other for the Lord's sake. We were permitted to live together only half a year, after which we were apprehended because we sought the salvation of our souls. Be not ashamed of us; it is the way which the prophets and the apostles went. Your dear father demonstrated with his blood that it is the genuine truth, and I also hope to attest the same with my blood, though flesh and blood must remain on the posts and on the stake, well knowing that we shall meet hereafter.

Hence, my dear Janneken, do not accustom your mouth to filthy talk, nor to

An Anabaptist goes to her death: one of many such scenes illustrating the original edition of The Martyrs' Mirror.

ugly lies, and run not in the street as other bad children do, rather take up a book and learn to seek there that which concerns your salvation. And now, Janneken, my dear lamb, who are yet very little and young, I leave you this letter, together with a gold *real* which I had with me in prison, and this I leave you for a perpetual adieu, and for a testament. Read it, when you have understanding, and keep it as long as you live in remembrance of me and of your father. Be not ashamed to confess our faith, since it is the true evangelical faith, another than which shall never be found.[1]

Anabaptists would wander through much of Europe before they finally found tolerance — they were to find it in the U.S.A. and Canada, but also in Holland. As small and self-isolating groups, for the most part pacifist, they always lived on sufferance in any place where they settled. But there was one Protestant minority in the sixteenth century powerful enough to demand tolerance. For a while it seemed perfectly possible that the Huguenots would win France for the Protestant cause, just as England, Sweden, Holland and many parts of Germany and Switzerland were won — at the level of affairs of state, or by warfare. They failed. But in the attempt they gained the first official guarantee of religious tolerance, the Edict of Nantes.

The story of the growth of Huguenot power, from secret beginnings as a radical group of heretics to the open recognition of the Edict of Nantes, is one of ever-increasing atrocity on both sides. It could hardly be more different from an

Anabaptist saga. The power of the Huguenots was far greater than their numbers (at their peak about one million out of twenty million in France), because a very high proportion of the nobility and middle classes were converted to the cause. It was a violent and often unscrupulous cause. Huguenot soldiers rampaged through the countryside, smashing church ornaments and hunting down priests. One captain wore a necklace of priests' ears; another made Catholic prisoners leap to their deaths from a high tower. The Catholics, whose efforts to suppress the Huguenots had sparked off the violence, were more than willing to reply in kind. Protestant prisoners were soon being pushed off battlements, and the massacre of St Bartholomew's Day can take its place in the front rank of Christian atrocities. During the night of August 24th, 1572, Huguenots in Paris were hauled from their beds and slaughtered, under orders from the young king, Charles IX. The Paris mob got out of hand in the streets, in an orgy of killing and pillage, while the king sniped idly with an arquebus from the windows of the Louvre. No city has such a barbarous record of butchering its own citizens as Paris. The years 1793 and 1871 were still far in the future. But in 1572 the killing lasted for two full days, and several thousands died.

The struggle between Catholics and Huguenots was political as well as religious, and the religious side of it was in the end solved with the easy cynicism of politics. In 1589 the heir to the throne was a Huguenot, Henry IV, but Paris would only accept a Catholic king. Changing his religion in the nick of time, Henry is credited with one of history's best-known throwaway lines (*Paris vaut bien une messe*, Paris is well worth a mass). But as king he was in a position to establish the Edict of Nantes in 1598.

Although the Edict guaranteed freedom of conscience and of worship to the Huguenots, together with certain military and legal rights, it was in fact little more than an agreed cease-fire line between two powerful groups. Such an arrangement, won by force, is liable to change when the balance of power changes. In the seventeenth century Richelieu and Louis XIV had no need to appease their Protestant minority. For a whole year (October 1627 to October 1628) Richelieu besieged the greatest Huguenot stronghold, La Rochelle. When it fell, after a heroic resistance, he removed all the military rights of the Huguenots but allowed them to retain their freedom of conscience. In 1685 Louis XIV withdrew even that when he revoked the Edict of Nantes, reintroducing persecution of any Huguenot who held to his faith. Within a few years of this remarkably retrograde act, France had lost some 400,000 of her most industrious citizens. Several thousand emigrated from La Rochelle alone, many of them going to America — where, in 1688, they founded the town of New Rochelle.

By then America had become the recognized haven for those in search of tolerance. The first group to have made the journey for that reason was the band of Puritans from England now known as the Pilgrim Fathers. From 1604 onwards English clergymen were forced to subscribe more precisely than ever before to the official doctrines of the Anglican church. The careful compromises of Elizabeth's reign were over. The penalty for dissent was excommunication for

The statue of Henry IV on the Pont Neuf in Paris, put up soon after his death.

the cleric, and harassment for his congregation. But on the borders of Lincoln-shire, Yorkshire and Nottinghamshire a number of villages had already formed themselves into congregations on the Calvinist pattern, with pastors and elders. From their ranks were to come the Pilgrim Fathers.

William Bradford, a leading pilgrim who later wrote the history of the whole adventure, said that persecution made their small group leave England for Holland:

> By a joint consent they resolved to go into the Low Countries where they heard was freedom of religion for all men; as also how sundry from London and other parts of the land had been exiled and persecuted for the same cause, and were gone thither and lived at Amsterdam and in other places of the land.[2]

In those days a licence was required to leave England. We are familiar with illegal immigrants paying vast sums to be smuggled into the country in small boats. The pilgrims were the opposite, illegal emigrants who had 'to seek secret means of conveyance, and to bribe and fee the mariners and give extraordinary rates for their passages'.[3] True to form, they were soundly cheated. They had hired an English ship at Boston, in Lincolnshire, and they waited at a secret meeting place for the captain to come and pick them up. When they were all safely aboard, he gave the signal to some officers to come and seize them. They were robbed of their valuables, rowed ignominiously into Boston in open boats, handed over to the magistrates and imprisoned for a month. That was in the autumn of 1607. Next spring they tried again, with a Dutch captain who turned out to be more reliable. It was far from the end of their troubles: a storm drove them almost up to Norway before the Lord stilled it, and it took them fourteen days to complete the crossing; but finally they arrived in Amsterdam.

Holland richly deserved its reputation for tolerance. In 1579 seven of Spain's provinces in the Netherlands had united to defend their liberty, and had specified that 'every citizen should remain free in his religion, and no man may be molested or questioned on the subject of divine worship'.[4] Soon Amsterdam was to be described, in a hostile but evocative phrase, as 'the fair of all the sects, where all the peddlers of religion have leave to vend their toys, their ribbons and fanatic rattles'.[5] And the city benefited greatly from the influx of energetic men of conscience, Jews as well as Protestants, fleeing from persecution elsewhere.

The one group that the Dutch could claim good reason for persecuting was the Roman Catholics, but even here their tolerance held firm. Holland's fight for independence had been against the repressive atrocities of Catholic Spain, and a young Catholic fanatic had assassinated the country's national hero, William the Silent. In the seventeenth century the law did in fact forbid the holding of Roman Catholic services in Amsterdam. Yet Roman Catholics continued to worship unmolested.

The clue lies behind the façade of an ordinary seventeenth-century house on one of Amsterdam's canals. From the outside a house like any other: but when a Catholic worshipper had climbed the rickety stairs to the top, he came out not into a normal attic but into a very handsome church. There were several of these roof-top churches in old Amsterdam. Today only one survives, known as Our Lord in the Attic. Actually our Lord has three attic floors running along the top of three separate houses, with the beams of the upper floors cut through in the

Our Lord in the Attic, in Amsterdam.

centre so that people in the galleries above could see and hear the mass. This is not the cramped little hiding-place of a persecuted sect: once up here the congregation is emphatically in church, complete with organ and high altar. It is a perfect case of the authorities turning a blind eye to a private but illegal practice in full swing: licensed deviation, a most civilized custom which the Dutch still believe in. In recent years, the private but illegal practices of minority groups have concerned not religion but drugs. Amsterdam has kept alive its fame as 'the fair of all the sects'.

The pilgrims who came to Amsterdam in 1608 settled down so quickly that within a year they felt sufficiently secure to quarrel among themselves. Some stayed in Amsterdam, others moved to Leiden. And it was the group at Leiden which decided, in 1620, that they would rather set up somewhere entirely on their own: not as one sect among many, but as the only sect. They had strong political reasons for leaving the Netherlands. The Inquisition was a few miles to the south in what is now Belgium, and was eager to move north. But I suspect they were also tired of merely receiving tolerance. In a place of their own theywould be free to go one stage better and try their hand at intolerance. New England was awaiting them.

They hired an English ship for the crossing: the *Mayflower*. She was only a little over 100 feet long, and in her narrow quarters 102 pilgrims were crammed for a journey which lasted nearly ten weeks. Already, on the voyage, there was a striking example of what the pilgrims liked to call God's providence. William Bradford later told the story with immense satisfaction. There was on board, he says, 'an insolent and very profane young man', a sailor, who enjoyed baiting the pilgrims, shocking them with obscene language, and telling them that on a crossing like this he expected to throw at least half of them overboard, as corpses, before the journey's end. 'But it pleased God,' says Bradford, 'before they came half seas over, to smite this young man with a grievous disease, of which he died in a desperate manner, and so was himself the first that was thrown overboard.'[6] Clearly God was watching over the settlers, who thought of themselves as his chosen people. It was a sense of conviction very necessary in the difficult times ahead.

Improvidently, the pilgrims had chosen mid-November to land, without any means of shelter, in a district now famous for its hard winters. What with exploring the coast, and hunting for food, it was December 20th before they had fixed upon a site for their village. And then they had, in a seventeenth-century phrase, 'all things to doe, as in the beginning of the world'.[7] They were to struggle through to the next autumn, when they would thank God that the harvest was safely home with the ceremony of Thanksgiving. But half the company had died in that first winter and spring. Only five of the eighteen married women survived. The list of names at the back of Bradford's *History* has a sickening refrain: 'Mr and Mrs Carver died during the first general sickness . . . Mr Winslow's wife died the first winter . . . Mrs Bradford died soon after their arrival', and so on, relentlessly.

The struggle and richly deserved success of the Pilgrim Fathers in building up their settlement was to become a cornerstone of the American dream, a shining example in the land of enterprise and hard work. Within less than two years of their landing, in 1622, a book was printed in London telling their story: and its title-page was able to speak, presumably without excessive exaggeration, of the colonists' 'difficult passage, their safe arivall, their joyfull building of, and comfortable planting themselves in the now well defended Towne of NEW PLIMOTH'.[8] Today a group of New Englanders are re-creating that well-defended but long vanished Towne. Following the details in the 1622 account, and using only tools and materials which were available to the settlers, they are building the simple street of wooden houses and the stockade to guard against Indians or wolves, which was the full extent of 'Plimoth Plantation'.

The characteristic village of New England still consists of wooden houses round a wooden church — more sophisticated now, but visibly deriving from that early tradition. I know of hardly any environment which looks more inviting than the white-painted houses of Massachusetts or Connecticut, sharing an open lawn with their elegant white church. But the early history of these

Plimoth Plantation; the reconstructed settlement of the Pilgrim Fathers at Plymouth, Massachusetts.

communities was less idyllic. The sense of being God's elect, so useful in times of hardship, turned all too easily to Puritan self-righteousness. At its comic extreme, it was seen in a series of resolutions said to have been debated and passed by one New England assembly. They went as follows:

1　The earth is the Lord's and the fullness thereof. Voted.
2　The Lord may give the earth or any part of it to his chosen people. Voted.
3　We are his chosen people. Voted.[9]

And when vast numbers of the local Indians died of smallpox, brought here by the settlers, the governor of Massachusetts wrote in his journal: 'God hath hereby cleared our title to this place'.[10]

In Massachusetts, which set the early pattern for New England, the strictest conformity was demanded both by church and state — the two being almost inseparable. The community was governed by a small minority, assumed (by themselves, at any rate) to be the lucky few whom God had singled out to join him in heaven. With this unique advantage, they set about supervising almost every aspect of other people's lives — even down to the length of their hair and the quality of their clothes. There were fines for not attending church services. A law was passed making idleness a crime. And if you behaved in an unseemly fashion on Sunday, the Sabbath, you were likely to find yourself being whipped on the Monday morning.

One of the most serious crimes was criticizing the ministers or disagreeing with what they preached. The normal penalty for this was expulsion from the colony. Mrs Anne Hutchinson courted disaster by holding seminars in her home at which she analysed the recent sermons and almost invariably found them lacking in correct theology. She was branded an 'opinionist' and was banished. To the infinite satisfaction of the puritan mind, she had a miscarriage soon afterwards: and at much the same time one of her friends, Mary Dyer, produced a still-born deformity. How the righteous gloated! All the worst characteristics of a closed and intolerant community came out in a pamphlet on the controversy:

> Then God himself was pleased to step in with His casting voice and bring in His own vote and suffrage from Heaven by testifying His displeasure against their opinions and practices, in causing the two fomenting women in the time of the height of the opinions to produce out of their wombs, as before they had out of their brains, such monstrous births as no chronicle (I think) hardly ever recorded the like. Mistress Dyer brought forth her birth of a woman child, a fish, a beast, and a fowl, all woven together in one, and without an head. Mistress Hutchinson being big with child, she brought forth not one (as Mistress Dyer did) but (which was more strange to amazement) thirty monstrous births or thereabouts at once, some of them bigger, some lesser, some of one shape, some of another, few of any perfect shape, none at all of them (as far as I could ever learn) of human shape.[11]

There can rarely have been a more repulsive combination of the smug, the vindictive and the credulous.

The most distinguished man to be banished from Massachusetts was himself a young minister, Roger Williams. He criticized the authorities for many things, including the way the colonists had taken land from the Indians. But above all he argued that the community had no right to punish people for private sins, errors of conscience which were a matter between themselves and their God. It was a principle which he would later define as 'soul-liberty'. The magistrates decided to ship him home on the next boat back to England. But he slipped away, and in the bitterly cold winter of 1635 he trudged south through wild territory until he reached the coast outside Massachusetts, and settled. Over the next few years other groups, unwelcome for various reasons in the older colonies, moved into the same area — including Anne Hutchinson and her friends. Together with Roger Williams they formed what became known as a haven of freedom, the new colony of Rhode Island. It was a community described by its opponents as 'the sink into which all the rest of the colonies empty their heretics',[12] 'the receptacle of all sorts of riff-raff people, and nothing else than the sewer or latrina of New England'.[13] But it was defined more aptly in its own early code of laws as a place 'where all men may walk as their consciences persuade them, every man in the name of his God'.[14]

The greatest test of Rhode Island's tolerance, which it passed with flying colours, was provided by a new group of Christians arriving from England: the Quakers. We think of Quakers now as eminently respectable, but in the early days they seemed rather closer to hooligans — inspirational, idealistic, infinitely

One of the white wooden churches of New England: at Norfolk, Connecticut.

courageous, but none the less hooligans. They reached New England in 1656. Soon one of them was smashing bottles in a Boston church and shouting at the congregation: 'thus will the Lord break your bones'. A woman streaked through the streets stark naked, another undressed in church under guidance from God. Massachusetts must have looked back with nostalgia at their minor troubles with Anne Hutchinson and Roger Williams. New laws were passed. The Quakers were banished, but they kept returning to testify to their faith. The first time back, the men lost an ear, the women were whipped. The second time back, the men lost the other ear, the women were whipped again. The third time, a hole was bored in the tongue of either sex. Still they returned, until the punishment was changed to death: and some returned even to be hanged. One of those hanged was Mary Dyer, who previously had been a follower of Anne Hutchinson and who had now found a new and more dangerous cause.

The Quakers were welcome on principle in Rhode Island. Roger Williams campaigned violently against their form of Christianity — their fondness for visions seemed, to his serious Bible-studying soul, like a cheap short-cut to God — but he hoped to persuade them, not restrain them. Like Voltaire in the next century, he could disapprove of what they said but defend to the death their right to say it.

The strange behaviour of the early Quakers had begun in England with the strange behaviour of their founder, George Fox. History is littered with visionaries who attracted for a while a band of followers, but whose cult faded. A generation after their death they are quite forgotten: at best they will later be rediscovered by academics and win a place in the history books as amusing or dangerous eccentrics. So it might have been with George Fox. His behaviour was

Quaker simplicity in place of the conventional church or 'steeple-house': their seventeenth-century meeting-house at Newport, Rhode Island.

The three spires of Lichfield cathedral, which struck at the life of George Fox.

of the classic pattern, being of a kind to impress a few but enrage many. His famous vision at Lichfield in 1651 is a good example:

> Walking with several Friends I lifted up my head and I espied three steeplehouse spires. They struck at my life and I asked Friends what they were, and they said, Lichfield. In a great field there were shepherds keeping their sheep. I was commanded by the Lord, of a sudden, to untie my shoes and put them off. I stood still for it was winter, and the word of the Lord was like a fire in me, so I put off

213

my shoes and was commanded to give them to the shepherds, and was to charge them to let no one have them except they paid for them. The poor shepherds trembled and were astonished.

Then I walked on about a mile till I came into the town, and as soon as I was got within the town the word of the Lord came to me again, to cry, 'Woe unto the bloody city of Lichfield!' So I went up and down the streets, crying with a loud voice, 'Woe to the bloody city of Lichfield'. It being market-day, I went into the market-place, and to and fro in the several parts of it, and made stands, crying as before, 'Woe to the bloody city of Lichfield'. And no one laid hands on me; but as I went thus crying through the streets, there seemed to me to be a channel of blood running down the streets, and the market-place appeared like a pool of blood.

And so at last some Friends and friendly people came to me and said, 'Alack, George, where are thy shoes?' I told them it was no matter. And returning to the shepherds, I gave them some money, and took my shoes of them again. [15]

Fox was often moved to interrupt preachers during church services and to engage in debate with them. He was a hard man to argue with. A favourite device was to ask his opponents if their words were their own. Of course, came the indignant reply. Very well, said Fox, but mine are from God. Yet when someone as intransigent as himself, a Ranter, tried to pester him with argument, he used a blunter tactic. 'Repent, thou beastly swine,' he yelled at him.

Highly theatrical preaching of Judgment Day was to remain for a while a Quaker characteristic, and a Quaker demonstration might erupt at any time and in any place. One day Pepys was in the crowd in Westminster Hall waiting for Charles II to appear and to address the assembly. He noted in his diary:

One thing extraordinary was, this day a man, a Quaker, came naked through the Hall, only very civilly tied about the privities to avoid scandal, and with a chafing-dish of fire and brimstone upon his head did pass through the Hall, crying 'Repent, repent!' [16]

If this had been the main aspect of the Quaker movement, the group would have had no more lasting effect than those who still cry doom on our city pavements. But at the centre of George Fox's vision was an idea which was also at the heart of the Reformation, but which had never been carried through to its logical conclusion. Luther had proclaimed the priesthood of all believers, a religion in which each man's personal relationship with God was his first concern: yet all the great churches of the Reformation, the Lutheran, the Calvinist, the Anglican, had their official pastors to guide the flock. Luther and Calvin had argued that no man could earn merit in the sight of God, who would choose the elect to join him in heaven for inscrutable reasons entirely his own: yet from this potentially egalitarian idea there had developed, in Massachusetts, the most self-righteous ruling clique known to history. George Fox cut through these contradictions. He dismissed all church buildings with the contemptuous phrase 'steeple-houses', arguing that the only real church is in men's hearts. The Calvinists had replaced the altar with the pulpit, but it was still the pastor's pulpit. George Fox would go further. His followers gathered not in a church but in a meeting-house, a plain room in which they sat facing inwards. There was no leader, no established form for the occasion. Anyone could speak if the spirit moved them: if no one felt moved to speak, silence. It was an arrangement which fulfilled in its purest form — far too pure for many — one of the ideals of the Reformation.

The two sides of George Fox's society are seen in its two names. His followers were called Quakers by their enemies because of their visionary antics, bidding others tremble before the Lord and themselves shaking in ecstasy. But their own name for themselves was and still is the Society of Friends. George Fox and his visions provided the poetry and brought immediate attention: but the more prosaic idea of a friendly society provided the long-term impetus of the movement, and was exemplified in William Penn. He could hardly have been more different from Fox. Penn was an aristocrat, the son of an admiral who was well acquainted with the royal family and was one of Pepys's superiors in the Navy Office. During the night of September 4th, 1666, Penn's father and Pepys dug a deep hole together in a London garden and lowered their wine into it to save it from the great fire: Pepys added his Parmesan cheese.

William Penn was drawn to the Quaker cause when he heard one of their wandering preachers. Within a year he found himself in prison for attending a Quaker meeting, and from then on he shared their difficulties in an England which was growing less tolerant as the century progressed. In the age of Nell Gwyn and Lord Rochester, the playboy king himself seems to have inclined to tolerance of all sorts (including religious), but the mood of the Restoration church and parliament was vindictive against the Puritans — who had, after all, killed a king, created a commonwealth, and driven out the Anglican bishops. Between 1661 and 1665 a series of Acts were passed in quick succession to limit the freedom of Dissenters. But they only put a new gloss of legality on a persecution that was already in full swing. In 1660 the Nonconformist preacher John Bunyan (hardly a firebrand of the George Fox variety) had been arrested for holding an unlicensed religious gathering. The offence landed him in Bedford gaol — for twelve years. He was only one of a vast number of victims around the country, and in the prison conditions of the day thousands died.

Here was a far stronger incentive to leave for America than the Pilgrim Fathers had experienced, and the greatest achievement of William Penn was in answer to this need. His dream of a religious settlement became possible when Charles II, who had borrowed £16,000 from Penn's father, offered to repay the son with a tract of land in the New World. Penn conceived it as an ideal Christian commonwealth, a place of refuge not only for Quakers but for any other persecuted people. 'There may be room there, though not here,' he wrote to a friend, 'for such an holy experiment.'[17]

It was not the first organized attempt at religious tolerance in America. The priority must go to Maryland, founded in 1632 by Lord Baltimore for Roman Catholics persecuted elsewhere. Baltimore pointedly welcomed Protestant settlers as well, and Maryland's Toleration Act of 1649, guaranteeing freedom of worship to all who believed in the Christian Trinity, is a milestone on the road to tolerance. But only five years later Maryland's tolerance proved its undoing, when Puritans gained the upper hand and immediately placed restraints on Anglicans and Catholics alike. And then there was Rhode Island: but that had developed almost accidentally among refugees from Massachusetts. Penn's colony was the first conscious blueprint for a tolerant society which both fulfilled its objectives and survived.

From the start it sounded an idyllic place. The name of the colony was to be Pennsylvania, Penn's woodlands. Its capital city, set in the angle between two pleasant rivers, was to be Philadelphia: the city of Brotherly Love. As to the limits of tolerance, you were expected to believe in one God, the creator of the universe — but that was about all.

The practical advantages of tolerance rapidly became apparent when a suspected witch was brought for trial before Penn. Ten years later the suspicion of witchcraft at Salem, in strict Massachusetts, would lead to mass hysteria and bloodshed. But when the witch appeared before Penn, he asked her: 'Art thou a witch? Hast thou ridden through the air on a broomstick?' 'Yes,' she said. There must have been a gasp in the court. Penn replied that if she could ride through the air on a broomstick, she had a perfect right to do so. He, for one, knew of no law against it. He recommended that she be set free; the jury agreed; and no more was heard of witchcraft in Pennsylvania.

People flocked into a place as sensible as Philadelphia. It grew, and with the Quaker example of hard work became prosperous. Today a city of more than two million people is presided over by a gigantic statue of William Penn. And in the skyscraper age they still follow a city rule which says that no one shall build higher than the brim of his hat.

Through their own policy of toleration the Quakers soon became, in Penn's phrase, 'dissenters in their own city'. Many of the new arrivals had a way of life offensive to Quaker ideals. A meeting of 1730 recorded that one particularly rowdy group had taken up residence. There had been 'firing of Guns and Revelling, occasioned by a Number of People under Pretence of Keeping a day to their saint, called Saint Patrick'.[18]

But George Fox had made a point of telling liars, drunkards and whoremongers that they too could find the inner light in themselves — a central message of the gospels much forgotten in Massachusetts. The Quakers accepted their changing city. Today, a tiny minority, they still gather for worship in the old meeting-houses, such as that of the Merion Friends, built in 1695 by a group of Quakers from Merioneth in Wales.

Around the rim of the famous Liberty Bell in Philadelphia there runs a quotation from the Old Testament: 'Proclaim Liberty throughout all the Land unto all the Inhabitants thereof.' The liberty in question is usually thought of as being America's freedom from Britain, because the bell hung at the top of Philadelphia's old State House: and it rang out when the Declaration of Independence was signed there in 1776. In fact the bell got its popular name from a later liberty, when it was chosen as a symbol in the fight to free the slaves. But the liberty it was cast for, the liberty of the quotation, was the original concern of Philadelphia: religious liberty.

The bell was commissioned for the fiftieth anniversary of Penn's Charter. It was cast in London, in Whitechapel, but it proved a bad advertisement for British workmanship. It cracked the very first time it was rung. With hindsight that was perhaps lucky. The bell was melted down and re-cast in Philadelphia: and later it would seem far better that the symbol of American liberty should have been home-made.

As a matter of fact, even the home-made version cracked: but not until 1835. By then the Liberty Bell had rung out loud and clear not only for independence, but also for the first occasion when an independent nation made religious freedom for all a matter of law. The American Constitution and the Bill of

Pennsylvania and the unchanging world of the Old Order Amish. Opposite: *Waiting for a lift in a buggy.* Overleaf: *Tilling the fields.*

Rights were both signed in the same group of state buildings at Philadelphia. The Constitution, in 1787, said that no religious test would ever be required for anyone holding office in the United States. The Bill of Rights added in 1791, in its First Amendment: 'Congress shall make no law respecting an establishment of religion, or prohibiting the free exercise thereof.' So Philadelphia's bell rang out for the final triumph of Philadelphia's principle. Tolerance had been found, and safeguarded.

The statue of William Penn which towers above Philadelphia, invaded only by aerials.

217

CHAPTER TEN

Politeness and Enthusiasm

I N the Bavarian church of Ottobeuren pink-faced cherubs peep round every corner, as often as not holding little gilded arrows, zig-zagged like lightning, which suggest a highly charged version of Cupid's darts. It seems an unusual ornament for a church, but this is no ordinary church. It is part of an abbey. This was the type of decoration thought suitable, in the eighteenth century, to lift the spirits of the better class of monk.

At much the same time as Ottobeuren was being built, Voltaire had written a description of the higher clergy in France which seems entirely in keeping with the baubles of the abbey:

> In France young men distinguished by their debaucheries, and raised to high positions in the Church by the intrigues of women, publicly make love and give luxurious suppers every day from which they rise to implore the light of the Holy Spirit.[1]

Four cardinals in one French family, the Rohans, demonstrate the point. Their good fortune began when the mother of the first was the mistress of Louis XIV. Her son Armand became a cardinal at the age of thirty eight. His great-nephew, also Armand, joined him in the Sacred College when he was only thirty. Another relation had to wait for his red hat until he was sixty four. But it was the fourth Cardinal de Rohan who became the best known of all, not so much for his Christian virtues as for his part in the Diamond Necklace Affair — a scandal which disclosed him in a secret midnight rendezvous in the gardens of Versailles with a disguised prostitute whom he took to be Queen Marie Antoinette. (He should have been forewarned: the scenario is remarkably like the final scene of *The Marriage of Figaro*, which had had a triumphant opening in Paris in the previous year.) The Rohan line of cardinals was ending in much the same milieu of sex and intrigue as it had begun.

No man was a more persistent scourge of the church in France than Voltaire. He was to find in England the only type of theology which appealed to him, and it was a quarrel with the powerful Rohan family which led to his discovery of English ways. He was already a leading Parisian dramatist, poet and wit when he was publicly insulted by the Chevalier de Rohan. Voltaire challenged him to a duel. The Chevalier responded by sending his servants to beat up this middle-class literary upstart, after which Voltaire was taken to the Bastille and then deported as an exile to England.

It was the English attitude to God which Voltaire would find attractive, rather than the English church as an institution. That was very different from its French equivalent, but he described it with the same incisive wit:

> The national religion — that in which fortunes are made — is the Episcopal, called the Church of England, or emphatically 'The Church'. You do not here see young men become bishops on leaving college; and moreover almost all the priests are married. The pedantry and awkwardness of manners, acquired in the universities, and the little commerce they have with women, generally oblige a bishop to be contented with the wife which belongs to him.[2]

Opposite: *Inside the eighteenth-century abbey church at Ottobeuren.*

Previous pages: *Enthusiasm in its modern form: a Pentecostalist preacher in Philadelphia exercises a powerful emotional spell over his congregation.*

The quizzical character of Voltaire: a statue in the village of Ferney.

If Ottobeuren stands as an image of the church in Catholic Europe, England must be represented by the massively complacent tombs with which the walls of her churches were lined in the eighteenth and early nineteenth centuries. Worthies in full wigs, or even dressed for the occasion in Roman costume, sit mourned by inconsolable ladies who often — it is not quite clear for whom — reveal one white marble breast. Below, an inscription lists the virtues of the departed. No other place or period has indulged in quite such monumental self-satisfaction. The rolling conventional phrases can be found in any church of the time. A stroll through part of Bath abbey provides a typical selection:

Unaffected Piety, uniform Benevolence and inflexible Integrity

It is incredible the sum of money he expended on Charity

Polished Manners, inflexible Integrity, and the warmest Benevolence of Heart

A public loss, a premature victim of an ardent and superior mind

Unaffected Piety, unassuming Manners, and unostentatious Benevolence

One of the most valuable women that ever liv'd, whose principal Happiness consisted (Altho' she was of some rank) in a real and unbounded Affection and Tenderness for her husband and children.

The English gentleman (or the would-be-gentleman who affected such unaffected Piety) was developing a new form of Christianity better suited to his civilized age. As if in readiness for the coming century, John Locke had published in 1695 a treatise entitled *The Reasonableness of Christianity*. A year later it was followed by John Toland's *Christianity not Mysterious*. The religion which had recently caused untold suffering and bloodshed through sectarian wars was preparing to enter the age of reason and optimism. Polite people would look back on religious warfare as an aberration caused by 'enthusiasm' — a word which they could discover from their Greek dictionary, elegantly bound in calf, to mean in its root form possession by a god, but which Samuel Johnson would soon define for them as 'a vain belief of private revelation: a rash confidence of divine favour or communication'. Brawling over theology was scornfully dismissed by Alexander Pope: 'For modes of faith let graceless zealots fight.'[3]

Monumental self-satisfaction: the tomb of Charles James Fox in Westminster Abbey.

223

'Everything is for the best in the best of all possible worlds' — when Voltaire later made that sentence famous, he did so in the bitterness of disillusion. But when he arrived in England, optimism was the most widely held philosophy. Everything seemed capable of improvement (the concept from which Capability Brown derived his nickname) and the gentlemen of England were as calm and confident in their religion as in their landscape gardening. 'Religion is a cheerful thing,' Lord Halifax explained to his daughter. And Lord Shaftesbury enlarged:

> Good Humour is not only the best Security against Enthusiasm: Good Humour is also the best Foundation of Piety and True Religion.[4]

For the proof of that religion, you had only to look about you. It was perfectly evident to anyone standing in the grounds of Stourhead that a discriminating gentleman had created them: how much more overwhelming the evidence of that even greater Gentleman above, who had so recently revealed to Sir Isaac Newton that his Estate too was run along rational lines. In an age of rapid scientific advance, the scientists saw each new discovery as further proof of God's guiding hand in the universe. Both Newton and Boyle wrote at length on theological matters. John Ray, who can claim to be the founder of the modern sciences of botany and zoology, wrote a book entitled *The Wisdom of God Manifested in the Works of Creation*. The classic statement of the eighteenth century's belief in God was made by William Paley in 1802, but precisely the same argument and example had appeared in theological works at least sixty years before (one of them named, appropriately enough, *A Gentleman's Religion, in Three Parts*).[5] Paley's proof, considerably reduced in length, went as follows:

> Suppose I had found a watch upon the ground, I should hardly think it had lain there for ever: for when we come to inspect the watch, we perceive that its several parts are put together for a purpose. This mechanism being observed, the inference we think is inevitable, that the watch must have had a maker: that there must have existed, at some time, and at some place or other, an artificer or artificers who formed it for the purpose which we find it actually to answer: who comprehended its construction, and designed its use.

To impress his reader more thoroughly with the wonder of God's handiwork, Paley asked him to suppose that the watch had a faculty which in another context we take for granted:

> Suppose it contained within it a mechanism — or a complex adjustment of lathes, files and other tools — for the purpose of producing, in the course of its movement, another watch like itself: the thing is conceivable.[6]

This great inventor, the landscape gardener of the universe, was the god of the English Deists. Voltaire found himself in agreement with their views:

> I believe in God; not the God of the mystics and the theologians, but the God of nature, the great geometrician, the architect of the universe, the prime mover, unalterable, transcendental, everlasting.[7]

Signs in the sky which had once shown the mystery of God now proved his skill as a mechanic. But the Gentleman who had created such a spectacular machine was hardly in keeping with the more popular aspects of Christianity.

224

Opposite: A cherub in the eighteenth-century abbey church of Ottobeuren, Bavaria.

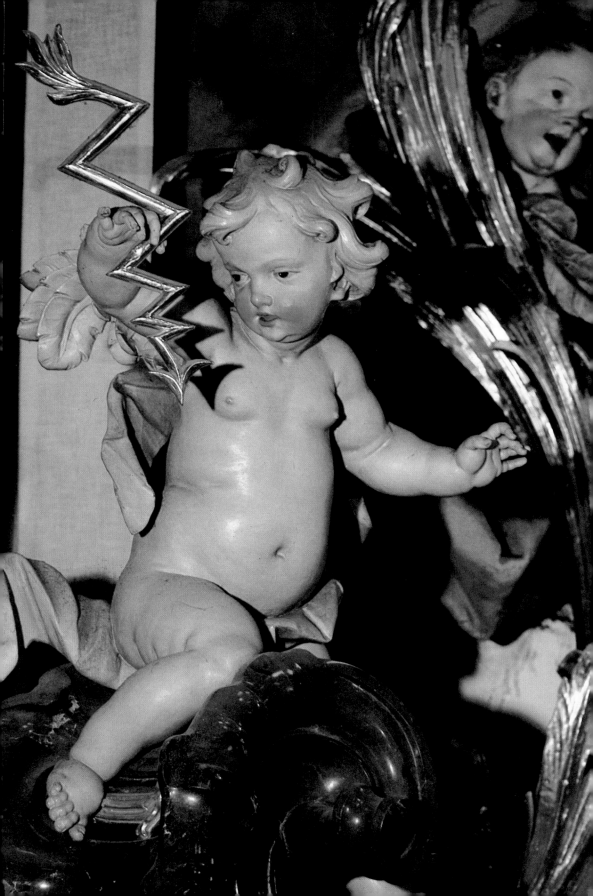

Miracles were contrary to his own natural laws. A son born to him of a virgin in the stables; a mysterious spirit with whom he was one in three and three in one; these hardly seemed part of his scenario. What was left was entirely rational; but for ordinary people slightly dull.

Sermons in the dignified churches of the day were read rather than preached. In Hogarth's *Sleeping Congregation* the parson has been droning on. The hour-glass, which stood on eighteenth-century pulpits to ensure a full sixty minutes of edification, has long since run dry. Only one person is awake — the clerk — and

The Sleeping Congregation: *engraving by Hogarth.*

Opposite: *The grounds at Stourhead, Wiltshire, and (below) a polite cleric of the time, the Rev. Carter Thelwell (by Stubbs, Holburne of Menstrie Museum, University of Bath).*

that for a reason which pre-dates even the most superstitious elements of Christianity, the pretty girl who unknowingly reveals her charms. The Church of England was clearly in need of a shock. 'The Christian World is in a dead sleep. Nothing but a loud voice can awaken them out of it.'[8] The loud voice was that of George Whitefield, who already in his twenties was to prove himself the most electrifying preacher of the century. His appearance was unprepossessing — Mr Squintum, the satirists would call him — but David Garrick said he would give 100 guineas to be able to say 'oh' with half the pathos that Whitefield put into it.

Oxford, sleepy Oxford, was the first to realize that something was up. The ancient universities were at a low ebb throughout the eighteenth century. Students were frivolous and idle. But it was here, in the 1730s, that John and Charles Wesley were running their famous Holy Club. Bible Moths, others preferred to call them. George Whitefield was slightly younger than the Wesley brothers (and of a class so much below theirs, being an inn-keeper's son, that according to the university rules they were not allowed to befriend him), but in 1733 he was welcomed into the Club. The young men split up their day between study, prayer and sober discussion; methodical they certainly were, Methodists they were mockingly named. John Wesley's journal reveals his own schedule one day, while the world went about its fashionable business:

> Four in the morning till five, private prayer; from five to seven we read the Bible together, carefully comparing it with the writings of the earliest ages. At seven we breakfasted. At eight public prayers. From nine to twelve I learned German, Mr Delamotte Greek, my brother writ sermons. At twelve we met to give an account to one another what we had done since our last meeting, and what we designed to do before our next. About one we dined. From dinner to four, public reading. At four, evening prayers. From five to six, private prayer. Six to seven, reading. Seven, public service. At eight we met again, to exhort and instruct one another. Between nine and ten to bed.[9]

Some found the new piety attractive, but the establishment was unimpressed. Oxford later expelled six Methodists who 'would not desist from publicly praying and exhorting'.

> BOSWELL. But was it not hard, Sir, to expel them, for I am told they were good beings?
> JOHNSON. I believe they might be good beings, but they were not fit to be in the University of Oxford. A cow is a very good animal in the field, but we turn her out of a garden.[10]

From the gardens of Oxford to the fields of the English countryside. This was precisely the path that Methodism took. It was in the fields near Bristol that the new pattern took shape. George Whitefield had been refused permission to preach in various Bristol churches — partly because of his undignified fervour, partly because he was often so critical of the resident clergyman. He therefore took the bold step, which was incidentally against the law, of preaching in the open air. His audience was a community of coal-miners who were widely considered to be the most barbarous heathens in England: and his success, as Whitefield often later remarked, could be seen in the white channels left by the tears on their coal-black cheeks. It was a success which he would repeat again and again, to audiences of five, ten, twenty thousand, both in Britain and America.

How did he do it? Everyone agreed that Whitefield was a great performer, with a magnificent voice which he knew how to float on the wind to reach a vast crowd. But above all he did it with the help of the fires of hell. The threat of hell, the promise of heaven; these two have always provided the most powerful impetus for religion. But they must go together. The eighteenth century had dropped hell (and so have we). George Whitefield re-introduced it with a vengeance. The following is an extract from one of his sermons which was heard and recorded by the philosopher David Hume:

> Come ye unconverted sinners, come and see the place where they laid the body of the deceased Lazarus: behold him laid out, bound hand and foot with grave-cloaths, locked up and stinking in a dark cave! View him again and again; go nearer to him; be not afraid; smell him, ah! how he stinketh. Stop there now, pause a while; and whilst thou art gazing upon the corpse of Lazarus, give me leave to tell thee with great plainness, but greater love, that this dead, bound, entombed, stinking carcase, is but a faint representation of thy poor soul in its natural state.
>
> I see hell opened, I see the damned tormented, I see such a one in hell. Can you live, think you, in everlasting burnings? Is your flesh brass, and your bones iron? What if they are? Hell-fire, that fire prepared for the devil and his angels, will heat them through and through.
>
> The attendant angel (*deep solemn pause*), the attendant angel is just about to leave the threshold of this sanctuary, and ascend to heaven. And shall he ascend, and not bear with him the news of one sinner, among all this multitude, reclaimed from the error of his ways? (*stamping foot, throwing eyes and hands to heaven, loud piercing voice*). Stop, Gabriel, stop, ere you enter the sacred portals, and yet carry with you the news of one sinner converted to God. [11]

The Duchess of Buckingham no doubt spoke for many in the polite classes when she commented on Whitefield:

> His doctrines are most repulsive and strongly tinctured with impertinence and disrespect towards his superiors. It is monstrous to be told that you have a heart as sinful as the common wretches that crawl on the earth. [12]

It was as shocking to respectable eighteenth-century Christians that a man should preach emotional sermons in the fields, as it is to many Europeans today that a preacher should sob on television, inviting the viewer to kneel with him in front of the set and accept Jesus now, at this very moment — or, in Whitefield's terms, before the attendant angel departs. Yet television evangelism, usually of an extremely emotional sort, is almost commonplace today in the United States. The motive is the same in both cases: to reach people who would not be reached in a church. And at least, with George Whitefield, there was no danger of falling asleep.

A very rare print by Hogarth, *Enthusiasm Delineated*, gives a satirical version of Whitefield preaching. The design is similar to that of *The Sleeping Congregation*, but the atmosphere could hardly be more different. Whitefield holds out the choice which he offered his congregation; God and the Trinity in his right hand, the devil with a gridiron in his left. In place of the hour-glass there is now a thermometer called Scale of Vociferation, going up to Bull Roar and Blood Heat at the top. Below there is another sort of scale: Extasy, Lust, Agony, Madness, Suicide. This takes the temperature of his audience, for in the public mind

Enthusiasm Delineated: *engraving by Hogarth on the preaching of George Whitefield.*

convulsions and fainting fits were a regular part of Methodist preaching. In fact Hogarth has muddled his preachers. Whitefield's congregations were invariably in tears. It was John Wesley's, in these early years, who tended to faint clean away. It was a spiritual phenomenon which the eighteenth century, including even most Methodists, regarded with extreme suspicion. And naturally such excesses horrified the Church of England, which has always taken its religion much as a gentleman takes his port — in dignified moderation, but with the enjoyment of a connoisseur.

But there was a more settled part of the new Methodism, which developed from the particular genius of the Wesley brothers. Whitefield, about to sail to America, had asked John Wesley to take over his open-air mission around

Bristol. Wesley was reluctant:

> I could scarce reconcile myself to this strange way of preaching in the fields, having been all my life so tenacious of every point relating to decency and order.[13]

But he did it, with great success, and he was to spend much of the rest of his life riding round the countryside with some edifying book propped up on his horse's neck. It has been calculated that he travelled 100 miles each week, 5,000 miles a year, the equivalent of nine times round the world in his lifetime — and that he preached some 40,000 sermons. Everywhere he left behind him new little groups and communities, larger versions of that original Holy Club in Oxford.

Within six weeks of his arrival in Bristol in 1739 Wesley had bought a patch of land, on which the first Methodist chapel was built. The name of the building suggests the informality of its beginnings. It is just the New Room — somewhere for Wesley's Society to meet with more convenience. It only took four weeks before the outer shell was ready to hold an inaugural meeting, and it was at this point that the skills of Charles Wesley came in. Until now the only singing in the Church of England had been psalms. Charles borrowed the use of hymns from the Nonconformists, and the opening of the New Room was the first occasion on which his hymn book was used. 'Arm of the Lord, awake, awake,' they sang that June evening in 1739:

> Arm of the Lord, awake, awake,
> Thine own immortal strength put on!
> With terror clothed, hell's kingdom shake,
> And cast thy foes with fury down!

Stirring words; rousing tunes; these hymns would remain a strong emotional experience linking all Methodists. Others at the time found them far too jolly to be counted as religion. Bristol's boy genius, Thomas Chatterton, lived but a few hundred yards away from the New Room. His comment was brief: 'You'd swear 'twas bawdy songs made godly.'[14]

The form of revivalism which began in England was to have its most lasting influence on America. The link between the two was George Whitefield. Like the more secular stars of today, he developed a huge following on both sides of the Atlantic. After handing over his Bristol open-air congregation to John Wesley, he had sailed for America in 1739. Philadelphia was the first large city he visited, and soon he was preaching to his usual vast audiences.

It is a well-known principle of history that all scientific experiments carried out in America in the eighteenth century were carried out by Benjamin Franklin. It certainly held good in the case of George Whitefield. One day, when Whitefield was preaching in Philadelphia at the junction of Market Street and Second Street, Franklin was standing at the back of the crowd on Market Street. He had read unscientific statements in the papers that Whitefield could preach to 25,000 people and be heard by every one of them — on the face of it impossible. So, being Franklin, he decided to test it.

> I had the curiosity to learn how far he could be heard by retiring backwards down Market Street towards the river; and I found his voice distinct till I came near Front Street, when some noise in that street obscured it. Imagining then a semi-circle, of which my distance from him should be the radius, and that it were filled with auditors, to each of whom I allowed two square feet, I computed that he might

well be heard by more than thirty thousand. This reconciled me to the newspaper reports of his having preached to twenty-five thousand people in the fields.[15]

As in England, Whitefield preached to the poorest classes, those neglected by other clergymen — in this case the Negro slaves, who were widely regarded as above beasts but below human beings and therefore undeserving of either the truth or the charity spelt out in the gospels. Christianity has produced few more heart-felt forms of music than the negro spiritual. It derives from the impact of eighteenth-century revivalism on the suffering and the musical genius of the slaves of America.

Whitefield's basic revivalist message was to offer his sinful congregation this one last chance to repent. (Franklin recorded that he told his Philadelphia audience they were half beasts and half devils.) This tallied with the message of certain very successful American preachers, such as Jonathan Edwards, and together they inspired the widespread eighteenth-century movement in America which became known as the Great Awakening. In a sense it has never ended. America became, and remains, the natural home of revivalism. Camp-fire meetings, involving many thousands, were a familiar feature of life on the frontier. Eventually the spark was carried back across the Atlantic to England, in a series of campaigns which run from Moody and Sankey to Billy Graham.

Even the ecstatic side of early Methodist experience lives on chiefly in America. Ecstasy has been part of Christianity from the start. It was implicit at Pentecost, and was popular among the Corinthians — for which they were rebuked by St Paul. But it had reached a new peak in the response, especially of women, to the warnings of John Wesley and the music of his brother Charles. Today one of the fastest growing branches of Christianity is Pentecostalism, which has its origins in the United States. I have seen white Pentecostalists in Los Angeles waiting in line to faint clean away, one after another, when the preacher's hand touches their forehead and the Holy Spirit enters them: and black Pentecostalists in Philadelphia lose themselves in a trance of music and dancing, coaxed on by the compelling voice of their pastor. Transplant either scene to a church in the English countryside, and the Anglican congregation would be amazed and, I would guess, deeply shocked — even today. But their response would be only a pale reflection of what the polite gentleman of the eighteenth century must have felt when he heard that young women had convulsions while listening to the sermons of Mr John Wesley. The distinguished Bishop Butler made his feelings plain in a memorable phrase: 'Sir, the pretending to extraordinary revelations and gifts of the Holy Ghost is a horrid thing, a very horrid thing.'[16] But horrid things do happen. And eighteenth-century Europe was about to be shocked by an even more basic form of convulsion.

In 1755 there occurred an event which disturbed the rationalism of Europe almost as much as it had shaken the earth of Portugal: the great Lisbon earthquake. First reports, 30,000 dead. How could the Supreme Being, until now such a reasonable person, do this? Voltaire immediately took up his pen:

> Now, when you hear their piteous, half-formed cries,
> Or from their ashes see the smoke arise,

Ecstasy as the pattern of religious experience: a moment in a Pentecostalist service in Philadelphia.

Penitence after the Lisbon earthquake: oil by Stromberle (Museu Nacional de Arte Antiga, Lisbon).

> Say, will you still eternal laws maintain,
> Which God to cruelties like these constrain?
> To nature we apply for truth in vain,
> God should his will to human kind explain.[17]

To the Methodists it was all very much simpler, for that was precisely what God was doing: explaining himself, in no uncertain terms. John Wesley was as quick into print as Voltaire, but he drew a different moral:

> Covetousness, ambition, various injustice, falsehood in every kind, the clergy themselves not excepted. God is not well pleased with this. You may buy intelligence where the shock was yesterday, but not where it will be tomorrow — today. It comes! The roof trembles! The beams crack. The ground rocks to and fro. Hoarse thunder resounds from the bowels of the earth. Now what help?

He even carried his theme into astronomy, that divine machine which had so recently been used to prove God's sense of order, and his vision took him to the very brink of science fiction:

> What think you of a comet? The late ingenious and accurate Dr Halley (never yet suspected of enthusiasm) fixed the return of the great comet in three years time. Probably it will be seen first, drawing nearer and nearer, till it appears as another moon in magnitude, though not in colour, being of a deep fiery red: then scorching and burning up all the produce of the earth, drying away all clouds, and so cutting

off the hope or possibility of any rain or dew, drying up every fountain, stream, and river, causing all faces to gather blackness, and all men's hearts to fail . . . Let us dare to own there is a God. Let us make this wise, this powerful, this gracious God our friend![18]

So the romantic image replaces the classical. Emotion, in religion, edges out reason. But old comforts die hard. The next century might belong to the fervent type of Christianity, but the more relaxed and self-indulgent sort would certainly last out this one. In the world of Jane Austen, young curates are mainly concerned to find those twin necessities of the clerical life — a well-endowed living and a well-connected wife. ('The parson knows enough who knows a duke,' commented William Cowper.)[19] There is no more typical example of a common-sense eighteenth-century Anglican parson than James Woodforde, who had a comfortable parish in Norfolk; and there are few documents more delightful, or more complacently of this world, than his diary. It is easy enough to quote tit-bits from any diary, and Woodforde provides them in abundance. For example:

> Very melancholy News on the Papers respecting the Ships wrecked and lives lost at Yarmouth. May those poor Souls lost be O Lord better off. And send thy divine Comfort to all their Relatives. Mr Custance sent us a brace of Partridges.[20]

But only a selection of ordinary days, chosen at random, can really suggest the flavour of Woodforde's life — in which food and good fellowship predominate, and the normal duties of a vicar are conspicuously absent. The following selection reveals what he was doing on the day the Bastille fell, and on the nearest date each month for the rest of that year of revolution, 1789:

> July 14, Tuesday. I caught a very fine Trout this morning about a Pound and a half. Mr Du Quesne was out with me a fishing but could not catch a Trout. We had for Dinner a fine Dish of Fish most of my catching, Ham and Chicken, Peas and Beans, a Leg of Mutton rosted, a Couple of Ducks, Currant and Apricot Tarts, Barberry Tarts and Custards.

> August 13, Thursday. Called at Dr Clarkes and my Brothers, both of whom went with me to Ansford Inn where we dined and spent the Afternoon till 9 at Night with ten other Gentlemen. We had for Dinner several Tureens of Turtle, as fine a Haunch of Venison as one would wish to see, also a large Venison Pasty and a Neck of Venison, Pies &c. The Turtle weighed 40 lb. Claret, Madeira and Port Wine at and after Dinner. We drank all the Claret that Wheeler had, which was only one Dozen. NB Another Meeting again on Wednesday next to decide some bets between 2 Horses running that Day. Each Gentleman betted a Guinea and the Winnings to be spent at Ansford Inn.

(On September 14th he was visiting London.)

> October 14, Wednesday. I took a little Rhubarb and ginger going to bed at night, being not right well.

> November 14, Saturday. Bespoke a Quarter of a Pipe of Port Wine and 4 Gallons of Rum of Mr Priest Senr. this Morning. My Brother and Wife slept in the Parlour Chamber. I think my Brother is grown very fat of late.

> December 14, Monday. Killed a Pig this Morning, weight $9\frac{1}{2}$ Stone. Between 11 and 12 o'clock I walked to Church and buried in the Church Miss Mary Girling of

Dereham aged 29 Years. She was brought in a Hearse with 4 Horses, a Mourning Coach and Chaise attending it. A great many People attended at the Funeral. I had a white silk Hatband, a pair of Beaver Gloves and also my Fee for burying her One Guinea. At Quadrille this Evening won a Shilling which Nancy owes me with much more. I was rather low the whole day long. Nancy recd. a Pair of white Gloves for Miss Girling.

In France things were very different. Instead of a complacent church threatened by an enthusiastic one, there was a corrupt aristocratic church whose very foundation had long been under attack from the standpoint of the Enlightenment — a movement of which Voltaire could lay a good claim to be the first cause, prime mover, or supreme being. It was a church which would be swept away, after 1789, on a wave of enthusiasm far more shocking than the Methodist variety.

By the time of the Lisbon earthquake Voltaire was the chief ornament of French literature, but the pen that brought him fame had also made him unwelcome at many of the courts of Europe. He had recently left Prussia after a row with Frederick the Great. Louis XV ordered him not to return to Paris. He had settled in republican Geneva, but soon an article was traced back to him which praised certain of the city's pastors for doubting Christ's divinity. In the ensuing uproar he moved again, this time to the house at Ferney which was to be his home for the remaining twenty-eight years of his life. It was poised delicately on the border between France and Switzerland, so that he could retire to safety on either side if the other found his tongue too sharp.

At Ferney, surprisingly, he renovated the church and from time to time preached in it. He had spent much of his life campaigning against the Church, which he referred to as *l'infame*, and his jibes at the expense of Christianity had been legion: 'If God did not exist, it would be necessary to invent him'; 'Let us worship God through Jesus if we must, if ignorance has so far prevailed that this Jewish name can still be spoken in all seriousness without being taken as a synonym for rapine and carnage'; 'Every sensible man, every honourable man, must hold the Christian sect in horror.'[21] But his quarrel was only with intolerance, superstition, fanaticism. On the façade of the church at Ferney he carved an inscription 'Deo Erexit Voltaire' (Voltaire built this for God), and it was not a joke. It seems that his own god, the reasonable god of the Deists, had survived the Lisbon earthquake. 'To believe in absolutely no god would be a frightful moral mistake, a mistake incompatible with wise government.' Religion should be 'pure adoration of a Supreme Being, detached from all superstition'.[22]

This strictly utilitarian god, so good for the people, would come into his own during the French Revolution — to which the Church, inseparable in its higher ranks from the nobility, fell an early casualty. In October 1789 the Assembly took over all ecclesiastical property. Later, as the revolution became more radical, an active policy known as 'de-Christianization' was launched. But a departing God can leave a dangerous vacuum. This was the gap which Robespierre intended to fill with the Supreme Being of Voltaire and the English Deists.

In its early years the revolution seemed to be moving towards a fully pagan form of ceremony based on the models of classical antiquity — a process in which the apotheosis of Voltaire himself was one of the landmarks. On his death in 1778 he had been forbidden burial in consecrated ground by the Paris clergy. After the downfall of the Church a plan developed to bring his body in triumph into the capital city. The building chosen to receive him was a church which had recently been built and which was about to be dedicated to St Genevieve. In 1790 it acquired, instead, the name which it still bears: 'Let us have the courage not to put this temple under the invocation of a saint. Let it be the French Pantheon.'[23] The remains of Voltaire were to be enshrined in the Pantheon on July 11th, 1791. The organizers employed Jacques-Louis David as the pageant master, and announced their intention 'to emulate the pomp and grandeur of the Greek apotheoses and the Roman consecrations'.[24] The procession set out from the demolished Bastille. The chariot bearing the sarcophagus with a recumbent image of the great man was drawn by twelve white horses, which in turn were led by men in antique costume. His collected works followed in a gilded cabinet. Musicians played instruments reconstructed from details on Trajan's column. Outside the National Theatre there was a special display devoted to Voltaire's innumerable works for the stage; everyone was moved to discover that sixty years earlier, in the opera *Samson*, he had written the line: 'People, rise up, break your chains.' Tens of thousands walked in the procession, and it was midnight before the sarcophagus was safely in the Pantheon. A newspaper commented that the day had witnessed 'the triumph of reason, the defeat of fanaticism'.[25] The phrase was apt enough for what Voltaire had stood for, but remarkably inappropriate to the real mood of Paris.

On its way from the Bastille to the Pantheon the procession passed beneath the windows of the Tuileries, where Louis XVI was now held prisoner. Many comments were made on the instructive contrast between the triumphant philosopher and the abject king. Eighteen months later Louis was dead. His execution (January 21st, 1793) was the greatest shock to Europe's established order since the death of Charles I. It took five days for the news to reach Parson Woodforde in Norfolk:

> January 26, Saturday. I breakfasted, dined, &c. again at home. Nancy breakfasted, dined, &c. again at home. Dinner today Souse, Veal Pye and Calfs Heart rosted. Billy Bidewells People brought our Newspapers from Norwich. The King of France Louis 16 inhumanly and unjustly beheaded on Monday last by his cruel, blood-thirsty Subjects. Dreadful times I am afraid are approaching to all Europe. France the foundation of all of it.

SERCOPHAGE qui a transporté les mânes de VOLTAIRE au PANTHÉON le 11 Juillet 1791.

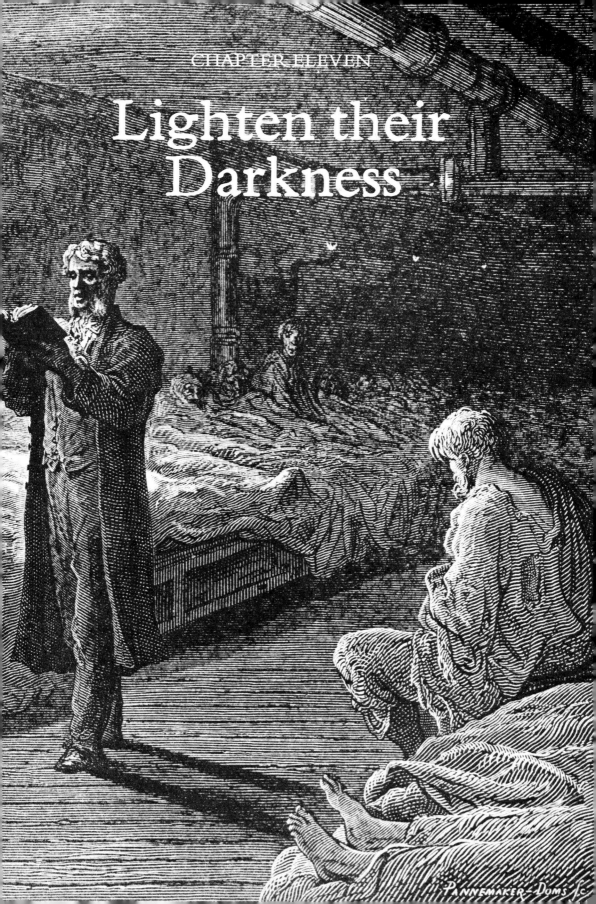

CHAPTER ELEVEN

Lighten their Darkness

ANY young man of tender conscience, if he happened to be a student at Cambridge between 1854 and 1857, was exposed to powerful pressures. As a freshman he could have heard the first ever bishop of New Zealand preaching in Great St Mary's:

> I go from hence to the most distant of all countries. There God has planted the standard of the Cross as a signal to His Church to fill up the intervening spaces, till there is neither a spot of earth which has not been trodden by a messenger of salvation, nor a single man to whom the gospel has not been preached. The voice of the Lord is asking 'Whom shall I send?' May every one of you who intends, by God's grace, to dedicate himself to the ministry, answer at once: 'Here I am, send me.'[1]

In his final year our undergraduate would have struggled to find a place in the Senate House, just over the road from Great St Mary's, when the hero of the moment spoke there in 1857. He was a presbyterian missionary, aptly described by a Frenchman as 'that indefatigable pedestrian'[2] — David Livingstone, who had just returned from his first long exploration deep into the heart of the unknown continent. His speech ended with a rousing appeal:

> I beg to direct your attention to Africa. I know that in a few years I shall be cut off in that country, which is now open; do not let it be shut again! I go back to Africa to try to make an open path for commerce and Christianity. Do you carry out the work which I have begun. I leave it with you.[3]

Previous pages: *'Scripture Reader in a Night Refuge': illustration in Doré's* London.

A postcard commemorating Livingstone's challenge to Cambridge.

" I go back to Africa to try to make an open path for commerce and Christianity. Do you carry on the work I have begun. I leave it with you. "

One of the boats with which Livingstone planned to steam into the heart of Africa: painting by Thomas Baines (Royal Geographical Society, London).

Such was the enthusiasm ('literally volley after volley of cheers'), both then and two weeks later at Oxford, that a Universities' Mission to Central Africa was set up the following year. The immediate purpose was to put an end to the slave trade of East Africa, glimpses of which had profoundly shocked Livingstone, and this added a pleasant sense of moral superiority to the crusade. 'Cambridge elevation and culture', wrote one member of the Senate House audience, 'came suddenly into contact with the mighty questions of African degradation.'[4] Slavery did also touch upon one slightly tender spot in England's elevation and culture. Until quite recently the British had been making a fortune by operating their own slave trade out of West Africa. In 1859, in another meeting in the Senate House, Cambridge was addressed by Samuel Wilberforce, whose father had led the campaign to end the English slave trade. Samuel was by now bishop of Oxford and his smooth eloquence had earned him the nickname of Soapy Sam. He told his audience that he could feel his father's ghost beckoning him

> to take up, in however feeble a manner, the work he so nobly began, and to witness to the next generation, that England can never be clear from the guilt of her long continued slave trade till Africa is free, civilized, and Christian.[5]

By the autumn of 1860 a small party of missionaries had been selected, under the leadership of the thirty-five-year-old Bishop Mackenzie, and once again it was Samuel Wilberforce who officiated at the parting ceremony. It was performed in the crypt of St Augustine's church at Canterbury, drawing a deliberate comparison between those about to take ship for Africa and the group of brave monks, led by Augustine, who had landed in Kent twelve centuries earlier to bring the faith to England.

The universities' expedition turned out to be as impractical as it was idealistic. The intention was to join up with Livingstone in East Africa, to steam up-river into the healthy and fertile highlands, and there to establish a self-supporting agricultural settlement as a centre from which to spread the faith and to lead the fight against slavery. But the steamer sent out for the purpose drew too many feet of water and had to be laboriously hauled over long stretches of rapids. And the very first glimpse of a party of eighty-four manacled slaves being herded by Arab traders made Livingstone and his colleagues forget their resolutions of non-violence; they cocked their rifles, routed the Arabs, and in a mood of high exhilaration cut the slaves free from their shackles. The missionaries eagerly took charge of them, and soon the boys were learning to march in step to a drum fashioned from an elephant's ear. But there was no serious chance of this little community surviving. The slaves were far from home, with no means of support. Contact with the coast was difficult, precautions against disease were inadequate, and many of the surrounding tribes were hostile. Within two years most of the missionaries were dead, including Bishop Mackenzie, and most of the freed slaves had been abandoned. A new bishop, sent out from England, withdrew the mission to the greater safety of the island of Zanzibar, twenty-five miles off the coast of Africa, which had long been under Arab control and was comparatively civilized. Livingstone was profoundly scornful of this tactical retreat, and he taunted the universities with the very analogy which they had themselves chosen: 'What would Gregory the Great have said if Augustine had landed on the Channel Islands?'[6]

In fact, since the main purpose of the mission had always been the ending of the slave trade, Zanzibar was a sensible place for its headquarters. It was the central market for the entire trade. It was calculated that some 50,000 slaves were

Opposite: *An African priest awaits the pope in front of St Peter's one Easter morning.*

A torn and patched photograph of Bishop Mackenzie, whose idealism ended in disaster.

240

brought each year to the coast (the only survivors of perhaps a quarter of a million who had been dragged from their villages deep in the interior), and they were nearly all brought across the final stretch of water to Zanzibar — the last public slave-market in the world. The Arab sultan made a handsome profit from his market, but he seems not to have understood the danger implied by the arrival of the missionaries. In 1863 he had welcomed to his shore a French order, the Holy Ghost Fathers, who also were concerned with freeing and converting slaves. In 1864 he rented a large house on the waterfront to the English mission and gave them five slaves as a nucleus for their little community. From their windows the missionaries could watch a horrifying spectacle. Arab slave ships sailed into the harbour, but they stopped just offshore. The reason was that the sultan charged customs duties on every slave imported into his island. Before landing, the slavers lifted their decks and inspected the people who were packed tightly below. They threw overboard the dead: and followed them with the dying, and with anyone who seemed too sick to fetch a good price at market. Now and then the missionaries managed to rescue a dying slave from the sea, just in time to give him a Christian burial.

The market was one of the few open spaces in the centre of old Zanzibar. Livingstone himself had visited it on an afternoon when three hundred slaves were being sold. The spectacle became something of a macabre tourist attraction for Europeans. An English visitor wrote that 'the chief object of attraction to every Englishman on first reaching Zanzibar is undoubtedly the slave market', and then continued in a frivolous tone which to us seems deeply shocking: 'There was a good deal of black cattle on hand this evening, but the market was apparently dull, and prices ranged low.' Only later came the obligatory note of outrage: 'It is of course impossible to see human beings sold like cattle without certain undefined feelings of nausea and disgust.' [7]

The Anglican cathedral of Zanzibar today stands triumphant on the site of the slave market. It was diplomatic rather than missionary pressure which had finally put an end to its daily transactions. In 1873 the British government persuaded the sultan to close the market, and to make sure that he kept his word there was soon a British admiral with nine warships standing off the coast: gunboat phil-anthropy. A rich Hindu merchant bought the disused site and gave it to the missionaries. To celebrate the completion of the church there was an inaugural service on Christmas Day 1879, with a congregation of freed slaves. The missionaries reported:

> Into the ante-chapel came groups of Arabs to see this strange sight, where so often they had bargained for slaves. The hymns, 'Hark the Herald' and 'While shepherds watched their flocks' were in Swahili. What a type of the change Christianity has made on the face of the earth was that church with its Christmas service! [8]

The moral affront of slavery had been only one of the many impulses to missionary work abroad. In his Cambridge speech Livingstone had talked of creating 'an open path for commerce and Christianity'. Christianity was the highest expression of Europe's civilization, and cheap manufactured goods were a measure of her practical achievements. It seemed obvious that both would be of use to the savages, and exporting them could benefit the pocket as well as the soul of Europe. In 1837 a missionary was able to point out an unexpected advantage

241

Opposite: *A saint in the making? Pope John XXIII held in affection by all creeds and nations (a statue at Loreto in Italy, see page 271).*

to Britain from the conversion of large numbers of South Sea islanders: 'at the lowest computation 150,000 persons, who a few years ago were unclothed savages, are now wearing articles of British manufacture'.[9] Such converts would also be taught a great many good British facts, intrinsically as alien to them as their garments. In the previous year an author had visited mission schools for Hottentot children in South Africa. He reported great progress with their lessons.

> In geography they had made creditable, and to my mind surprising, advances. They were able to tell, without the least hesitation, the name of each county, with that of its capital, when pointed to on the map of England and Wales.[10]

Behind such teaching lay the absolute conviction that European ways were best. Livingstone informed his assistants, during one of his voyages out to Africa: 'We come among the Africans as members of a superior race and servants of a Government that desires to elevate the more degraded portions of the human family'.[11] Even Cardinal Newman announced that western civilization could be considered 'as the representative society and civilization of the human race, as its perfect result and limit'.[12] A British colonial administrator in the later years of the century asked a missionary to translate the following message for a native audience at the mission station:

> Tell them how interested the Queen is in their welfare, how she wants them to improve themselves and their country. We were like you long years ago, going about naked with our war paint on, but when we learnt Christianity from the Romans we changed and became great. We want you to learn Christianity and follow our steps and you too will be great.[13]

The author of those remarks, Sir Harry Johnston, personified many of the more extreme attitudes of nineteenth-century colonialism — except that he added an unusual dash of cynicism, for he was an atheist who nevertheless regarded missionaries as an essential part of colonial expansion:

> As their immediate object is not profit, they can afford to reside at places till they become profitable. They strengthen our hold over the country, they spread the use of the English language, they induct the natives into the best kind of civilization, and in fact each mission station is an essay in colonization.[14]

Johnston described himself as devoted to 'the scheme of universal British dominion',[15] a process which he considered a natural part of evolution. A character in one of his novels (Johnston was a man of many talents, painter, author, journalist, explorer) muses on European superiority:

> I suppose it is all due in some way to the glacial periods, which made us what we are, able to lay down the law to the coloured peoples, who kept snug in the tropics while we were battling against the cold.[16]

In 1886, before the carve-up of Africa had got fully under way, Johnston sent to the Foreign Office a map headed 'How Africa Should Be Divided'. It showed which areas should be allotted to England, France, Portugal, Germany, Italy, Spain, and Belgium. The remarkable fact was that not a single square inch of the

A missionary with freed slaves in Zanzibar.

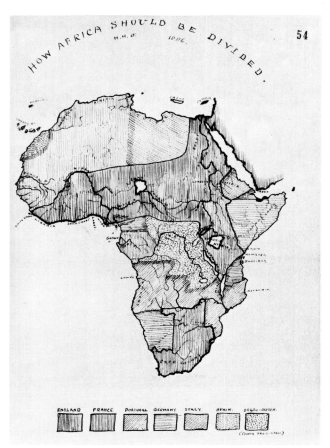

The map which Johnston sent to the Foreign Office in 1886 (Public Record Office, London).

continent was unallocated. Even more remarkable, by 1911 his vision had almost entirely come true. In that year the only two areas of Africa to retain any independence were Ethiopia and Liberia, and Christian missions had long been working the length and breadth of the continent — in the profusion of Protestant sects and Roman Catholic orders which can still be found there today.

It had been a romantic and stimulating ideal to carry the light of Christian truth, at great personal risk, into heathen Africa — the 'dark continent', in that phrase which subtly combines hints of both racial and moral superiority. Then, late in the century, a reaction set in.

> As there is a darkest Africa is there not also a darkest England? The lot of a negress in the Equatorial Forest is not, perhaps, a very pretty one, but is it so very much worse than that of many a pretty orphan girl in our Christian capital?[17]

> In these pages I propose to record the result of a journey into a region which lies at our own doors — into a dark continent that is within easy walking distance of the General Post Office. The wild races who inhabit it will, I trust, gain public sympathy as easily as those savage tribes for whose benefit the Missionary Societies never cease to appeal for funds.[18]

The theme of a journey into the unknown land of the working classes, with its attendant thrills and dangers, was one which was frequently used. In 1872 the brilliant French illustrator, Gustave Doré, provided fashionable London with a book about itself. There were visits to the boat race and the Derby, to Westminster Abbey and to a garden party at Holland House, but there was also an expedition into Whitechapel:

> You put yourself into communication with Scotland Yard to begin with. You adopt rough clothes. You select two or three companions who will not flinch even before the horrors of Tiger Bay: and you commit yourself to the guidance of one of the intelligent and fearless heads of the detective force. He mounts the box of the cab about eight o'clock: and the horse's head is turned — east.

> At dark corners, lurking men keep close to the wall; and the police smile when we wonder what would become of a lonely wanderer who should find himself in these regions unprotected. 'He would be stripped to his shirt' was the candid answer.[19]

Darkest England: a slum area on the hillside below St Paul's; from Doré's London.

Two years later an East End missionary gave a rather endearing account of just such a thing happening.

> A gentleman walked down one of these streets, and while leaning against a lamp post looking up at the houses, some girls who were skipping twisted their ropes round him, and in a moment men and women rushed from the door, emptied his pockets, and stole his watch and hat.[20]

These quotations are from the 1870s and 1880s, by which time the scandal of heathen England was a fashionable topic. It was presented to the public, by W. T. Stead in his *Pall Mall Gazette*, with the full sensationalism of modern crusading journalism. But to specialists it had long been clear that the industrial working classes had slipped out of reach of the churches. It was a process which became inevitable with the growth of the cities. People moved from villages where, however poor, they had formed part of a conventionally church-going community — one small enough for absentees from church to be identifiable, and for acquaintanceship with a good vicar to be a potential source of comfort. They came instead to a city so vast that different classes could live in separate districts and never see each other. As the population of the towns doubled and then quadrupled, the number of churches and chapels remained at first almost static. If there did happen to be a church near a poor man's house, its internal arrangement stated all too clearly that it was not intended for the likes of him. The plush box pews, with their doors, carpets and cushions, were rented or owned by individual families in exactly the same way as a box at the opera. Newspapers of the time, offering items for auction, would calmly include church pews and canal shares in the same lot. In principle there were always some free benches available, but in 1821 in the whole of Sheffield, with a population of more than 60,000, the Anglican churches offered only 300 seats in which somebody could worship without paying. The free places were likely to be in a remote part of the building (there are many arch references to the distance that smell can travel or a flea jump), or else on benches down the central aisle, where a poor family would feel embarrassingly open to inspection and all too aware of the contrast between their own clothes and those of their neighbours to either side. It was hardly surprising that the working classes, after six exhausting days in the factory, did not spend Sunday in church.

> All the writers of the bourgeoisie are unanimous on this point, that the workers are not religious, and do not attend church. Among the masses there prevails almost universally a total indifference to religion. The clergy of all sects is in very bad odour with the working men.[21]

These observations, made as early as 1844, were from the shrewd pen of a young foreign visitor. At the remarkable age of twenty-four Friedrich Engels wrote *The Condition of the Working Class in England*, the earliest attempt at an overall picture of the suffering and attitudes of the industrial poor. He pointed out the physical separation of the classes, with the sordid areas of Manchester tucked safely away out of sight from the main thoroughfares; he went into the appalling realities of sweated labour and of back-to-back houses, and listed differing life expectations (in Liverpool in 1840 the average age of death in the families of professional people was 35, of higher craftsmen 22, and of labourers only 15); he described the way the poor were automatically swept aside for each new advance of industry or science (his account of a railway being driven through a pauper's graveyard is medieval in its macabre imagery, with putrid flesh oozing beneath the pile-drivers); he emphasized the identification of the churches with the middle classes, and even quoted a complaint by labourers about parsons who constantly appealed for money to help the unfortunate of distant lands. But Engels's book was not translated into English for more than forty years. For the moment the middle classes were able to turn a blind eye to the situation, or to put trust in their own favourite remedies.

During the first half of the century the best hope had been considered to lie in building more churches. Between 1821 and 1850 the Church of England alone constructed more than 2,500 churches in England and Wales, and the various Nonconformist groups provided an even greater number of new chapels. But in 1851, the very year of the Great Exhibition in which Britain showed the world her technical and commercial achievements, it was brought forcefully home that all these new churches were still not answering the need. On March 30th of that year, a Sunday, there was someone counting heads at every church and chapel in the country. No doubt each congregation was at its largest possible level, for the census had been announced long in advance. The resulting figures showed that just over 40 per cent of the population attended a religious service on that day — a massively high level by our standards, but it seemed low then. What also emerged with absolute clarity was that this 40 per cent included very few members of the working class. The organizer of the census commented, when he published his findings, that the recent spate of church-building had gone a long way towards providing sufficient places for worship but that this no longer seemed to be the answer:

> Teeming populations often now surround half-empty churches, which would probably remain half-empty even if the sittings were all free. It is evident that absence from religious worship is attributable mainly to a genuine repugnance to religion itself.[22]

He argued that a more aggressive form of Christian preaching was required. 'The people who refuse to hear the gospel in the church must have it brought to them in their own haunts.'[23]

For some years the City Missions had been sending lay missionaries into those haunts. Their approach was what they called 'conversational evangelism', visiting from house to house to interest people in the Bible. Gustave Doré had found a Scripture Reader walking between the crowded beds of a Whitechapel doss-house, with his eyes firmly on the printed page. It was all a little distant and patronizing, as the engravings seem unconsciously to admit in a volume published by the London City Mission. It was entitled *The Man with the Book*, and the man with the book remains distinctly separate from the people he is visiting.

It is true that there was a quite remarkable ignorance of the tenets of Christianity. A government commissioner inquiring into education asked a sixteen-year-old youth who Jesus Christ was: 'a king of London long ago', came the answer.[24] But the London City Mission's account of an eight-year-old boy's criminal record does suggest that arriving in the East End with a Bible was an inadequate response to the problems of the slums. These were his convictions during 1834:

Feb. 13	For possession of seven scarfs, etc.	2 months' imprisonment
May 10	Rogue and vagabond	1 month's imprisonment
July 10	Possession of half a sovereign	1 month's imprisonment
Sept. 13	Simple larceny	1 day's imprisonment, and whipped
Sept. 27	Rogue and vagabond	2 months' imprisonment
Dec. 31	Simple larceny	1 month's imprisonment, and whipped.[25]

People considered the problem one of sin as much as poverty. A best-selling pamphlet of 1883, *The Bitter Cry of Outcast London*, complained that the missionaries were not achieving enough, and printed in capital letters the alarming conclusion: 'THIS TERRIBLE FLOOD OF SIN AND MISERY IS GAINING UPON US.'[26] Sin and misery, in that order — a Methodist appealing two years later for missionaries to the slums had the same priorities. 'The essential qualities are a profound sympathy with the poor in their sin and suffering, and an equally profound conviction of the power of the Gospel to save them.'[27] The same author vigorously resisted a suggestion that the missionaries should actually live in the poor areas of London. To do so would endanger the health of themselves and their families. Instead they 'should have homes in a healthy, bracing neigh-

Illustrations from John Weylland's The Man with the Book, *1878.*

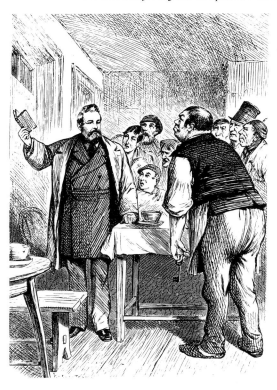 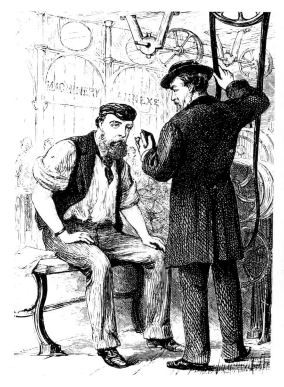

bourhood, and thus be able to come to their sphere of work each morning fresh and strong'.[28] The slums were morally as well as physically poisonous. 'Adam and Eve were created and placed in a garden', wrote a popular religious novelist: 'cities are the result of the fall'.[29]

From 1865 there was a new and flamboyant figure on the mission scene, one who could match anybody in his horror of sin, but whose experience of the slums would eventually lead him to reverse the old priorities and to see suffering as the more urgent problem. He was William Booth, founder of the Salvation Army. The arrival of his Hallelujah Lasses with their brass bands brightened any dark street and gave evangelism a new lease of life. The Army developed its characteristic approach only gradually, but every one of its ideas was in reaction against the genteel and class-conscious churches which had made so little impact. Booth decided early on that the working classes would be more likely to listen to people of their own kind, and some of his most successful missionaries were illiterate. Unlike the Methodists, they were under orders to live in the roughest districts. Booth described what his followers sang as 'songs' because he considered the word hymn 'too churchy', and it was typical that they consisted of new words set to existing popular tunes. Meetings were held not in church buildings but in coffee houses, theatres, music halls. The technique was what Booth's son described as 'rollicking for the Lord', and its great advantage was that it 'helps to keep us free from the shackles of respectability'.[30]

The Salvation Army combined two distinct elements, the military and the theatrical — a powerful combination. The missionaries were graded in military ranks, with Booth at their head as the General of the Army, and he expected an absolute obedience characteristic of those other soldiers of Jesus, the Jesuits. The book of *Orders and Regulations* was based on a manual originally devised for the real army. Prayer was commonly referred to as Knee Drill, and when on parade the order 'Fire a Volley' was the signal for a rousing cry of Hallelujah. But within this structure there was great scope, in the early days, for imagination. It was often his assistants who dragged Booth further into 'vulgarity' than he intended. A printer was asked for a poster announcing the arrival of 'Two Lady Preachers' on Tyneside. He considered the phrase dull and substituted 'The Hallelujah Lasses'. Booth was profoundly shocked, until the startling success of the phrase won him round. In the same vein advertisements appeared in the 'Rewards Offered' columns, stating that The Lord wanted to recover his Property — which turned out to refer to his Lost Sheep. Salvationists stood in the markets beside stall-holders who were crying out cheap prices for their wares, and in competition offered salvation 'cheaper still'. Famous characters emerged from among the saved — Sarah McMinnies the Saved Barmaid, or Happy Hannah the Reformed Smoker. A drunken escapologist, having seen the light, adapted his Houdini act to accompany a sermon on the Trap Doors to Hell.

Naturally this type of approach caused more of a stir than the arrival of a solitary Man with the Book. Here was the aggressive evangelism which the organizer of the 1851 census had called for, but it was equally natural that it should in its turn provoke more hostility. Meetings in the street were often conducted under a barrage of missiles as well as insults. One young woman died after being knocked down and kicked, and in one year alone — 1882 — some sixty Salvation Army buildings were assaulted by mobs and 669 Salvationists were violently attacked. One of them, who had the advantage of being an ex-pugilist as well as an ex-sweep, filed a report of a 'good meeting':

> We were set upon by a band of ruffians shouting, howling and pulling us about. Some of the sisters were very roughly handled indeed. They pelted us with all sorts of things, flour in abundance. I was as white as a miller. We had a good meeting, and one man professed to be saved.[31]

To save people — this, as in any revivalist mission, was the basic object of such flamboyant activity, and each new convert knelt at a penitents' bench to acknowledge his guilt and to pledge himself to a new life. Sin, however glittering the show, was still the central theme. But in 1890 William Booth published a book, *In Darkest England*, in which he acknowledged a change of emphasis. People's sufferings, he argued, must be dealt with before you could get at the root of their sin:

> What is Darkest England? For whom do I claim that urgency which gives their case priority over that of all other sections of their countrymen and countrywomen? I claim it for the Lost, for the Outcast, for the Disinherited of the World. Who are the Lost? I reply, not in a religious, but in a social sense, the lost are those who have gone under, those to whom the prayer to our Heavenly Father, 'Give us day by day our daily bread,' is either unfulfilled, or only fulfilled by the Devil's agency: by the earnings of vice, the proceeds of crime. Why all this apparatus of temples and

Show business in the service of the Lord.

meeting-houses to save men from perdition in a world which is to come, while never a helping hand is stretched out to save them from the inferno of their present life?[32]

Booth outlined a wide-ranging scheme for providing the poor with work, with training, with opportunities to emigrate, and he called the type of salvation he was now proposing Social Salvation. His proposals led to his being accused of Socialism, a charge very far from the truth, but the accusation was relevant in one indirect sense. The role which Booth was now suggesting for the missions, seen at its very simplest level in the famous Salvation Army soup kitchens, was one which the state would eventually take over in developed countries under the gradual influence of Socialism — the protection of all citizens from the worst effects of poverty. It is a task which the state can perform not only on a much wider scale, but also with greater dignity. There is an inevitable ambiguity about religious charity in a non-religious age, as captured neatly by Bernard Shaw in *Major Barbara*. When a Hallelujah Lass asks Snobby Price if he has had a piece of bread, he replies: 'Yes, miss; but I've got the piece that I value more; and that's the peace that passeth understanding.'[33]

History has shown that it is almost impossible to run a successful mission which offers nothing but the Truth. Some more concrete benefit must be provided as well, whether it be soup, soap, education, agricultural know-how, a bed for the night, medical assistance or even freedom from slavery. Since the nineteenth century western societies have become increasingly irreligious, and yet the extent of mission work — on the face of it more needed than ever — has declined dramatically. The welfare state, free education, increased opportunities for leisure have all spoilt the missionaries' chances. At one stage the churches made some headway by organizing games and outings for the poor, but others have taken on that task as well. How many in the vast crowds roaring their support for Queen's Park Rangers, Everton, Fulham, Wolverhampton Wanderers, Bolton Wanderers or Aston Villa, know that their favourite club started life as the team of a Sunday school or chapel? The fame of these particular teams is in one sense a lasting achievement on the part of the clergymen who founded them, but is hardly a contribution to Christian faith in the twentieth century.

Many attempts have been made to find a form of mission appropriate to modern times, including even the 'silent witness' of missionaries working full-time at the factory bench without necessarily revealing their motive for being

Increased prosperity has made it harder for the Salvation Army to win attention:
working-class children queue at a soup kitchen in about 1900,

there. There could hardly be a more total change from marching into a slum area with trumpets and banners. Charity work continues also in the older style of mission, side by side with the more impersonal efforts of the state — caring for old people, for the mentally disturbed, for unmarried mothers, for tramps. But the great assault on the disbelief of the working class often consists now of little more than youth clubs and coffee bars run by the churches in competition with the pub. It seemed an almost impossible task in the nineteenth century to reach the Home Heathen and the Poor. It has proved even harder to say anything meaningful to the indifferent and the not so poor.

In Africa the practical work of the missions, particularly in education, has continued to provide them with a more valid presence. Missions of all types can be found, from those still in the nineteenth-century mould (implicitly, but often unconsciously, bringing the superior white man's religion to the savages) to others where the Europeans take subordinate roles in the developing of an essentially African church. A remarkably high proportion among the leaders of the new independent countries are Christian, and the pattern has continued among the politicians fighting for majority rule in Rhodesia. Bishop Abel Muzorewa and the Reverend Ndabaningi Sithole are self-evidently committed Christians, but Joshua Nkomo also is a Methodist lay preacher and Robert Mugabe a devout Catholic. Christianity also plays an important role on the European side. The political injustices in Rhodesia and South Africa are glaring

and spend their holidays on the beach in the 1960s.

enough to provoke specifically Christian protest against ostensibly Christian governments. Garfield Todd has spent many years of his life working as a missionary, and the Roman Catholic Bishop Donal Lamont was at one time sentenced to ten years in prison for failing to report the whereabouts of guerrillas.

The independent African churches which have developed from European missionary effort over the past hundred and fifty years are now referred to internationally as the Younger Churches, and are widely regarded as having more of the fire of early Christianity than many of their senior colleagues in the Christian fold. In May 1977 a black Anglican priest from Tanzania, Martin Mbwana, came to visit various industrial parishes in Britain. He had been invited as a missionary who might, it was hoped, inspire the natives with some of his Christian zeal.

Opposite: A mission in the King's Road, London, in the 1960s.

Missionaries in the Church Army, which was the Church of England's answer to the Salvation Army.

CHAPTER TWELVE

The Roots of Disbelief

NTIL recent times all people that on earth do dwell have believed in gods of some sort, and always for remarkably similar reasons. Whether the believer is primitive or sophisticated, whether he sits beside a fire in the jungle or the fire in his study, religion has answered his needs in two main areas. It has explained the mystery of what he can observe but not understand — the beauties of nature, the fury of the elements, the unpredictability and injustice of pain, disease, death, the dark obsessions within himself and others, the very existence of all that is. And it has provided the group in which he lives with its identity, its framework, its ethics, backed up by priestly ritual or sacred texts deriving from distant and heroic times. However much different religions may vary, they all fulfil these two basic purposes — answering questions about the universe, and providing a structure for society.

In western societies, during the last two centuries, the Christian god has been gradually deprived of these functions. Science has found alternative explanations for physical mysteries, and a fashion for liberty has rejected the church as the preordained framework for society. The results of this slow process have been startling. They have introduced an element completely new in the history of established Christian communities: what one might call conventional atheism. Any atheist of the nineteenth century regarded his non-belief as a matter of passionate commitment. He would fight, as Charles Bradlaugh did, for the right not to swear on the Bible. A hundred years later an agnostic or atheist will often disregard his freedom to affirm (a freedom won only after a desperate struggle), and will calmly swear upon a Bible in which he does not believe. He regards the act of swearing as the indication of his good faith, making the truth or untruth of the book in his hand unimportant. This is not insincerity about the claims of Christianity: it is something far more threatening to the Christian faith, indifference to those claims. It is a state of affairs which has caused certain Christians to describe the societies they live in as 'post-Christian'. Whatever the future may hold (and Christianity has proved itself irrepressible often enough in the past), a sense of aftermath is certainly appropriate to the present. The dust has long settled on the great religious controversies of the nineteenth century, but in them lie the origins of present disbelief. If this chapter seems to be largely about England, that is not purely a case of local bias. England is widely regarded, with some justification, as the most secular country in the west. And England shows most clearly the nineteenth-century background to such a state of affairs.

The early discoveries of modern science had seemed to reinforce the biblical image of God as the great architect. The famous seventeenth-century clash between science and the church had been about authority as much as truth. Admittedly the solar system of Copernicus and Galileo did contradict Genesis (an earth moving round the sun would burst through the 'firmament' which separated the waters above from the waters below), and the Roman Inquisition arrested Galileo for teaching what was 'contrary to Holy Scripture'. But his real crime was in contradicting what the church had always taught, and what any

Images by William Blake of God the Creator (Whitworth Art Gallery, Manchester) and of Isaac Newton (Tate Gallery, London).

man's senses could confirm — that the earth was at the centre of the universe and that the sun went round it. The pope, Christ's vicar on earth, had no intention of finding himself on a minor planet. But Protestant northern Europe, not being saddled with fifteen hundred years of clerical opinion to add to the authority of the scriptures, found it easy enough to accept the new system. Evidently Genesis was considered vague enough in this area to accommodate the realities of science, and Newton would soon develop the partnership further. He offered his newly discovered force of gravity as additional evidence of God's design. When he could discover no physical law to keep the planets precisely in their orbits, he argued that God himself intervened from time to time to make whatever minor adjustments might be necessary.

But if Genesis was a little vague about the firmament, it was extremely precise on the age of the earth and how it began. Adding up the life-span of the patriarchs provides an obvious ladder back to the beginning. The difficulty is that although the lives of the old men were surprisingly long, the resulting life of the earth is astonishingly short. It was not only the nineteenth century which protested. Calvin had ridiculed the sceptics of the sixteenth century, dismissing them with the scorn typical of a man wielding an established dogma:

> Obstinate people will not refrain from guffaws when they are informed that but little more than five thousand years have passed since the creation of the universe, for they ask why God's power was idle and asleep for so long.[1]

In the following century biblical mathematics became even more precise. Archbishop Ussher worked out his famous chronology (which can still be found printed in certain twentieth-century Bibles) and announced that God began that first hectic week of creation on the morning of Sunday, October 23rd, 4004 B.C.

The two sciences which were to clash most severely with biblical authority had their beginnings in the eighteenth century: geology, which would unearth   259

Adam and Eve and Queen Victoria, at opposite ends of the river of time (from Sebastian Adams's Synchronological Chart of History*).*

from the rock strata a long succession of fossilized creatures, many of them extinct; and modern zoology, in which the first serious attempts to classify animals as species would soon lead to theories of evolution. But the age of enlightenment, which was busy looking for rational explanations for all the miracles in the gospels, was not likely to offer a very sturdy defence of the even more improbable events of Genesis. Fourteen pious students at the university of Innsbruck did on one occasion complain to the emperor Joseph II that their professor had told them the world was much older than was stated in the Bible, but his characteristic response was to sack the students: 'Heads as poor as theirs cannot profit from education.'[2]

It was in the more aggressively self-confident nineteenth century that the conflict became inevitable. Both sides were almost equally complacent. While missionaries were exporting to Asia or Africa a form of Christianity which involved imitating European ways, the lesser scientists were finding in evolution equally encouraging proof of the white man's natural superiority. One of the century's best-selling books on evolution was published fifteen years before *The Origin of Species*. It was entitled *Vestiges of the Natural History of Creation*. The author, Robert Chambers, explained the development of the human foetus during the months of pregnancy:

our brain goes through the various stages of a fish's, a reptile's, and a mammifer's brain, and finally becomes human: more than this, after completing the animal transformation, it passes through the characters of the Negro, Malay, American and Mongolian nations, and finally is Caucasian.[3]

Chambers's version of evolution made much of the effect of environment on species, so he was able to point to an even more satisfactory development:

Peculiar features of the most repulsive kind, projecting jaws with large open mouths, depressed noses, high cheek bones, and bow legs, together with an extremely diminutive stature, are the outward marks of a low and barbarous condition all over the world. On the other hand, the beauty of the higher ranks in England is very remarkable, being, in the main, as clearly a result of good external conditions.[4]

The pattern of evolution is largely optimistic, even if not carried to these extremes, and it had an immediate appeal to many in a confident age. Five years after the appearance of Chambers's book an author urged the Christian churches to study science so as to refute

a form of error at once exceedingly plausible and consummately dangerous, which is telling so widely on society that one can scarce travel by railway or in a steam boat, or encounter a group of intelligent mechanics, without finding decided traces of its ravages.[5]

The Origin of Species arrived late on the scene, but no previous work had offered such a wealth of argument and it turned the debate into a subject of ferocious public controversy. Darwin himself wrote, 'I see no good reason why the views given in this volume should shock the religious feelings of anyone',[6] and he went on to point out that God could just as well have created the world by setting in motion the process of evolution. He could, and many Christians today believe that he did so. But the price of such a belief is to regard Genesis as just one more creation myth, and that was harder to accept in 1859 than now. Darwin himself drifted gradually into agnosticism (a phrase coined by his disciple, T. H. Huxley), but the debate immediately escalated into those higher reaches of idiocy which have remained notorious ever since. When the British Association called a meeting at Oxford in 1860 to discuss the matter, and Bishop Wilberforce asked Huxley whether he traced his descent from an ape on his grandfather's side or his grandmother's, the distinguished bishop made the Church's response to the problem seem alarmingly superficial. Had he asked the same of Darwin, his question might well have appeared offensively personal. One of the more delightful accidents of history is the resemblance of the great scientist to a genial old ape.

Genesis was not the only part of the Bible under attack by mid-century, and science had other shocks in store for the faithful — including some from a fifth column, the biblical scholars themselves. Any attentive reader of the Bible is

The gratifying sequence: the Negro, American, Mongolian and Caucasian races (from Georges Cuvier, The Animal Kingdom, *1849).*

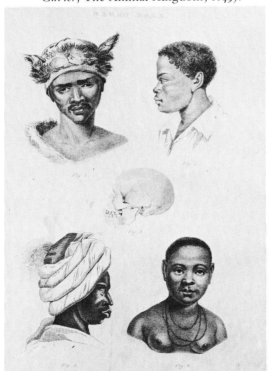
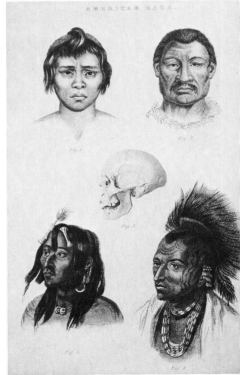

bound to notice certain inconsistencies. Thomas Hobbes had pointed out in 1651 that Moses, the author of Deuteronomy, could not have written that part of the book which said the whereabouts of Moses's grave remained unknown. This humble level of detective work was to blossom in the nineteenth century into a detailed analysis of which parts of the Bible were reliable and which were not. Techniques which had been developed for the study of Homer (separating original passages from later additions) were applied to the Old and New Testaments with alarming results. Soon everything was being doubted, and in 1835 there appeared a *Life of Jesus* which argued that all the supernatural details in the gospel stories were myths which had grown up around someone who must have been an undoubtedly persuasive religious leader, but about whom very little of an historical nature could be reliably discovered. The author, David Strauss, was promptly dismissed from his university post. Society does not lightly modify its beliefs, but it was soon to find itself fighting on many fronts. In England, in the year 1853, a professor of King's College in London and a railwayman at Swindon were both sacked for the same reason — that they did not believe in hell. Ten years later the Anglican bishop of Natal, John Colenso, was convicted of heresy and deprived of his bishopric. He also had doubted the doctrine of eternal punishment for sinners (and, equally shocking to the Victorians, had tolerated polygamy among the Zulus), but his central offence had been very much more startling — particularly in a bishop. He had argued, in

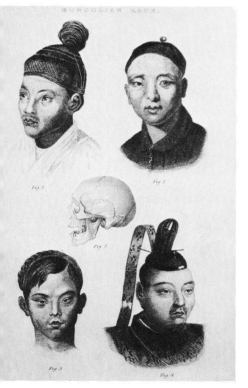

A photograph of Darwin in 1878, and a caricature of him in The Hornet, *1871.*

print, that although the Bible says its first five books were written by Moses not a word of them so much as dated from his period, the entire sequence being a later Jewish forgery. The bishop added, moreover, that there were so many impossibilities in Genesis that the entire Bible might have to be rejected. It was an alarming sign of the way things were going.

Another new area of threat became evident with the publication in 1841 of Ludwig Feuerbach's *Essence of Christianity*, in which he argued that God had been invented by men as a specific answer to their needs and hopes (George Eliot, with a fine instinct for the controversial, translated both this and Strauss's *Life of Jesus* into English). Feuerbach's thesis would later be developed in different ways by psychologists — particularly by Sigmund Freud, whose *Future of an Illusion* presents religion as an expression of a communal neurosis, in which man has provided himself with a much needed father–figure and some reassuring wish-fulfilment:

> It would be very nice if there were a God who created the world and was a benevolent Providence, and if there were a moral order in the universe and an after–life; but it is a very striking fact that all this is exactly as we are bound to wish it to be.[7]

The study of comparative religion provided further dangers. Believers in any religion naturally need to feel that they are right, and they prefer to be uniquely right. But the rightness of any one religion implies the wrongness of all the others, and the more that is known about the others the harder this becomes to maintain. As word came back from the distant corners of empire about primitive religious rituals, it was noticed that they shared many characteristics with each other and even with Christianity. In his massive compilation, *The Golden Bough*, James Frazer assembled the oddities of religious ritual as industriously as Darwin had pieced together the oddities of animal and plant behaviour, and he came up with a similar evolutionary conclusion. In the closing paragraph of his twelve volumes, he describes himself standing in what had once been a sacrificial grove of Diana. He hears the Angelus ring out from a near-by church. '*Le roi est mort, vive le roi*' is his final comment. Christian ritual follows the basic pattern of birth, death and rebirth. It is, he implied, higher on the evolutionary scale than primitive religions, but not intrinsically different — nor necessarily at the top of the scale, for evolution goes on and the pattern of development which Frazer himself found in his material was that of magic, replaced by religion, replaced by science (it is a scheme which anthropologists no longer accept, but it was symptomatic of its time). Naturally Christianity's more sophisticated rivals now also came under the same kind of scrutiny. There was a growing interest in the sacred books of the east and Frazer himself praised Christ and Buddha in the same breath, in a manner highly shocking to the conventional Christian: they were 'two of those beautiful spirits who appear at rare intervals on earth like beings come from a better world to support and guide our weak and erring nature'.[8]

'Why may not the supernaturalism of China, or India, or of Arabia have as good a claim to divine character as the supernaturalism of Europe?'[9] The question, very moderate of its kind, was asked in 1841 by the *Oracle of Reason* — one of the many free-thinking magazines which sprang up during the century. The scientists themselves were not concerned with disproving Christianity, but their researches were eagerly seized upon by those who were. A journal entitled *Freethinker's Information for the People* aimed to provide atheist lecturers with the latest information on geology, zoology and comparative religion. It held out the highest hopes:

> We may, in future articles, be enabled to show that Apollo, Adonis, Bacchus, Jesus, Osiris, Isis, Christ, Creeshna, Cyrus, Moses, Aaron, Miriam, Mary, Abraham, Isaac, Jacob, Noah, Brahma, Jehovah, Jupiter, Jove, and the whole heavenly host of them, are but different personifications of the sun.[10]

Unfortunately the magazine folded before the proof was forthcoming.

The tone of the atheist campaign was shrill and inflammatory. The editor of the *Oracle of Reason* had in his London window a poster which would certainly cause offence even today: 'The Existence of CHRIST, alias the Baby God, disproved'.[11] The same man later opened a bookshop in Edinburgh with the name Paterson's Blasphemy Depot, where books were sold with such challenging titles as *The Bible an Improper Book for Youth*.[12] The immorality and violence of the Bible was a theme older than any of the new sciences, but it was particularly well suited to shock Victorian sensibilities and it provided the atheists with easy opportunities:

> That revoltingly odious Jew production, called BIBLE, has been for ages the idol of all sorts of blockheads, the glory of knaves, and the disgust of wise men. It is a

history of lust, sodomies, wholesale slaughtering, and horrible depravity, that the vilest of all other histories, collected into one monstrous book, could scarcely parallel.[13]

Only four women are named in the genealogy of Christ: Thamar, who seduced the father of her late husband; Rachel, a common prostitute; Ruth, who, instead of marrying one of her cousins, went to bed with another of them; and Bethseba, an adultress, who espoused David, the murderer of her first husband.[14]

If God did not require the shedding of blood for his satisfaction, how came Christ to offer it, and God to accept it? He who should require or permit the death of another, because of the offence of eating an apple, would be counted ferocious among men to this hour.[15]

Writing, printing and selling such matter was dangerous, but spells in prison made martyrs for the cause. The author of the third quotation, George Holyoake, spent six months in goal in 1842 for blasphemy, having said in a public debate that in times of economic hardship he would 'place the Deity on half-pay'.[16]

The struggle to change the laws against blasphemy was a natural task for the atheists, but it formed only one part of their practical programme. The movement known as Secularism, which laid the basis for our modern largely secular societies, was dedicated to ending the control exercised by official religion over everyday life. In Britain, with its established church, there was a very great deal to be dismantled. Until 1828 no man could hold public office unless he assented to the doctrines of the Church of England; until 1836 no couple could be married except by an Anglican parson, no matter whether they happened to be Roman Catholic, Methodist or anything else; until 1871 all teaching posts at Oxford and Cambridge were reserved for those who professed the Anglican faith. The campaign against compulsory payment of church taxes and tithes was part of the same long struggle. So was the insistence on affirming instead of taking a Christian oath, which reached its climax in the efforts of Charles Bradlaugh to enter the House of Commons after being elected a member. On numerous occasions he was physically ejected from the chamber. His constituency was offered at by-elections and he was re-elected. It took six expensive years of law-suits and protests before a new Speaker allowed him to take his seat. In 1888 he had the final satisfaction of promoting the bill which made it legal to affirm both in the House of Commons and in courts of law.

The sounds of battle have died down now. The ancient fury about the age of the earth or the taking of an oath seems like distant history. Most Christians have adjusted quite happily to evolution, most juries will not think less of a man who affirms. Yet the struggles have led to two extreme responses by certain Christians, which are diametrically opposed to each other but which are both surprisingly influential.

One response has been to accept gracefully the gashes made by science in the fabric of conventional religious belief, and then to argue that the real truth of Christianity or of the Bible lies elsewhere. It was a process which began very early, in the desperate efforts to reconcile Genesis with the age of the world suggested by geology and fossil remains. The solutions were various. Some said that we had misunderstood the Hebrew word *yom* in translating it as 'day' in the

Charles Bradlaugh about to be ejected from the House of Commons (Illustrated London News, *1880*).

six days of Creation: it meant something nearer to a 'creative epoch', and the six creative epochs had lasted some 30,000 years. Others maintained that Genesis only described God's creation of the part of the world that he intended for Man, which was roughly western Asia. It was argued that we had wrongly interpreted the phrase 'in the beginning' to mean the same as the first day of Creation: there had in fact been a long period between the two (a period described in Genesis 1:2), during which the rocks now being chipped away at by geologists were gradually forming; the fossils in these rocks were of animals which had become extinct before the third verse. Simpler minds insisted that all the fossils had got into the rocks in the 1,600 years between the Creation and the Flood, and that extinct animals — such as the dinosaur — were those which had missed the ark. The boldest solution was that of a man who had the misfortune to be both a leading naturalist and an energetic supporter of the Society for Promoting Christian Knowledge. He was Philip Gosse, and he announced his own particular compromise in *Omphalos*, published in 1857 (two years before *The Origin of Species*). God, said Gosse, had created the world precisely as Genesis described. But he had built into it scientific evidence of a long previous existence.

The habit of retreating to new positions is a dangerous one (as a child, when my belief in Father Christmas was threatened by a scientific calculation that no man with four reindeer could visit every child in Britain in one night, I was able to retain my faith for a little longer by imagining a separate Father Christmas for

A creature that missed the ark? Or created by God as a fossil? Remains of a giant marsupial (Natural History Museum, London).

each county), and certainly the definitions of God offered by some Christians today would appal those who began the process of accommodation. Paul Tillich, one of the most influential of modern theologians, has defined God as the 'infinite and inexhaustible depth and ground of all being':

> That depth is what the word *God* means. And if that word has not much meaning for you, translate it, and speak of the depths of your life, of the source of your being, of your ultimate concern, of what you take seriously without any reservation. Perhaps, in order to do so, you must forget everything traditional that you have learned about God, perhaps even that word itself.[17]

This implies that there can be no such thing as a serious atheist (for if he takes anything seriously, he knows God), but to atheists it will seem to admit something rather different — that the Baby God (to borrow the atheistical phrase of a hundred years ago) finally has gone out with the bath water. By the 1960s there was even a movement among American theologians known as the 'death of God' or 'Christian atheist' school.

In Britain the new theology became the subject of a public debate almost as passionate as the great nineteenth-century controversies after a small book by a bishop became a best-seller; it was John Robinson's *Honest to God*, published in 1963. Robinson described how he had found inspiration in the ideas of Tillich and others (particularly Dietrich Bonhoeffer, who had argued that Christianity might have to drop its 'religious premise' if it wishes to convince modern man, who seems increasingly able to carry on without a need for God, without a sense of sin, without a desire for salvation). Robinson himself argued that we must give up trying to believe in some supreme and separate Being outside ourselves: 'assertions about God are in the last analysis assertions about Love — about the ultimate ground and meaning of personal relationships'.[18] The Church of England as a whole seems to have been moving in the same direction. Its Doctrine Commission has recently produced a report entitled *Christian Believing*. A member of the Commission singled out as the central conclusion of their inquiries the statement that Christian life is 'an adventure, a voyage of discovery, a journey sustained by faith and hope, towards a final and complete communion with the Love at the heart of all things'.[19]

Inevitably such bland and tactful claims have provoked an opposite response, a hankering for the old certainties and severities. The type of modern Christianity referred to as Fundamentalist began specifically as a response to the threat of scientific discoveries. It developed in America during the late nineteenth century, and acquired its name from five 'fundamentals' which were held to be essential to Christianity. The first was the absolute and detailed truth of the Bible. In the turmoil of the modern world many have found a welcome anchor in such uncompromising simplicity. Fundamentalism has found new converts more easily than other forms of modern Christianity. Its appeal was widely demonstrated in the crusades of Billy Graham, who has said about the Bible:

> Its critics, who claimed it to be filled with forgery, fiction, and unfulfilled promises, are finding that the difficulties lie with themselves, and not the Bible. Greater and more careful scholarship has shown that apparent contradictions were caused by incorrect translations rather than divine inconsistencies. It was man and not the Bible that needed correcting. It is the blueprint of the Master Architect. The true Christian denies no part nor attempts to add anything to the Word of God.[20]

Brave Victorian defenders of the Bible might be put to shame by the faith of some of their modern successors. In a book published in 1972 the Professor of Theology and Old Testament at an American theological college solemnly calculates the capacity of Noah's ark as 1,400,000 cubic feet, then explains that this is equivalent to 522 modern railroad box cars: two of all the air-breathing creatures in the world 'could be comfortably carried in only 150 box cars', leaving plenty of space for all the extinct animals and the necessary food. The same author achieves the ultimate in Fundamentalist self-confidence by accusing those who doubt the factual accuracy of Genesis of 'seeming to imply that God is not a trustworthy witness of what happened at the time of creation'.[21]

These two directly opposed responses, the over-accommodating and the intractable, are not (as outside observers might suspect) merely the comic extremes of modern Christianity in western societies. They are two of its most lively areas, and they are relevant in two different ways to the problem of disbelief. Both are responses to the nineteenth-century developments which have steered many others into disbelief. And both, I suspect, contribute to present disbelief by making it increasingly difficult for Christianity in either of these forms to be taken seriously.

The Christian churches have suffered the same pressures and challenges as their individual members, and nothing shows the result more clearly than the change in the Roman Catholic church over the past hundred years — or, more precisely, between the first and second Vatican Councils. A single pope, Pius IX, ruled for thirty-two years in the middle of the nineteenth century, the longest pontificate in history. When he mounted the papal throne in 1846 he was the type of pope familiar for a thousand years — spiritual head of all Roman Catholics, but also absolute sovereign of a large slice of central Italy, the papal states. At this time he had decidedly liberal views, but they perished in the year 1848, when a revolution made him flee for his own safety from Rome. By the time Pius died, the papal states were part of the new nation of Italy, Rome was her capital city, and Pius himself was the type of pope with whom we are familiar today — still the spiritual head of the entire Roman Catholic world, but sovereign now only over one-sixth of a square mile, the Vatican City. As his temporal power had declined, so his claims to spiritual authority had increased. And the nature of that authority was increasingly reactionary. At precisely the time when liberal theologians were beginning to classify the Virgin Birth as a myth, Pius elevated to the status of a dogma the equally magical concept of the Immaculate Conception. This idea (that Mary, alone of all human beings since Adam and Eve, had been born free from original sin) had long been part of the popular and specifically Roman Catholic cult of Mary: by giving it at this late stage the authority of dogma, the pope was making a deliberate gesture both against Protestantism and against scientific rationalism. He followed this up with a more precise broadside, his famous *Syllabus* of eighty modern errors. These included such things as socialism, civil marriage, and secular education; the final error on the list was the view that 'the Roman Pontiff can and should reconcile himself to and agree with progress, liberalism, and modern civilization'.[22] Pius completed the high defences round his diminished state by presiding over a Vatican Council in 1869–70 (the first such council for over 300 years) at which he made a dogma of another long-standing but unspecified tradition — that the pope, when speaking *ex cathedra* on a matter of faith or morals, is infallible.

The Roman Catholic church maintained this high authoritarian stance for nearly a century. As recently as 1950 Pius XII put out an encyclical, *Humani Generis*, warning against false teaching in schools. No one was to maintain, for example, that there had been any human being on earth since the Garden of Eden who was not directly descended from Adam and Eve. (Behind this insistence lay the need to safeguard the doctrine of original sin: 'original sin is the result of a sin committed, in actual historical fact, by an individual named Adam, and it is a quality native to all of us, only because it has been handed down by descent from him').[23] But twenty years later there had been the most profound transformation. It was as though a fairy wand had miraculously translated the church of Rome from one side to the other in all the old arguments.

The man who had wielded the fairy wand was himself a most improbable piece of casting. In the conclave which followed the death of Pius XII there were twelve ballots before a decision was reached. Clearly the seventy-seven year old Cardinal Roncalli was no more than a compromise candidate, mainly acceptable because his reign was certain to be short: and it was equally obvious from his very conventional past career that he would do nothing unusual as pope. Instead, in his brief five years, John XXIII changed the Roman Catholic church almost out of recognition — and incidentally endeared himself to the entire world in a way that no other religious leader has ever done in his own lifetime. By preserving the simple virtues of warmth and openness among the baroque trappings of high office, he gave even the non-religious a sense of what religion should perhaps be about. There was a feeling that we were watching something never before seen by so many, the living reality of a saint. The process is now under way in the Vatican which will lead almost certainly to his being canonized.

The act of John's which brought about such changes within the church was his entirely unexpected calling of a council. From the start it was evident that this would be a different sort of council. In Vatican One the papacy had dictated; in Vatican Two it would listen, and there was a great deal to listen to. Pope John had evidently kept liberal ideas to himself during a lifetime of obedience, and so — it turned out — had many others. The resulting upsurge of free debate will have repercussions for many years to come. The most startling result so far, to the ordinary Catholic, has been the changes in the form of worship. Services are in the vernacular. Lay people play a large part in them and on occasion receive the wine as well as the bread. The Reformation has finally reached Rome. But the Protestant Reformation refused to stop where Luther intended: the new sense of inquiry and of self-responsibility led inevitably to the hundreds of Protestant sects with which we are familiar today. Change, once it is in the air, will always be too fast for some, too slow for others. The followers of Archbishop Lefebvre resent being deprived of their Latin mass (there were many in Protestant lands who felt the same in the sixteenth century), while liberal

John XXIII at the summer residence of the popes, Castel Gandolfo.

Catholics in northern Europe fail to see why an elderly bachelor in Rome should dictate to them on birth control. The interesting question of the coming years will be whether the massive church of Rome, held together for so long by a rigid structure of authority, can survive its Reformation intact.

The Protestant churches have altered less over the same period, but the general direction of their change has been similar — from nineteenth-century aggression to twentieth-century conciliation. It can be seen chiefly in their attitude to each other. In the nineteenth century Protestant sects were constantly splitting into smaller ones; chapels of different denominations stood side by side, inside their iron railings, isolated in their own particular self-righteousness; small villages in England would even have one shop for the Anglicans and another for the Nonconformists. In the twentieth century the pattern has been reversed. The process can be seen if one follows the fortunes since the turn of the century of just one small American church, the German Evangelical Synod of North America. In 1934 it merged with the Reformed Church in the United States to form the Evangelical and Reformed Church. In 1957 this in turn merged with the General Council of Congregational Christian Churches (itself a merger of the National Council of the Congregational Churches and the General Convention of the Christian Church) to become — and the name suggests a sigh of relief — the United Church of Christ. But even the United Church of Christ has less than two million members.

The international centre of this new togetherness, known to Christians as the ecumenical movement, is the World Council of Churches — an organization with headquarters at Geneva which was founded in 1948 and now has nearly three hundred member churches (Eastern Orthodox as well as Protestant), from over eighty countries. Like all such organizations, its activities are not exactly inspiring to outsiders; but the Protestants do point with pride to various ecumenical experiments which succeed on a more personal level. The place most often mentioned is Taizé, in France. It is a monastery founded after the last war for monks from different Protestant churches, but its ecumenical commitment goes further than that. Services are held for Roman Catholic and Eastern Orthodox congregations, as well as Protestants. Each Easter huge numbers of young people, inspired by the idealism of the place, camp in the open air and join in a liturgy which as far as possible transcends sectarian differences. The sense of togetherness is clearly infectious, but then so is it in that somewhat similar type of gathering, the pop festival. Enthusiasts believe that this lowering of the barriers is the way forward for Christianity. Maybe. But there is something reminiscent of the humble prayer which Thomas More wrote for the people of Utopia:

> O God, I acknowledge Thee to be my creator, my governor, and the source of all good things. I thank Thee for all Thy blessings, and especially for letting me practise what I hope is the truest religion. If I am wrong, and if some other religion would be better and more acceptable to Thee, I pray Thee in Thy goodness to let me know it. [24]

One of many forms of liturgy tried out in Holland (home of the most radical Christian experiments) even includes the words: 'Lord, if you exist, come among us.' [25]

The turmoil of the last hundred years has left many strange reversals among the Christian churches. In England, for example, there are now more Roman

Opposite: The Virgin Mary, on the column put up in 1857 to commemorate the dogma of her Immaculate Conception: Piazza di Spagna, Rome.

Catholics than Anglicans in church each Sunday morning; and while the Catholic priest faces the congregation to break the bread, the Anglican parson may choose to turn his back on the people and devote himself to the altar. To what end now all the pain and martyrdom of the sixteenth century? But the upheavals have also left Christians in an entirely new and potentially encouraging position. The nineteenth-century pressures towards disbelief, which have prompted new defensive theologies and re-alignments within the churches, have also removed the unworthy reasons for professing Christianity. For the first time since Constantine, Christianity is now no advantage in anyone's career, or the lack of it no drawback. Social disapproval of those who do not go to Church has vanished in most western communities. The old handiwork reasons for believing ('each little flower that opens, each little bird that sings, He made their glowing colours, He made their tiny wings') have been largely explained away. Even the old ethical reasons have been removed. The Victorians were convinced that atheism would spell the end of all morality, but it would be a bold man who claimed today that the average Christian was more moral than the average atheist. Although many Christians do still regard good behaviour as synonymous with Christian behaviour, greater familiarity with other religions has largely removed Christ's monopoly on his ethical precepts.

Stripped of all these supports, faith becomes once more what it always should have been — an act of faith. Christians in western societies are back in the position of the church of the first three centuries, a minority whose only binding link is a shared faith in Christ and his promises. They are back with the intrinsic benefits of that situation, but without its chief drawback. They are not, in most countries, persecuted for their faith.

Opposite: *The certainties of simple faith: outside a church in Russia.*

Problems of the Church in an age of mass communication.

CHAPTER THIRTEEN

The Godless State ?

For almost 1,500 years, from the conversion of Constantine to the late eighteenth century, a partnership of some sort between church and state was normal in those parts of the world which had adopted Christianity. Emperors and popes might struggle to dominate each other, kings and bishops might clash over politics, parliaments and Nonconformists might disagree about liberty of conscience, but these were all quarrels within the Christian family. It was inconceivable that the rulers of any Christian community should not join with the church in a public commitment to Christianity: or, as has happened in our own century, that ancient Christian countries should find themselves committed, at the level of state policy, to the proposition that there is no god.

The change began with the Enlightenment, although the light was then considered suitable only for a minority. Voltaire wrote to Frederick the Great, on the subject of Christianity:

> Your majesty will do the human race an eternal service in extirpating this infamous superstition, I do not say among the rabble, who are not worthy of being enlightened and who are apt for every yoke; I say among the well-bred, among those who wish to think.[1]

Both Voltaire and Jean-Jacques Rousseau, who between them formed almost every fashionable opinion of the late eighteenth century, believed that the people required religion of some sort if they were to be effectively governed. In Rousseau's blueprint for an ideal political structure, as outlined in *The Social Contract*, the ruler will insist that each of his subjects believe in a 'civil religion'. Its theology was devised by Rousseau so as to promote the highest level of social and patriotic behaviour. There were to be five compulsory articles of belief:

> the existence of an omnipotent, intelligent, benevolent divinity that foresees and provides; the life to come; the happiness of the just; the punishment of sinners; the sanctity of the social contract and the law.[2]

No further explanation must be given, no flesh added to these abstractions, but anyone who could not assent to them was to be banished. If any citizen accepted these beliefs, but then 'behaved as if he did not believe in them', the punishment was death.

Rousseau's dreary compromise offered neither the warmth of religion nor the light of reason. The real excitement lay to either side, in the two extremes between which Rousseau so awkwardly dangled — in the vision of a future republican world of reason, equality, science, or in nostalgia for a glorious past, glowing with the richness and mystery of medieval art in a hierarchy made apparently secure by the twin protection of throne and altar. During the nineteenth century and into the twentieth the battle would rage between these two ideals, each equally unrealistic. The French Revolution and the subsequent empire, like a curtain-raiser to the modern world, had already offered a full preview of the various permutations.

The changes in the French calendar showed how the Revolution intended to sweep away the cobwebs of ancient superstition. Gods were found to be lurking in every corner of the old system. Years were numbered from the birth of one deity; week-days were named after several others, from a different religion; the pattern of the week, with its day of rest, was based on the working habits of a

Previous pages: *A packed congregation in one of the monastery churches of Zagorsk, in Russia.*

divine creator; public holidays were in honour of saints. The Revolution proposed, instead, to date the years from its own beginning. The week went decimal — both more rational and more demanding — with each day known by a number, but with rest allowed only on the tenth. Public holidays would celebrate not saints but Nature and Reason.

In 1793 all the churches in Paris were ordered to be closed, and the same year saw two examples of the new type of festival. August 10th was the first anniversary of the day on which the Paris mob had stormed the Tuileries and had put an effective end to the monarchy. The occasion was celebrated with a Festival of Regeneration, also known by the even more uninspiring name of Festival of the Unity and Indivisibility of the Republic. Among the ruins of the Bastille Jacques-Louis David had built a huge figure of a seated woman. She was Mother Nature. From her breasts there spurted two jets of water, at which delegates filled their cups and drank libations. Three months later there was a Festival of Reason, in which an actress from the opera played the Goddess of Reason and was enthroned in the cathedral of Notre-Dame — with the red bonnet of Liberty on her head and a crucifix beneath one of her elegant feet.

This was all part of the policy known as de-Christianization, but the most powerful man in the Convention considered such charades tasteless and the policy itself dangerous. He was Maximilien Robespierre. He was an enthusiastic disciple of Rousseau and was himself a deist, believing in 'an Eternal Being that guides the destinies of nations and appears to watch with particular vigilance over the Revolution in France'.[3] In a report to the Convention Robespierre pinpointed the dilemma which was to recur again and again, whenever revolution found itself confronted by religion:

> There are people who are superstitious in perfectly good faith. They are sick people whom we must restore to good health by winning their confidence. A forced cure would drive them to fanaticism. Priests have been denounced for saying the Mass. They will continue to do so all the longer if you try to prevent them. He who wants to prevent them is more fanatical than the priest himself.[4]

Robespierre persuaded the Convention of Rousseau's thesis — that the people needed something higher than Reason to venerate and fear — after which he set about establishing a new and official Cult of the Supreme Being. Robespierre was both the mastermind and the star of its inaugural ceremony on June 8th, 1794. David, pageant-master of the Revolution, built a hill on the Champ de Mars — where the Eiffel Tower now stands. In front of a large crowd Robespierre climbed the hill to perform a ceremony at its summit. There were those who felt that the scenario exalted Robespierre as much as the Supreme Being. If so, he was prefiguring a cult of personality which would later seem almost inseparable from revolutions, but there is no way of telling whether this was Robespierre's intention — because in less than two months, in a reversal equally characteristic of the revolutionary pattern, his own neck was beneath the guillotine.

The cult of personality was soon to be raised to giddy heights by the man whom Mme de Staël called Robespierre on horseback. Her phrase acknowledged the remarkable way in which Napoleon's image encompassed both sides of the question. He was a product of the Revolution, but in less than five years he transformed France from a republic to an empire. He had an almost professional   277

The Festival of the Supreme Being, June 1794 (Musée Carnavalet, Paris).

disinclination to believe in any Being more supreme than himself, yet his view of religion was the utilitarian one (that it is good for women and servants) which derived from Voltaire. His remarks on the subject were eminently practical:

> What is it that makes the poor man take it for granted that ten chimneys smoke in my palace while he dies of cold — that I have ten changes of raiment in my wardrobe while he is naked — that on my table at each meal there is enough to sustain a family for a week? It is religion, which says to him that in another life I shall be his equal, indeed that he has a better chance of being happy there than I have.[5]

Reason offered no such hopes, the Supreme Being had made no promises: it was essentially Christianity which advised the poor to wait. Notre-Dame was witness to the change of direction. Eleven years after the actress had been enthroned there as Goddess of Reason, this far greater actor was being crowned emperor of the French on the very same spot. To echo the coronations of the Holy Roman Empire, Napoleon brought the pope from Rome to officiate — but at the last moment, as if clinching the long struggle for supremacy between emperors and popes, he took the crown from the hands of Pius VII and placed it on his own head. 'So far as the pope is concerned', he later wrote, 'I am Charlemagne.'[6] Ingres painted him in his coronation robes with the sceptre of Charles V and a sword which was supposed to have belonged to Charlemagne. When David showed Napoleon crossing the Alps on his charger, it was noticeable that Charlemagne had passed that way also and had idly scrawled his name on a rock by the wayside.

278

Napoleon appreciated the political value of religion, no less than of publicity. The Roman Catholic church had been officially disestablished in 1795, but Napoleon made a Concordat with Pius VII. The familiar Christian trappings of everyday life came back to France. Nuns and monks returned, and so did Sundays and saints' days and the calendar dating from Anno Domini. Napoleon had even accepted the pope's demand that French children should only be christened with the names of saints, but it was not long before a new saint was discovered: St Napoleon, a Roman officer who had been martyred for his faith in the third century. Fate had dealt the emperor one trump card in his scheme for using Christianity in the service of the state. His own birthday, August 15th, happened to be the principal feast day of the best-loved figure in the whole Christian hierarchy; it was the Feast of the Assumption of the Blessed Virgin Mary. It now became, in addition, the saint's day of the newly discovered St Napoleon, and it was declared to be a day of national festivity. Meanwhile an Imperial Catechism had been issued. Its purpose was to 'bind by religious sanctions the conscience of the people to the august person of the Emperor'.[7]

A Christian empire evolving peacefully from an atheist republic was an astonishing combination of the themes which would dominate extremist politics for the next century, but then 1789 to 1815 in France had been astounding years. With Napoleon at long last out of the way, Europe was free to settle down to a more clear-cut version of the contest. The contenders could separate and become identifiable: atheism in the red shorts in the left corner, Christianity in the white shorts on the right. The czar immediately invited the princes of Europe to join with him in a Holy Alliance against revolution. The alliance's three leading members, Russia, Austria and Prussia, had all been ruled — in the years just before the French Revolution — by monarchs much influenced by the Enlightenment. Their successors had no wish to see any more enlightenment or any more revolution. To safeguard against either they pledged themselves to stand together as 'members of a single Christian nation'.[8]

The Middle Ages were the period when Europe had seemed to be a single Christian nation, and the medieval yearnings of the Romantic Movement played a large part in the political dreams of the right. In 1799 Novalis had anticipated the mood in an essay called *Christendom or Europe*. He advocated returning to a rather vaguely defined medieval structure of society, of which the virtues were 'respect for antiquity, attachment to spiritual institutions, a love for the monuments of our ancestors, and the old glorious state families, and the joy of obedience'.[9] Of all these merits, the joy of obedience was undoubtedly the most attractive to the Christian rulers signing the Holy Alliance. The only prince to abstain was the English prince regent, who was advised by Castlereagh that the alliance was 'a piece of sublime mysticism and nonsense'[10] (the strictly utilitarian Jeremy Bentham had an even more pungent phrase for such matters, 'nonsense on stilts').[11] The Christian princes wasted no time in reviving certain ancient institutions which had been abolished under the Enlightenment or by Napoleon. The Index of Prohibited Books and the Inquisition were restored; and the Jesuits, who for two centuries had been a symbol of papal influence throughout Europe, were re-established.

It was in France, home of the Revolution, that the clash between the two competing sides was most clearly seen. The returning Bourbons were among the

first to sign the Holy Alliance. After twenty years in exile, there were still two brothers of the guillotined Louis XVI to inherit the throne: Louis XVIII and his successor, Charles X. Charles had learnt nothing from the recent upheaval, and his greatest wish was to set the clock back to the days of the *ancien régime*. His coronation in 1825 was the high point of the Christian–royalist reaction. By returning to the correct details of the medieval rite, with a prince of the blood royal, the ceremony seemed to cancel out the travesty of Napoleon's charade in Notre-Dame. It took place in the cathedral at Rheims, the traditional setting for the coronation of every French king in the thirteen centuries since Clovis. Each king had been anointed with oil which was supposed to have been brought from heaven by a dove for the coronation of Clovis, and which was kept in a precious vial known as the *sainte ampoule*. In 1793 a republican had smashed the bottle against a statue of Louis XV, spilling the liquid. But just as Napoleon had found his St Napoleon, so Charles was relieved to hear that faithful royalists had rescued a few drops of the precious oil. On May 29th the king lay on the ground in Rheims cathedral while the archbishop inserted the oil through seven slits in the royal robe. The next day, rather reluctantly, Charles touched 121 people who were afflicted with scrofula. They had been extremely indignant when he offered them money in place of the ancient ceremony. They were not interested in an updated version of the Middle Ages.

Like most pieces of propaganda, the coronation impressed Charles's supporters but enraged his opponents. His legislation was to prove even more provocative, favouring all too openly the *émigré* nobility and the church. A law was even passed making sacrilege a capital offence. Hostility to the régime finally exploded in the next of France's series of revolutions, that of 1830. Delacroix painted *Liberty Guiding the People* in that year, and his picture shows that revolution too had by now acquired its own romance — which it has never since lost. Liberty, as well as having burnt her bra (a foretaste of the more limited aims of Women's Lib), carries aloft the sacred *tricolor*. It had been the symbol of the Revolution and the empire, but had not been seen in France since the restoration of the Bourbons — who had grievously underestimated all that it meant to the French. Now, in July 1830, a distant cousin of Charles X walked to the Hôtel de Ville draped in the sacred flag. His accession as Louis Philippe seemed to represent a new beginning, a middle way between the two extremes. His father, quick on to the revolutionary bandwagon, had changed his name in 1792 from the duke of Orléans to Philippe Egalité and had even voted for the death of his cousin, the king. The son, in keeping with this tradition, was to be known as the Citizen King. But his régime turned out to be almost as conservative as that of Charles X, with the difference that it favoured the middle classes rather than the nobility. Within the very first year of the new reign Victor Hugo wrote that he heard 'the dull sound of revolution, still deep down in the earth, pushing out under every kingdom in Europe its subterranean galleries from the central shaft of the mine which is Paris'.[12] It was to surface again throughout Europe in 1848. There were two separate revolutions in Paris that year. The first, in February, arose from agitation by the middle classes for parliamentary reform. On that occasion the return to the barricades swept away the Citizen King and

Napoleon in his imperial robes, by Ingres (Musée de l'Armée, Paris).

led to the Second Republic. But red flags as well as *tricolors* were seen on the streets, and in May de Tocqueville described an alarming mood in Paris:

> I saw society split in two: those who possessed nothing united in a common greed; those who possessed something in a common fear. No bonds, no sympathies existed between these two great classes, everywhere was the idea of an inevitable and approaching struggle.[13]

The struggle became violent with the uprising of the poorer districts of Paris in June. After six days of gruesome street fighting the bourgeoisie was victorious — and exacted brutal reprisals. Reaction was setting in once more. It had taken the First Republic twelve years to turn into an empire. It took the second only four.

Two young men were watching the events of 1848 with the closest interest. In the first few weeks of the year they had published an analysis of what they believed lay in store for Europe, though hardly anyone read it at the time. Fifty years earlier Novalis had said 'where there are no gods, spectres rule'.[14] Now Marx and Engels identified the spectre and set it in opposition to a holy alliance, in the opening words of *The Communist Manifesto*: 'A spectre is haunting Europe — the spectre of communism. All the powers of old Europe have entered into a holy alliance to exorcise this spectre.'[15] *The Communist Manifesto* had little to say about religion. It accused the bourgeoisie of having turned the priest into one of 'its paid wage labourers', and in supplanting the old feudal society of having 'drowned the most heavenly ecstasies of religious fervour, of chivalrous enthusiasm, of Philistine sentimentalism in the icy water of egotistical calculation'.[16] It was remarkable that Marx was not more obsessed with religion. When he was a student in Prussia, church and state had been so intertwined that political comment was often expressed in theological terms: Marx's university friends, for example, felt that they were attacking the very structure of society when they argued that the gospels were largely myth. But Marx himself saw different religions as 'nothing more than different stages in the development of the human spirit, as snake-skins cast off by history, and man as the snake which wore them'.[17] Before 1848 he had already written his most famous comment on religion, and it was far from being as hostile as is usually imagined:

> Religion is the sigh of the oppressed creature, the heart of a heartless world and the soul of soulless conditions. It is the opium of the people. To call on them to give up their illusions is to call on them to give up a condition that requires illusions. Criticism of religion is criticism of that vale of tears of which religion is the halo.[18]

The revolutions of 1848 brought Marx back first to France (from which he had been expelled in 1845) and then to Germany, where his writings had been suppressed by the censors. But the liberties of 1848 were short-lived. In 1849 Marx moved to the country which was to remain his home for the rest of his life, England. It was ideal for his purposes. Britain had the most fully developed capitalist economy, together with a useful habit of appointing solemn government commissions to compile Blue Books on the fearful conditions of the working classes; it offered Marx a magnificent library in the British Museum; and it had no government censor.

Since 1789 England had been in as much of a jitter about revolution as any other country, and had placed similar faith in religion as the most effective answer. The author of *An Enquiry into the State of the Public Mind amongst the*

The spire of a Gothic church rises above the industrial landscape: at Runcorn in Cheshire.

Lower Classes had begged parliament in 1798 to build more churches in the thickly populated areas, arguing that 'the true Christian will never be a leveller, will never listen to French politics, or to French philosophy'.[19] In 1818 the government voted £1 million for the building of churches, largely as a precaution against revolution. It was the beginning of a spate of neo-Gothic church building. The style was the result of a rather mundane consideration, economy — it was discovered that a large quantity of brick could be concealed beneath Gothic frills, whereas the uncompromising lines of classicism required more expensive stone — but it did also chime with the romantic appeal of the Middle Ages and of an authoritarian church.

The simplest way of shoring up society with a Christian buttress was to emphasize that God had intended the obscene inequalities of nineteenth-century life. A best-selling book of the 1840s, *Chartism Unmasked*, put the case in its most naked form:

> Another Chartist doctrine opposed to the Word of God is that poverty is not the result of the everlasting purpose of a Sovereign God but is only the result of unjust human laws. This is disposed of by the Bible which says 'The poor shall never cease out of the land'.[20]

The doctrine was immortalized by Mrs Alexander, though her pretty lines look more brutal when printed as ordinary prose: 'The rich man in his castle, the poor man at his gate, God made them high or lowly and *ordered* their estate'.[21] She wrote those words in that remarkable year of 1848.

But perhaps the revolution could be tamed rather than opposed? In that same year of 1848 an Englishman wrote from Paris to his friend, F. D. Maurice, in London. He argued that Socialism 'must be Christianized or it would shake   283

Christianity to its foundation, precisely because it appealed to the higher and not to the lower instincts of the men'.[22] Maurice sent back a letter agreeing that there had to be 'an English theological reformation, as the means of averting an English political revolution'.[23] The result was the movement known as Christian Socialism, which aimed to promote Christian principles in industry. Marx and Engels had already used precisely the same phrase in *The Communist Manifesto* when ridiculing such efforts ('Christian socialism is but the holy water with which the priest consecrates the heartburnings of the aristocrat'),[24] and some of the ideas of Maurice's Christian Socialists did seem to justify those harsh words. The group launched a magazine in 1848 called *Politics and the People*, which was intended for the working man. Its opening words stated the wish to join hands across the gulf:

> WORKMEN OF ENGLAND, we who have started this Paper do not work with our hands: we are not suffering hardships like many of you. Therefore you may think that we shall not understand you. Possibly we shall not altogether at first, but you can help us. You are in contact with the realities of life; you can help to make all our studies and thoughts more real.

A few pages later it became all too clear how far the Christian Socialists were capable of drifting from the realities of life. The Reverend Charles Kingsley, later to reach a more suitable audience with *The Water Babies*, suggested to the workmen of England that their gloom might be relieved if they paid a visit to the National Gallery:

> Pictures raise blessed thoughts in me — why not in you, my brothers? Believe it, toil-worn worker, in spite of thy foul alley, thy crowded lodging, thy ill-fed children, thy thin, pale wife — believe it, thou, too, and thine, will some day have *your* share of beauty. God made you love beautiful things only because He intends hereafter to give you your fill of them. That pictured face on the wall is lovely — but lovelier still may the wife of thy bosom be when she meets thee on the resurrection morn! Those baby cherubs in the old Italian painting — how gracefully they flutter and sport among the soft clouds, full of rich young life and baby joy! — Yes, beautiful indeed, but just such a one at this very moment is that once pining, deformed child of thine, over whose death-cradle thou wast weeping a month ago; now a child-angel, whom thou shalt meet again, never to part.[25]

Marx arrived in London the year after those words were written, and he was plunged straight into the realities of city poverty. He and his wife lived in two rooms in the squalid district of Soho. Three of his children died there, and on one occasion Marx hadn't even enough money to pay for the coffin. But Marx had only to walk a few hundred yards from the squalors of Soho to find himself in the British Museum. In its great domed Reading Room, which was completed in 1857, a temple to Reason, was hatched the first practical political system to do without God. The first volume of *Das Kapital* was published in German in 1867, and the following year the International Workingmen's Association voted it 'the Bible of the working class'.[26] It was certainly almost as long, and considerably harder to read.

The nearest thing that Marx and Engels ever saw to Communism in practice was the Paris Commune of 1871. It emerged accidentally from the Franco-Prussian war. In a Paris exhausted and embittered after a siege by the German

Pining deformed children turned into baby cherubs: detail of Adoration of the Shepherds *by Guido Reni (National Gallery, London).*

army, the National Guard joined forces with the radicals and rose against a reactionary national assembly. The government forces withdrew to Versailles, and for two exhilarating and muddled months Paris indulged in what Lenin later described as a 'festival of the oppressed'.[27] A characteristic element of the festival was its anti-clericalism. The archbishop of Paris was arrested as a hostage. When he protested that his concern as a churchman was only to pacify the situation, a leader of the Commune cut him short with: 'That's enough, you have been doing that to us for the last eighteen centuries, it won't wash any more.'[28]

When the Versailles troops stormed the city, massacring many of those they captured, a group of Communards lined up and shot six hostages, including four priests and the archbishop of Paris. The final battle between the two sides took place in a strangely appropriate setting — the cemetery of Père Lachaise, with its row upon row of pompous or sentimental monuments to bourgeois piety. The left-wing political parties in France still hold a memorial ceremony each year at the cemetery wall, where the defeated Communards were shot. They at least died close to a field of battle. During the next savage week thousands were dragged into the street and killed, often on the merest pretext. In an orgy of revenge, the ruling classes saw themselves as wiping out an evil which stretched right back through 1848 to 1793. The *Figaro* set the tone, saying that it was essential 'to purge Paris':

> Never has such an opportunity presented itself for curing Paris of the moral gangrene that has been consuming it. Today, clemency equals lunacy. What is a

republican? A savage beast. We must track down those who are hiding, like wild animals. Without pity, without anger, simply with the steadfastness of an honest man doing his duty.[29]

For most of his life Marx expected the revolution to occur in an industrialized country (at first he had high hopes of France, then later of Germany), but in the event the first country to adopt the red flag was the most backward in Europe, one which was just clambering out of the Middle Ages and in which the serfs had been freed only as recently as 1861. In the chaos of world war, the Bolsheviks — a handful of dedicated revolutionaries — were able to seize power in 1917 in the vast peasant empire of Holy Russia, a country which was fervently Christian and in which the Church was closely identified with the emperor. Naturally one of their first acts was to seize the Church's extensive property (as with Henry VIII and the English monasteries, there were also pressing economic arguments for this), and as soon as possible they tackled the much harder task of undermining the popular religion. An intriguing example of their methods was described by a priest in the early 1920s. Some hungry children in Georgia were told to ask God to give them their daily bread. Three times they asked and nothing came. Then they were told to make the same request to Lenin, and lo and behold, a truck-full of food came round the corner.

It was Lenin who gave Marx's 'opium of the people' its harsher meaning:

Religion is the opium of the people. It is a kind of spiritual gin in which the slaves of capital drown their human shape. Every idea of God is unutterable vileness, vileness of the most dangerous kind, contagion of the most abominable kind.[30]

Opposite: *A tomb in the cemetery of Père Lachaise.*

Communards lying numbered in their coffins.

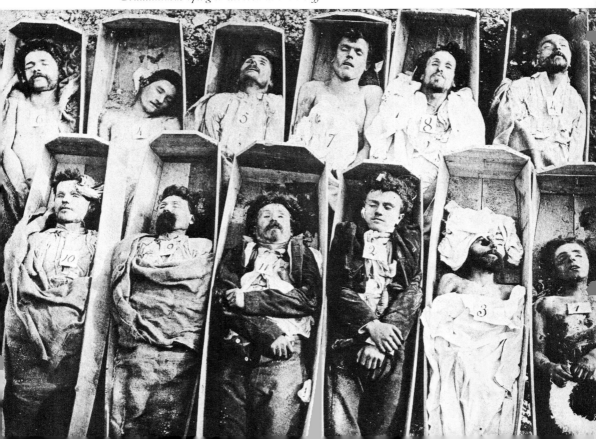

On the feast day of St Sergius at Zagorsk. Waiting for the crowds to gather. Opposite: Spectators on the gallery of one of the churches, and (below) a gathering of bishops for the open-air ceremony.

There has been over the years a continuous campaign in the Soviet Union to discourage people from believing in this unutterable vileness. Sometimes it has been violent: during 1922 more than 8,000 priests, monks and nuns were killed, a horrifying number but one which should be set against the millions of party officials who were purged and of peasants who were deported to their deaths in labour camps for resisting collectivization. More frequently the assault on religion has been on the level of propaganda — through the League of Militant Atheists set up in 1925 or the Congress of the Godless ten years later, through films specially made to ridicule the very idea of God, through exhibitions such as are on show in the Museum of Atheism at Leningrad, and — at the most naïve level — through the report that in outer space Yuri Gagarin had found no trace of a deity. Naturally Christians around the world are outraged to hear of such campaigns, violent or not, against their faith. But they need hardly be surprised. Christian countries, throughout history, have not been famous for tolerating other religions in their midst. The surprising fact is that Albania is so far the only Communist country to have made religious worship illegal.

The legal position in the Soviet Union has been unchanged since 1929. Article 124 of the Constitution says: 'the freedom to hold religious services and the freedom of anti-religious propaganda is acknowledged to all citizens'.[31] It's a strange phrase, but it means exactly what it says. Anyone may worship any god within any four walls that have been registered for worship, but public propaganda is reserved for those who say there is no god. There is therefore a legal right to practise an acquiescent form of religion — a permission quite inadequate to any evangelical Christian, committed to converting others. There are half a million Baptists in the U.S.S.R., many of whom feel an active obligation to spread the word. The Baptist sect reached Russia in 1884 and was persecuted by the czars, but it reached the amazing level of five million members during a liberal period in the 1920s. In harsher times the number has dwindled, but Baptist evangelism — being contrary to the letter of the law — still leads today to gaol sentences and persecution.

The majority of Christians in the Soviet Union are Russian Orthodox, with a long tradition of quietly obeying the state. Over the years many Orthodox churches have been closed, but those that are open are frequently full. On a feast day at the ancient monastery of Zagorsk I saw scenes of religious fervour such as it would be hard to find in southern Italy, and the ceremony was like a window on to the Middle Ages — with its rich vestments, the ecclesiastical jewels, and the virtuoso bass passages of the Russian Orthodox liturgy. Even the Soviet authorities admit that forty million people are still believers. A recent government report complained that fourteen tons of iron supplied to one factory had been diverted to a clandestine trade in Christian ornaments. The report even allowed itself what must surely be classed as a hint of bureaucratic humour:

A. Galichansky, a worker of this factory, has been welding in the firm's time crosses at 25 roubles a time. He also paints the crosses with the State's paint in the required colour. Other workers have been casting little statues reflecting the likeness of a citizen called Christ, who, according to rumours, has been dead since A.D.33.[32]

Opposite: *Sunset in Rome: St Peter's.*

The Soviet Union was the first state in the history of the world to make a dogma of the non-existence of God, but its leaders rushed in to fill the gap — as if admitting that society abhors a theological vacuum. The queue slowly filing past the tomb of Lenin in Red Square can only be described as undergoing a religious experience; Djilas wrote that he saw women in shawls crossing themselves as they approached the embalmed body, which itself is in the direct tradition of saints' relics in the crypts of cathedrals. In one poster of the thirties Stalin was to be seen smiling benevolently in the night sky above the Kremlin. Marx would no doubt have been horrified to see his face mounted on gigantic placards beside Stalin or Mao, but in North Korea — where the cult of personality has been carried to its furthest extremes — Marx, Engels and Lenin have all been dropped from the pantheon. The theoretical basis of the creed is now referred to not as Marxism but Kimilsungism, and Kim Il Sung appears alone on the hoardings. It is arguable that all Communist countries have merely replaced old gods with new, but so far only North Korea has achieved monotheism.

The twentieth century has seen many variations in the long struggle between the ideals of the French Revolution and those of the Holy Alliance. In Spain and Portugal the pendulum swung briefly to the atheist left before returning more forcefully to the Catholic right. Today two countries, Poland and Italy, offer a fascinating contrast and suggest that compromise is possible. In Poland, a Communist country, 80 per cent of the population are church-going Roman Catholics. In Italy, the historic centre of the Roman Catholic faith, the largest single political force in all the main cities is now the Communist party. Bologna has had a Communist administration since 1946, followed later by Milan, Turin, Genoa, Venice and Florence. In 1976 Rome went the same way.

After the war Pius XII threatened severe measures against any Catholic who collaborated with the Communists, and ever since then the pulpits of Italy have resounded with political sermons at election time. But the two sides coexist. In a poll taken during 1976, the group of people who described themselves as 'very religious' turned out to include an almost equal number supporting the Christian Democrats and the Communists. The leader of the Communist party, Enrico Berlinguer (responsible for the recent 'historic compromise' of power-sharing with the Christian Democrats), has a wife who is a practising Catholic and children who are prepared for confirmation by a Jesuit. And no doubt the Umbrian Communist party were not entirely cynical when they claimed St Francis of Assisi as one of their predecessors in the region.

The Eternal City has its first Communist mayor, and it is not beyond the bounds of possibility that sooner or later it will have its first Communist pope. Christianity and Communism share many of the same ideals, and once the power struggles are over they may come to recognize as much. It is the strength of any great religion that it is capable of finding within itself an almost infinite variety of new forms. They are not necessarily true to the origins of the religion, nor are they inevitable results of those origins. They are reflections of their own times. Stalin followed no more unavoidably from Marx than the Renaissance popes from Jesus Christ.

When planning this book and television series, I read the New Testament straight through — as if it were the scripture of an unknown religion, or as a Buddhist might read it. I found it impossible to believe that a stranger, coming to the Bible for the first time, would receive from it any clear idea of what Christ or Christianity stood for — so varied and self-contradictory are its messages and parables — and yet I was able to recognize the sources of all the different Christianities which twenty centuries have produced. Christ the King for the imperial churches; suffering for the Middle Ages; quietness and humility for those who find that path to God; a note of radical protest for the revolutionaries; the Apocalypse for the apocalyptic. In recent years, when the western world has made almost an alternative religion of personal relationships, we have emphasized — with justification, but more than any age before us — that the message of the gospels is Love. If our countries move gradually into a Socialist form of society, we shall hear rather more — again with justification — that the central theme of Christianity is sharing. This is not a cynical point, nor would such a development be cynicism on the part of Christians. To be able to adapt is strength in a religion as much as in a species. It is something which two thousand years of Christianity have amply proved.

Popular print put out by the clerical party in France in 1848.

Acknowledgments

The Team

Reducing history to the dimensions of a television screen is a fascinating task. It makes writing a book seem child's play. A powerful quotation or a significant fact, which would be of immediate use in a chapter, must pass a daunting series of tests before earning a place in a film. A wonderful idea, yes, but is it visual? Even if there is a suitable location, are we certain that a block of flats has not been built there since the photograph was taken? How far is the nearest airport? Can we afford to get there with a crew of seven? The clever notion may take all these obstacles in its stride, but will the government let us in? Has Granada's *World in Action* recently exposed torture there, or corruption, or military matters, and so queered the pitch for innocent Christians? Innocent Christians! As likely as not the new régime is fanatically Muslim. More chance of filming torture, corruption or the military than anything to do with Christianity. And then, once on location, is the weather right? Has scaffolding gone up since the director did his recce? Will the traffic never stop? And how, how on earth, can our small and gallant party hold back for a moment the ocean of tourists (at the very best they will be yelling at each other to keep quiet), hold them back just long enough to tell our brief story in an apparent oasis of quiet?

But somehow the few nuggets of treasure are brought back, from which, in darkened rooms, the story will be pieced together – often in a quite different form from the original plan, but not necessarily any the worse for that. Every stage of this painful and totally absorbing process involves many different people, whether arguing about what to go for, how to get it, or what to do with it. The making of a long television series is most emphatically a team effort. And looking back over three crowded years, it is often impossible to remember which idea was whose or whose idea went where.

The nucleus of our team was formed in the summer of 1974. Norman Swallow (executive producer), Mike Murphy (producer) and I were invited by Granada to consider turning Christian history into thirteen hours of television (thirteen is a magic number in television schedules, not because of the Last Supper, but because it represents three months, a quarter of the broadcasting year). We responded with enthusiasm. Like civilization or the ascent of man, Christianity provides a historical thread through a vast and varied tapestry — and one which is of personal importance to an even greater number of people. It seemed amazing that no one had so far attempted the story on television. So we reinforced ourselves with a researcher and a secretary, Steve Timmins and Frankie Glass, and the five of us set about clearing a path into our vast subject. Soon we had sufficiently detailed plans to involve our first two directors, Mike Houldey and Carlos Pasini. By the following spring we were on the road, pursuing skeletons in a dance of death in the early hours of Good Friday in Spain, dashing over to Rome to join the crowds on Easter morning of Holy Year in St Peter's Square, and on Monday watching pilgrims climb each step of the Scala Santa on their knees. We were in business.

The team was still growing and soon it had doubled: two more directors (Peter Plummer and Baz Taylor), a production manager (first Keith Thompson, then Peter Cuff), another researcher (Jane Taylor), a film researcher (Avril Warner), another secretary (Sue Hogan). This was headquarters, the platoon who were daily on parade in the long battle with intractable material or intransigent officials. In support we had a battalion of experts, headed by Granada's three religious advisers: the Reverend Dr Arthur Chadwick, Father Vincent Whelan and Canon Frank Wright. Others who were kind enough to help us with suggestions are too numerous to mention, but I must single out Professor Robert Markus on whom we leant more than most, and who many times extracted me from the thickets of early church history. When rushes began coming in, we acquired an editor-in-chief (David Naden), in overall charge of making films from the fragments. Later we were delighted to be joined by Richard Rodney Bennett, who was to compose music for each of our completed films, and by Marcus Dods as conductor. And for the last lap there were two more directors (John Sheppard, John Pett), two more researchers (Anthea Boulton, Maxine Baker).

But that, in itself, was only the Home Front. Whenever we flew away for the actual filming, there were new teams and a new range of challenges. I am grateful, first of all, to the directors for having coached me patiently in a type of television performance that was entirely new to me. It is a difficult craft to confide in the lens of a camera, chatting with it casually about early heresies or the fall of Constantinople. There is a tendency to become transfixed by that cold eye, like a rabbit in the headlights of a car, whereas the viewer would rather welcome into his living-room someone who feels at home there. I was greatly helped too by the encouragement and enthusiasm of Granada's film crews. George Turner, Mike Thomson and Ray Goode were the cameramen who, between them, covered our main trips abroad. The sound recordists were Alan Bale, Phil Taylor, John Muxworthy and Phil Smith (only one of whom subscribed to the sadistic theory that for perfect sound the microphone must be taped to the performer's chest). The assistants and the electricians who came with us on our longer trips are listed below. To all of them, and to others who were with us for shorter periods, I am most grateful: not only for making our many travels so enjoyable, and the work as easy as possible, but also for sharing the opportunities in a most generous way with a rival. My wife Christina was always with us, in cramped places or at crowded events, trying to capture the same moments on a still camera for this book. The possible clash of interests was never a problem. The team merely expanded to include her too.

To everyone, our thanks.

Assistant cameramen: Ken Garroway, Daf Hobson, Mike Lemmon, David Odd, Andy Stephen.
Assistant sound recordists: Harry Brookes, Martin Kay, Ken Reynolds, Nick Steer, Andy Wyatt.

Electricians: Jimmy Camp, Alistair Crumlich, Dave Duffy, Fred Edwards, Jimmy Green, Brian Jones, Alan Longshaw, John O'Neil, Peter Pennington, Bill Riley, Charlie Shoreman, David Ratcliffe, Stan Vayro, Bob Webley, Les Wood, John Yates.
Editors: Jack Dardis, Don Kelly, Tony Smith.
Assistant editors: Roland Coburn, John Eden, Andy Sumner.
Dubbing: John Whitworth, Andy Wyatt.

Finally, our thanks also to the much smaller team with whom we worked on the book, under great pressure to meet the deadline of the series: Gwen Godbold, who typed it; John Brown, who gathered in photographs from museums and art galleries; Elizabeth Cowen, who edited it; John Crabb, who was in charge of production; and Ian Craig who has the ultimate merit of a designer, providing marvellous ideas of his own and yet welcoming suggestions from his author or photographer.

Photographs

The author would like to thank the following for permission to reproduce photographs: Bibliothèque Publique et Universitaire, Geneva, p. 166; the British Library, p. 67; the British Museum, p. 228; J. E. Bulloz, p. 280; Camera Press Ltd, pp. 55, 271; Church Army, London, p. 254; *Daily Express*, p. 257; Tony Evans, p. 256; Foto Marburg, p. 165; Foto Mas, pp. 45 right, 177; Fratelli Alinari, pp. 42, 158, 170 left, 188; Dr Georg Gerster and the John Hillelson Agency Ltd, p. 54; Kunstmuseum, Basel, p. 164; the Mansell Collection, pp. 136, 139, 153, 225, 264 left; Museo Civico di Carpi, p. 190; Museu Nacional de Arte Antiga, Lisbon, p. 232; National Gallery, London, pp. 15, 18, 147, 285; National Gallery of Art, Washington, D.C., p. 92; National Portrait Gallery, London, p. 170 right; Public Records Office, p. 244; reproduced by gracious permission of Her Majesty the Queen, p. 172; Radio Times Hulton Picture Library, pp. 36, 192; Royal Geographical Society, p. 239; Salvation Army, London, pp. 251, 252, 253; Scala, p. 45 left; Städelsches Kunstinstitut, Frankfurt-am-Main, p. 163; Städtisches Suermondt-Museum, Aachen, p. 146; Tate Gallery, p. 259 right; Thames & Hudson Ltd, p. 264 right; United Society for the Propagation of the Gospel, London, pp. 238, 240, 242; University Library, Utrecht, p .72; Whitworth Art Gallery, University of Manchester, p. 259 left.

Sources of Quotations

This is not a bibliography. It merely lists in alphabetical order the sources from which quotations have been used. The quotations were chosen for a dramatic purpose — being spoken aloud on television — so they have often been abbreviated from their original form, sometimes drastically. Biblical passages are taken from the Authorized Version, when the words are already familiar in that form: or from the New English Bible on occasions where it offers greater clarity in a less-well-known passage.

Anderson-Moreshead, A. E. M., *The History of the Universities' Mission to Central Africa, 1859–1909*, 1955.
Aston, Margaret, *The Fifteenth Century: the Prospect of Europe*, 1968.
Athanasius, *Life of St Anthony*, trans. Robert T. Meyer, 1950.
Augustine, St, *The City of God*, trans. John Healey, 1945, 2 vols.
Bainton, Ronald, *Here I Stand*, 1950.
Baynes, Norman, *Byzantium*, 1948.
Bede, *A History of the English Church and People*, trans. Leo Sherley-Price, 1955.
Belden, Albert, *George Whitefield*, 1953.
Benedict, St, *The Rule*, trans. Oswald Hunter Blair, 1906.
Berlioux, Etienne, *The Slave Trade in Africa in 1872*, 1872.
Bernard, St, *Letters*, trans. B. Scott James, 1953.
Besterman, Theodore, *Voltaire*, 1969.
Bieler, Ludwig (ed.), *The Irish Penitentials*, 1963.
Boase, T. S. R. , *Boniface VIII*, 1933.
Booth, William, *In Darkest England and the Way Out*, 1890.
Bourdeaux, Michael, *Religious Ferment in Russia*, 1968.
Bowie, Theodore, *Studies in Erotic Art*, 1970.
Bradford, Ernle, *The Great Betrayal*, 1967.
Bradford, William, *History of Plimoth Plantation*, 1901.
Bridget, St, of Sweden, *The Revelations*, ed. William Cumming, 1929.
Briggs, Asa, *Victorian Cities*, 1968.
Carpenter, S. C., *Eighteenth-century Church and People*, 1959.
Caxton, William, *Mirror of the World*, 1913.
Cellini, Benvenuto, *Autobiography*, trans. George Bull, 1956.
Chadwick, Owen, *The Reformation*, 1964.
Chambers, Robert, *Vestiges of the Natural History of Creation*, 1844.
Cobban, Alfred, *A History of Modern France, 1799–1871*, 1965.
Cohn, Norman, *The Pursuit of the Millennium*, 1957.
Colomb, P. H., *Slave-Catching in the Indian Ocean*, 1873.
Columbus, Christopher, *Four Voyages*, trans. J. M. Cohen, 1969.
Conquest, Robert (ed.), *Religion in the U.S.S.R.*, 1968.
Coulton, G. G., *Five Centuries of Religion*, 1925–50, 4 vols.

Coulton, G. G., *A Medieval Garner*, 1928.
Coulton, G. G. *The Medieval Village*, 1925.
Cragg, Gerald R., *The Church and the Age of Reason*, 1960.
Crocker, Lester G., *The Age of Enlightenment*, 1969.
Dallimore, Arnold A., *George Whitefield*, 1971.
Daniel, Norman, *Islam and the West*, 1960.
Darwin, Charles, *The Origin of Species*, 1971.
Dawson, Christopher, *The Making of Europe*, 1932.
Delort, Robert, *Life in the Middle Ages*, 1974.
Dickens, A. G., *The English Reformation*, 1967.
Dillon, Francis, *A Place for Habitation*, 1973.
Doré, Gustave, *London*, 1872.
Dowd, David L., *Pageant-master of the Republic*, 1948.
Downey, James, *The Eighteenth-century Pulpit*, 1969.
Droz, Jacques, *Europe between Revolutions, 1815–1848*, 1967.
Dunn, R. S., *Puritans and Yankees*, 1962.
Edwards, Stewart, *The Paris Commune*, 1971.
Encyclopaedia Britannica, 1972.
Encyclopaedia Britannica, 1976.
Engels, Friedrich, *The Condition of the Working Class in England*, 1969.
Erasmus, *Julius Exclusus*, trans. Paul Pascal, 1968.
Evans, Joan, *Life in Medieval France*, 1957.
Fawcett, J., *Eighteen Months at the Cape*, 1836.
Foote, Peter, and Wilson, David, *The Viking Achievement*, 1970.
Fox, George, *Journal*, 1924.
Frazer, James, *The Golden Bough* (abbrev. ed.), 1923.
Freethinker's Information for the People, 1842–3.
Frend, W. H. C., *The Early Church*, 1965.
Freud, Sigmund, *Works*, trans. James Strachey, vol. XXI, 1964.
Graham, Billy, *Peace with God*, 1954.
Green, V. H. H., *Medieval Civilization in Western Europe*, 1971.
Gregory of Tours, *The History of the Franks*, trans. Lewis Thorpe, 1974.
Guicciardini, Francesco, *The History of Italy*, trans. Sidney Alexander, 1969.
Hanke, Lewis, *Aristotle and the American Indians*, 1959.
Harris, Ronald W., *Reason and Nature in the Eighteenth Century*, 1968.
Hebblethwaite, Peter, *The Runaway Church*, 1975.
Herbert, Robert L., *David, Voltaire, Brutus, and the French Revolution*, 1972.
Hillerbrand, Hans J., *The Protestant Reformation*, 1968.
Hillerbrand, Hans J., *The Reformation in its own Words*, 1964.
Hobsbawm, E. J., *The Age of Revolution*, 1973.
Hook, Judith, *The Sack of Rome, 1527*, 1972.
Huizinga, J., *The Waning of the Middle Ages*, 1955.
Hull, E., *Early Christian Ireland*, 1905.
Huxley, Elspeth, *Livingstone*, 1974.
Ignatius of Loyola, St, *Autobiography*, trans. Joseph F. O'Callaghan, 1974.
Ignatius of Loyola, St, *Spiritual Exercises*, trans. Thomas Corbishley, 1973.
Inglis, Kenneth S., *Churches and the Working Classes in Victorian England*, 1963.
James, M. R., *The Apocryphal New Testament*, 1924.

Janney, Samuel, *The Life of William Penn*, 1852.

Kendrick, T. D., *The Lisbon Earthquake*, 1956.

Knox, John, *History of the Reformation in Scotland*, 1949, 2 vols.

Larousse Encyclopedia of Byzantine and Medieval Art, 1968.

Las Casas, Bartolomé de, *Selection of his Writings*, ed. George Sanderlin, 1971.

Laven, Peter, *Renaissance Italy*, 1966.

Livingstone, David, *Cambridge Lectures*, 1858.

Lyles, Albert M., *Methodism Mocked*, 1960.

McCulloch, John A., *Medieval Faith and Fable*, 1932.

Mallett, Charles E., *A History of the University of Oxford*, 1927, 3 vols.

Mallett, Michael, *The Borgias*, 1969.

Mann, Horace, *Sketches of the Religious Denominations of the Present Day*, 1854.

Markus, R. A., *Christianity in the Roman World*, 1974.

Marx, Karl, *Early Writings*, trans. Rodney Livingstone, 1975.

Marx, Karl, and Engels, Friedrich, *Basic Writings on Politics and Philosophy*, ed. Lewis Feuer, 1969.

Meiss, Millard, *Painting in Florence and Siena after the Black Death*, 1961.

Miller, Hugh, *Foot-prints of the Creator*, 1849.

Mitchell, R. J., *The Laurels and the Tiara*, 1962.

More, Thomas, *Utopia*, trans. Paul Turner, 1965.

Niebuhr, Richard, *Christ and Culture*, 1952.

Norwich, John Julius, *A Christmas Cracker*, 1974.

Novalis, *Christianity or Europe*, trans. John Dalton, 1844.

Oliver, Roland, *Sir Harry Johnston*, 1957.

Oliver, Roland, *The Missionary Factor in East Africa*, 1952.

Oxford Dictionary of Quotations, 2nd edn, 1953.

Padover, Saul K., *The Revolutionary Emperor*, 1967.

Paley, William, *Natural Theology*, 1802.

Parkes, Henry B., *The Divine Order*, 1970.

Parry, J. H. *The Age of Reconnaissance*, 1973.

Pastor, Ludwig, *The History of the Popes*, 1886–1933, 16 vols.

Pepys, Samuel, *The Diary*, 1893–9, 10 vols.

Pius II, *The Tale of Two Lovers*, trans. Flora Grierson, 1929.

Pius XII, *Humani Generis*, trans. Ronald Knox, 1950.

Poliakov, Leon, *The History of Anti-Semitism*, 1966–74, 2 vols.

Politics and the People, 1848.

Prescott, Orville, *Princes of the Renaissance*, 1970.

Relation or Iournall of the English Plantation settled at Plimoth in New England, 1622.

Reynolds, Ernest E., *Thomas More and Erasmus*, 1965.

Ridley, Jasper, *John Knox*, 1968.

Robinson, John, *Honest to God*, 1963.

Rousseau, Jean-Jacques, *The Social Contract*, trans. Maurice Cranston, 1968.

Royle, Edward, *Victorian Infidels*, 1974.

Rudé, George, *Revolutionary Europe, 1783–1815*, 1964.

Rudé, George, *Robespierre*, 1975.

Runciman, Steven, *The Fall of Constantinople*, 1965.

Rutman, Darrett B., *Winthrop's Boston*, 1965.

Sandall, Robert, *History of the Salvation Army*, 1947–68, 5 vols.

Sherley-Price, Leo, *Little Flowers of St. Francis*, 1959.
Sims, George R., *'How the Poor Live' and 'Horrible London'*, 1889.
Southern, R. W., *Western Views of Islam in the Middle Ages*, 1962.
Spence, Jonathan, *Emperor of China*, 1974.
Stevenson, J. (ed.), *A New Eusebius*, 1957.
Stevenson, J. (ed.), *Creeds, Councils and Controversies*, 1966.
Symondson, Anthony (ed.), *The Victorian Crisis of Faith*, 1970.
Synge, Edward, *Works*, 1756, 4 vols.
Tacitus, *The Agricola and the Germania*, trans. H. Mattingly, 1970.
Talbot, C. H., *Anglo-Saxon Missionaries in Germany*, 1954.
Thurston, H., *The Holy Year of Jubilee*, 1900.
Tillich, Paul, *The Shaking of the Foundations*, 1962.
Toller, Frederick B., *Meeting House and Counting House*, 1948.
Tozzer, Alfred (ed.), *Landa's Relación de las Cosas de Yucatan*, 1941.
Van Cleve, Thomas, *The Emperor Frederick II*, 1972.
Vaughan, Alden T. (ed.), *The Puritan Tradition in America*, 1972.
Vidler, Alec R., *The Church in an Age of Revolution*, 1961.
Voltaire, *Works*, trans. William F. Fleming, 1927, 22 vols.
Voltaire, *Voltaire's England*, ed. Desmond Flower, 1950.
Wesley, John, *Journal*, 1938, 8 vols.
Weylland, John, *Round the Tower*, 1891.
Whitcomb, John C., *The Early Earth*, 1972.
Wildes, Harry E., *Voice of the Lord*, 1965.
Wilson, David D., *Many Waters Cannot Quench*, 1969.
Winslow, O. E., *Master Roger Williams*, 1957.
Wohl, Anthony S. (ed.), *The Bitter Cry of Outcast London*, 1970.
Woodforde, James, *The Diary of a Country Parson*, 1924–31, 5 vols.

Chapter One (pages 12–33)

1 Stevenson, *Eusebius*, 2.
2 Ibid., 3.
3 Ibid., 137; and Frend, 74.
4 Stevenson, *Eusebius*, 135.
5 Ibid., 13–14.
6 Niebuhr, 30.
7 Isaiah 40: 3.
8 Luke 5: 4–10.
9 James, 476–7.
10 Acts 18: 6.
11 Ibid., 19: 2–5.
12 Ibid., 15: 31.
13 Galatians 3: 28–9.
14 Acts 24: 5.
15 Stevenson, *Eusebius*, 2–3.
16 Ibid., 143.
17 Markus, 87.

Chapter Two (pages 36–55)

1 Stevenson, *Creeds*, 160.
2 *Larousse*, 14.

3 Frend, 186–7.
4 Ibid., 149–50.
5 Gregory, 5.
6 *Encyc. Brit.*, 1972, XI, 618.
7 Ibid.
8 Stevenson, *Eusebius*, 213.
9 Exodus 20: 4.
10 Baynes, 290.
11 Runciman, 178.
12 Athanasius, 22–8.

Chapter Three (pages 59–81)

1 Dawson, 23.
2 Ibid., 88.
3 Augustine, I, 14–15.
4 Bieler, 75.
5 Ibid., 215.
6 Ibid.
7 Hull, 224–5.
8 Benedict, 8–44.
9 Bede, 99–100.
10 Ibid., 106.

11 Tacitus, *Germania*, 134.
12 Talbot, 75–8.
13 Norwich, 10.
14 Foote, 14–15.
15 Coulton, *Medieval Garner*, 72.
16 Bernard, 8.

Chapter Four (pages 85–103)

1 Green, 56–7.
2 Coulton, *Medieval Village*, 519.
3 Huizinga, 61.
4 Delort, 97.
5 Caxton, 106–8.
6 Bridget, 108–16.
7 Coulton, *Medieval Garner*, 333.
8 Meiss, 83.
9 Coulton, *Five Centuries*, I, 35 and 41.
10 McCulloch, 107.

11 Sherley-Price, 199–200.
12 Ibid., 196.
13 Thurston, 25.
14 Boase, 233.
15 Indulgence posters for Holy Year, 1975.

Chapter Five (pages 106–27)

1 Koran 42: 13.
2 Ibid., 4: 171.
3 Poliakov, II, 47–8.
4 Ibid.
5 Southern, 21.
6 Daniel, 113.
7 Cohn, 70.
8 Ibid., 68.
9 Bradford, Ernle, 184.
10 Southern, 31.
11 Evans, 93.
12 Koran 13: 35; 36: 56; 47: 15; 52: 20.
13 Daniel, 149.
14 Van Cleve, 304.
15 Columbus, 37.

Chapter Six (pages 130–52)

1 Mitchell, 174.
2 Pastor, II, 198.
3 Parkes, 365.
4 *Hamlet*, act II, scene ii, ll. 323–7.
5 Mitchell, 55.
6 Pius II, 120–22.
7 Pastor, I, 360.
8 Prescott, 329.
9 Mallett, Michael, 255.
10 Prescott, 4.
11 Pastor, v, 193.
12 Ibid., 196.
13 Laven, 209.
14 Reynolds, 261.
15 Erasmus, 45–90.
16 Hook, 165.
17 Cellini, 71.
18 Ibid., 76.

Chapter Seven (pages 156–73)

1 Guicciardini, 320–21.
2 Bainton, 115.
3 Ibid., 80.
4 Romans 3: 28.
5 Bainton, 147.
6 Chadwick, 56.
7 Bainton, 217.
8 Ibid., 223.
9 Ibid., 226.

10 Ibid., 228–9.
11 Hillerbrand, *Reformation in own Words*, preface.
12 Dickens, 275.
13 Ridley, 338.

Chapter Eight (pages 176–96)

1 Aston, 46.
2 Parry, 35.
3 Hanke, 26.
4 Ibid., 47.
5 Las Casas, 200–202.
6 Ibid., 165.
7 Ignatius, *Autobiography*, 23.
8 Ignatius, *Exercises*, 58.
9 Ibid., 67–70.
10 Ibid., 112.
11 Ignatius, *Autobiography*, 106ff.
12 Bowie, 231.
13 Spence, 81.
14 Tozzer, 116.

Chapter Nine (pages 200–217)

1 Hillerbrand, *Protestant Reformation*, 147–52.
2 Bradford, William, 15.
3 Ibid., 16.
4 Dillon, 94.
5 Wildes, 388.
6 Bradford, William, 91.
7 Rutman, 40.
8 *Relation*, title page.
9 Hanke, 99–100.
10 Dunn, 12.
11 Vaughan, 217–18.
12 Ibid., 300.
13 Winslow, 259.
14 Ibid., 219.
15 Fox, for the year 1651.
16 July 29th, 1667.
17 Janney, 175.
18 Toller, 232.

Chapter Ten (pages 220–35)

1 Voltaire, *Works*, IV, 180.
2 Ibid., 178–9.
3 *Essay on Man*, Epistle 3, l. 305.
4 Harris, 91.
5 Synge, II, 1–301.
6 Paley, ch. 1.
7 Cragg, 237.
8 Belden, 1.
9 Lyles, 82–3.

10 Mallett, Charles, 123.
11 Downey, 161–72.
12 Wilson, 69.
13 Wesley, March 31st, 1739.
14 Lyles, 93.
15 Dallimore, 439.
16 Carpenter, 204.
17 Crocker, 83 and 87.
18 Kendrick, 151.
19 *Oxford Dict. Quot.*, 164: 9.
20 November 7th, 1789.
21 *Oxford Dict. Quot.*, 557: 7; Voltaire, *England*, 87–8; *Encyc. Brit.*, 1976, vol. 6, 889.
22 Besterman, 217 and 221.
23 Herbert, 142.
24 Dowd, 48.
25 Herbert, 86.

Chapter Eleven (pages 238–54)

1 Anderson-Moreshead, 2.
2 Berlioux, 51.
3 Livingstone, 24.
4 Ibid., intro.
5 Anderson-Moreshead, 5.
6 Oliver, *Missionary*, 15, n.2.
7 Colomb, 390–402.
8 Anderson-Moreshead, 68.
9 Symondson, 63.
10 Fawcett, 40.
11 Huxley, 108.
12 Symondson, 65.
13 Oliver, *Johnston*, 297.
14 Ibid., 182.
15 Ibid., 175.
16 Ibid., 134.
17 Booth, 11–13.
18 Sims, 1.
19 Doré, 141–2 and 146.
20 Weylland, 50.
21 Engels, 155.
22 Mann, 96.
23 Ibid., 97.
24 Engels, 143.
25 Weylland, 40.
26 Wohl, 56.
27 Ibid., 106.
28 Ibid., 105.
29 Briggs, 28.
30 Sandall, I, 203–4.
31 Ibid., 202.
32 Booth, 16–18.
33 *Major Barbara*, act II.

Chapter Twelve (pages 258–73)
1 Hillerbrand, *Protestant Reformation*, 183.
2 Padover, 155.
3 Chambers, 306.
4 Ibid., 280.
5 Miller, 19.
6 Darwin, 455.
7 Freud, 33.
8 Frazer, 361.
9 Royle, 113.
10 *Freethinker's*, vol. II, no. 2.
11 Royle, 82.
12 Ibid., 83.
13 Ibid., 76.
14 Ibid., 110.
15 Ibid.
16 Ibid., 78.
17 Tillich, 63–4.
18 Robinson, 105.
19 *The Times*, Feb. 14th, 1976.
20 Graham, 15–17.
21 Whitcomb, 82 and 36.
22 *Encyc. Brit.*, 1976, vol. 14, 485.
23 Pius XII, 21.
24 More, 128.
25 Hebblethwaite, 39.

Chapter Thirteen (pages 276–91)
1 Cragg, 241.
2 Rousseau, 286.
3 Rudé, *Robespierre*, 122.
4 Ibid., 123.
5 Vidler, 19.
6 Cobban, 56.
7 Ibid., 32.
8 Droz, 17.
9 Novalis, 26.
10 Rudé, *Revolutionary*, 285.
11 Hobsbawm, 287.
12 Ibid., 371.
13 Cobban, 143.
14 Novalis, 24.
15 Marx and Engels, 48.
16 Ibid., 51.
17 Marx, 213.
18 Ibid., 244.
19 Inglis, 6.
20 Vidler, 94–5.
21 *Oxford Dict. Quot.*, 3: 15.
22 Vidler, 96.
23 Ibid.
24 Marx and Engels, 72.
25 *Politics and the People*, vol. I, no. I.
26 Marx and Engels, 23.
27 Edwards, 277.
28 Ibid., 213.
29 Ibid., 340–41.
30 Conquest, 7.
31 Bourdeaux, 110.
32 *Sunday Times*, Feb. 2nd, 1976.

Index